797,885 Books

are available to read at

www.ForgottenBooks.com

Forgotten Books' App
Available for mobile, tablet & eReader

ISBN 978-1-333-36639-1
PIBN 10495683

This book is a reproduction of an important historical work. Forgotten Books uses state-of-the-art technology to digitally reconstruct the work, preserving the original format whilst repairing imperfections present in the aged copy. In rare cases, an imperfection in the original, such as a blemish or missing page, may be replicated in our edition. We do, however, repair the vast majority of imperfections successfully; any imperfections that remain are intentionally left to preserve the state of such historical works.

Forgotten Books is a registered trademark of FB &c Ltd.
Copyright © 2017 FB &c Ltd.
FB &c Ltd, Dalton House, 60 Windsor Avenue, London, SW19 2RR.
Company number 08720141. Registered in England and Wales.

For support please visit www.forgottenbooks.com

1 MONTH OF
FREE
READING

at

www.ForgottenBooks.com

By purchasing this book you are eligible for one month membership to ForgottenBooks.com, giving you unlimited access to our entire collection of over 700,000 titles via our web site and mobile apps.

To claim your free month visit: www.forgottenbooks.com/free495683

* Offer is valid for 45 days from date of purchase. Terms and conditions apply.

English
Français
Deutsche
Italiano
Español
Português

www.forgottenbooks.com

Mythology Photography **Fiction** Fishing Christianity **Art** Cooking Essays Buddhism Freemasonry Medicine **Biology** Music **Ancient Egypt** Evolution Carpentry Physics Dance Geology **Mathematics** Fitness Shakespeare **Folklore** Yoga Marketing **Confidence** Immortality Biographies Poetry **Psychology** Witchcraft Electronics Chemistry History **Law** Accounting **Philosophy** Anthropology Alchemy Drama Quantum Mechanics Atheism Sexual Health **Ancient History Entrepreneurship** Languages Sport Paleontology Needlework Islam **Metaphysics** Investment Archaeology Parenting Statistics Criminology **Motivational**

FAITH AND ITS EFFECTS:

OR,

FRAGMENTS FROM MY PORTFOLIO.

BY MRS. PHŒBE PALMER,

Author of
"The Way of Holiness," "Present to my Christian Friend," &c.

HIS NAME IS CALLED THE WORD OF GOD.—ST. JOHN.
ALL THINGS ARE POSSIBLE TO HIM THAT BELIEVETH.—JESUS.
BY WORKS WAS FAITH MADE PERFECT.—ST. JAMES.
HOW CAN YE BELIEVE WHO RECEIVE HONOR ONE OF ANOTHER?
JESUS.

10th Thousand.

New-York:

PUBLISHED FOR THE AUTHOR, AT 200 MULBERRY-STREET.

JOSEPH LONGKING, PRINTER.

1850.

996407A

COPYRIGHT SECURED.

TO

REV. BISHOP JANES AND LADY,

WHOSE EXPERIENCE AND PRACTICE FURNISH,

TO THE PRAISE OF GOD,

A DAILY EXHIBITION OF FAITH AND ITS EFFECTS,

THIS VOLUME

IS AFFECTIONATELY DEDICATED

BY

THE AUTHOR.

PREFACE.

What is faith? This is a question, which by the pious of all ages has been regarded as pre-eminently important. And surely the magnitude of the inquiry cannot be estimated beyond what its merit demands. What question can be more momentous to one who would secure the divine approval, since without faith it is *impossible* to please God? Yet the subject of faith has been so ably discussed by theologians of deep piety, that the author of this work has no intention of entering upon this ground as the revealer of any new theory. She may not speak of a higher anticipation than that of bringing forth truths as old as the Bible, with the humble hope that the Holy Spirit may cause them to be presented to the reader with vitality and freshness.

And why write a book, if nothing new to communicate? We answer, with the hope that some sincere inquirer, who may have been long looking for some new revelation, or that some great thing be wrought, may cease the vain endeavor, and in lowliness of mind ask for the old paths.

Few, perhaps, have been more perplexed in relation to faith than the writer was in early life.

She has since discovered that the religion of the Bible does not require great powers of mind to reach it, but deep humility of spirit to come down to its simplicity. That the Bible is the word of God, is a truth with which from infancy she had been familiar, yet from a want of a proper realization of this fact her difficulties mainly arose. For years past she has in experimental verity apprehended the Divinity of the Word, and consequently her difficulties about faith have all vanished.

Meeting with many who inquire the heavenly way, and yet have been hindered by similar perplexities, the author, in her frequent communications with such, has in her directions pointed to the law and the testimony as an infallible guide, and a sufficient rule for faith and practice. Her endeavor has been to meet these diversified cases, (which have ranged from the unawakened sinner to the traveler in the way of holiness,) on the ground of Bible truth; and it is hoped that something which has been presented may instruct and interest a few in each class of experience. If the work may be in any degree instrumental in the awakening and ultimate salvation of souls, the author's highest ambition will have been reached, and the glory shall be ascribed to the Father, Son, and Holy Spirit.

CONTENTS.

No I.—To Mr. M——. Mr. M—— acknowledges himself unawakened—What is faith?—Interview with a Hicksite friend—Displeasure incurred—Doings and sayings at a class meeting—An unlikely subject of prayer presented—Mrs. W.'s inquiry—The sinner condemned already—The culprit C——; his agony when under condemnation, the effect of his faith in man—Mr. M—— not a believer in the Bible as the word of God—Influential friends cannot save—Mr. M—— under condemnation—Why the word of God has not the same effect as a voice from heaven   Page 13

No. II.—To Mr. M——. Mr. M. inquires the way—Inquires the effect of faith—Evidences of the inbeing of faith—Perilous condition acknowledged—Hardness of heart confessed and bemoaned—Not required to save ourselves—Sinful to stay away from the Saviour—A letter to a sincere inquirer—Difficulties in the way of salvation—Repentance known by its fruit . . 21

No. III.—To Mr. M——. Mr. M—— inquires whether the power to believe may not be withheld—The power to exercise faith never withheld from the truly sincere—Difficulty with one who had been seeking the Lord four years, and how removed—Man possesses the awful power of pronouncing his own blessings and curses—Five individuals converted the same day on which they were awakened—Difficulty with Mr. S.—Of one who thought it was too late 28

No. IV.—To Mr. M——. Sincerity and earnestness not sufficient to insure salvation—An illustration of how faith is the gift of God—How to show fruit meet for repentance—An error in presenting petitions for awakened persons—Lad on the roof of a building—The man near a cataract—Not saved by doing *nothing* 34

No. V.—To Mr. M——. A matter of surprise with Mr. M——Reasons for delay wholly with the creature—Singular case of a lady where conviction followed conversion—Late Rev. S. M. relates a similar case—God ever meets us on the ground of his word—How to keep a new heart—Progression required—The Bible; its excellence—The scheme of salvation conditional . . 40

No. VI.—To Mr. M——. Condemned and justified at the same moment impossible—Case of a young lady who mistook a state of condemnation for one of justification; not intentionally hypocritical—How the mistake may imperceptibly be made—Condition upon which a state of justification is retained—How soon may perfection be attained? 47

No. VII.—To Mr. M——. The summit of Christian attainment may never be reached in time—Paul not perfect in attainment—He professes perfection, and in what sense—A state of perfection requiring progression urged—*Christian*, not Adamic, perfection, the object 51

CONTENTS.

No. VIII.—To Mr. M——. Inquiries relative to the length of time intervening between a state of justification and entire sanctification—Mr. Wesley's views on the subject—How backslidings might be less frequent—Another inquiry from my Hicksite friend—How unholy professors encourage skepticism—The case of a young man whose friends were professing Christians—Salvation from sin may be obtained *now*—How a housekeeper obtained it Page 54

No. IX.—To Mrs. W——. Fruits of holiness partially enjoyed—Work of the Spirit, and tenderness of conscience at an early age—Regret—Difficulties—The cost counted—Activity required—Intense breathings—A wrong standard of experience—A darling object—Great things anticipated 61

No. X.—To Mrs. W——. A sacrifice contemplated—The surrender is made—The seal of consecration enstamped—Apprehends a state of holiness—Exults in the knowledge of the sanctification of body, soul, and spirit—Scruples removed—Christ all in all 70

No. XI.—To Mrs. W——. The bliss of dwelling in God—Blessings are received for the good of others—Confession contemplated—What had been a hinderance for years—Hearty submission to the order of God 75

No. XII.—To Mrs. W——. The adversary foiled—Unbroken quiet—Tempted in a dream—Sweet repose—Encouragement given during sleep—Peace, the heritage of the believer . . 78

No. XIII.—To Mrs. W——. Temptation relative to retaining the blessing—Mental conflict—Peace—Confession—Desires to know the precise foundation of faith—A statement of the way in which prayer was answered—The consequences of turning out of the way apprehended 83

No. XIV.—To Mrs. W——. Heaven begun below—Holiness the believer's strength—"If I get it I cannot keep it"—Remark of Dr. B—— Mysticism—Consecration a simple act—Holiness maintained by constant faith—The Scriptures a medium of communion with God—The way of the cross—A new existence—Effect on the world of universal holiness in the church . . . 88

No. XV.—To Mrs. R——. Questions—Unreasonable not to be holy—Danger of slighting convictions—Sad remembrances—A fearful state—Count the cost—Decision—Self-sacrifice—The martyrs—The offense of the cross not ceased—Self-distrust—The way opened to the holiest—Temptations 94

No. XVI.—To Mrs. R——. Power of faith—Terms of the covenant—Unsanctified resting in creature-good—Self-denial—A Jewish offerer—The Christian's altar—The altar greater than the gift—Self-sacrifice reasonable ; our duty ; its benefits—The offering must *touch* the altar—The will must be resigned . 98

No. XVII.—To Mr. K——. An impression confirmed—Religious joy—Temptation succeeds—Unwise inference—Holiness a state of character, not of emotion—The disciple with Jesus in the wilderness, and on the mount—The disciples on Tabor—The unwise request—The crown coveted, not the cross . . . 105

No. XVIII.—To Mr. K——. Questions—Mr. K——'s resolution—Inconsistency of Mr. K——'s position—May the sanctification of the soul be achieved gradually?—"God's word its own evidence"—Correspondence between faith and confession—"Have

I lost my will?"—Illustrations—The obedient child—The Saviour—Family government—Ruling by love—Daily intercession—Household dedication—Restraint—Abraham's family—Joshua—Eli . . . . Page 110

No. XIX.—To Mr. K——. Remarkable visit of the Spirit—A new heart given to a little child—"I want to pray more"—An accusation of the tempter—Little W—— Infantile anticipation . 118

No. XX.—To Mr. K——. Faith receives Christ in all his offices—Distrustfulness—Illustration—A specific kind of unbelief pointed out—The Bible the voice of God to man—Reference to 2 Pet. i, 21—Profession on the authority of the WORD urged—Waverings in faith sinful—Triumphs of Satan—Loss to the church—Slight notions of the sin of unbelief lamented 123

No. XXI.—To Mr. K——. "*Only* unbelief"—Ancient Israel—Borders of the promised land reached—Met and vanquished by an enemy—Who was it ?—God dishonored by unbelief . 129

No. XXII.—To Rev. Mr. P——. Difficulties in the distance—Humility and decision—Divine protection—Daniel—Workers together with God—Witness of the Spirit—Distinction between faith and sight—Abraham; his *patient* faith—The wavering one . . 133

No. XXIII.—To Rev. Mr. P——. Premature application of the promises—Not willing to be holy—Paul's concise statement of the way to holiness—Distinction between consecration and sanctification—Obedience must precede appropriating faith—Wickedness of removing a sacrifice from the altar—Thomas—Of one who gave up his will 137

No. XXIV.—To Rev. Mr. P——. Temptation as to the genuineness of faith—"Man-work"—Faith without works—"Workers together with God"—Queries about self-sanctification—Answers—Scriptural test 142

No. XXV.—To Rev. Mr. P——. Baptism of the Spirit—The just shall live by faith—Witness of the Spirit—Answer delayed—Need of patience—My sister—Interview with Rev. T. Merritt—Confession—Steadfastness—Zeal 146

No. XXVI.—To Rev Mr. P——. Mr. P.'s singular statement of his case—Conclusions questioned—Illustration—The effect of my faith in Mr. P—— Witness of the Spirit—"The Spirit speaketh expressly"—The Bible the voice of the Spirit—The blessing apprehended in the promise—Faith in a dark hour—Resignation 150

No. XXVII.—To Bishop and Mrs. H——. Separated friends—Day of my espousals—Judge W——, and Judge R—— Happiness without holiness—A forty years' seeker obtains the blessing in a few hours—An evening on the camp ground—Struggles of a minister for holiness; his confession—Full salvation in five minutes—Brother and sister B—— "This *now* salvation"—Decision—Self-denial—Sweet peace 155

No. XXVIII.—To Rev. T. M——. The "Third Monday evening meetings"—Rev. Mr. C—— Our calling—Mrs. —— The testimony of a maid in Israel—Searching the Scriptures—"It is all here"—A pious visit—Interrogations—An object of great desire—Withstood by Satan—The vow—The victory—Delay—Trial—A hearty profession of full salvation 165

No. XXIX.—To Rev. Mr. K——. E—— street Church—One hundred witnesses—Revival—A local preacher—Long-continued efforts to obtain holiness—Remark of Dr. —— Sixty persons set apart for God—The camp prayer meeting—A passer-by arrested—A searching preacher—Revival in Baltimore—The work of God in A—— street in 1831—Morning meetings—Men and angels—Holiness the strength of the church—Satan's favorite instrument—A reproachful compliment . . . Page 175

No. XXX.—To Mrs. B——. Mark xi, 24—1 John v, 14, 15—An illustration—Answers to prayer—"The Faithful and True"—"In God will I praise his word"—The bank bill—The infidel minister—Faith and sense—The word personified—An end of the difficulty 183

No. XXXI.—To Mrs. B——. Presumption taken for faith—Doctrines abused—The assertion, "Believe that you have it, and you have it," not Scriptural—Importunate prayer unanswered—An unauthorized petitioner—The lame and blind offered in sacrifice—The backslider's prayer—Divine direction sought in vain—Meddling with secret things—Why some parents cannot believe—Unholy hands lifted up 189

No. XXXII.—To the Members of the —— Church. The church is a family—Intercessions—Revival prevented—The sin of one man—A reproach to Christ—Social gatherings *versus* class meetings—A wonderful deception—The convicted—Cruel friends—"Who ruined that soul?"—God's decree nullified—A revival in God's order—Death busy and the church idle—"Curse ye Meroz" 195

No. XXXIII.—To the Members of the —— Church. Neglect of the stated means—A remark of Mr. Wesley—An engagement to meet a friend—Who broke it?—One in three at class—What Thomas lost—All strong, and all at work—"Begin at my sanctuary"—Six left of three hundred—An estimate—Nursing fathers and mothers 201

No. XXXIV.—To Rev. ——. Memoir of Mrs. —— The common people—Good news—A commanding post—Ability equal to duty—Our calling as a church—"The high doctrines of our creed"—Mysteries—A popular young minister—Mr. Wesley's last advice—How others regard us—A dilemma—Professor —— Disappointment—A Presbyterian's opinion of a Methodist congregation—"What do ye more than others?" 206

No. XXXV.—To Mr. J——. Disposition of property—Inequalities of human condition—Responsibility graduated by possession—Prudent foresight recommended by Solomon—Of those who heap together riches—Comparative liberality—Censoriousness—"Are rich men required to give up all?"—Community of goods—A debate 213

No. XXXVI.—To Mr. J——. A stumbling block—"One hundred dollars instead of six"—The wealthy father and his two sons—Jacob's vow—Large income for the Lord's treasury—A broken vow—Obstacle to religious prosperity—Tests of fidelity—David's view of liberality—Systematic mode of giving—The tenth devoted—"Giveth and yet increaseth"—Missionaries . . . 218

No. XXXVII.—To Rev. ——. "Why cannot I believe?"—Plain dealing—Our reputation belongs to God—Expulsions from the ministry—"Why insist on terms?"—A resolve to stand or fall with truth—Ashamed of Christ's *words*—The sin of ignorance—Objection to Scripture phraseology—Paul's conduct—Reputation not resigned—"How can ye believe?"—Christ's benediction on the outcast 225

CONTENTS. 11

No. XXXVIII.—To Rev. Mr. H——. Heaven's nobility incog—Views presented by the Spirit on the subject of confession—A sanctified soul hails from heaven—The force of the clause, "in earth as in heaven"—An angel on earth; his singleness of purpose; his heroic zeal . . . . Page 234

No. XXXIX.—To Rev. Mr. M——. "What is the witness of the Spirit?"—Wesley's definition—"He that believeth hath the witness"—A promissory note—Ten years' experience—Whether we believe or not is matter of consciousness—"What are the evidences of entire sanctification?"—"The Spirit itself beareth witness"—"By what marks may we know that we are entirely sanctified?" 239

No. XL.—To Miss S——. The divine image borne and reflected—The doctrine of entire sanctification at conversion considered—It is anti-Wesleyan—Unscriptural—Christians urged to go on to perfection—Desires for holiness the result not of backslidings, but of an active and growing faith—Humiliating confession of an errorist 246

No. XLI.—To Miss S——. Mr. Wesley's views—The author's habit of mind—Evidence of justification previous to entire sanctification—Movement of the denominations toward the unity of the faith—Tuesday meeting—A charming sight—Quotations from Wesley—Experience of David—The apostles—A cloud of witnesses—Caleb and Joshua—The danger of refusing to go on to perfection 251

No. XLII.—To Mr. C——. Profession and practice—The cross—"I will guide thee by mine eye"—Lessons of experience—The importance of immediate action in the use of present grace—A temptation not to speak *definitely* yielded to—Sad effects—Reproved, but not rejected—Holiness may be forfeited by neglect—A strange testimony—Lingering in duty—Its consequences—Views of personal obligation 258

No. XLIII.—To Mrs. D——. Establishing grace—God's worthies—Few excel—Instability—Unlike God—Let your yea be yea, and your nay nay—The seal of the Spirit—Our Father's testament—Spiritual ambition—Ann Cutler 269

No. XLIV.—To Mrs. E——. Disappointment—Our recent interview—Sad change—Fault-finding *versus* prayer—Ministers need encouragement—"Our minister is not popular"—Harmful effects of speaking evil of ministers—A false light—Confession—A stumbling block—"Touch not mine anointed"—A family regulation with respect to the reputation of ministers . . . 274

No. XLV.—To Mr. K——. Solicitude—A twenty years' seeker—The longer and the shorter way—Remarkable experience in the steam cars—A meeting established for the promotion of holiness—How holiness sustains in the hour of trial, exemplified—The difference between willingness and obedience—A quotation from Mr. Wesley 279

No. XLVI.—To Miss D——. A little child learning to walk—The Divine sympathy proportioned to our feebleness—"I will hold thy right hand"—Shrinkings from duty—"I have ordained you"—The weak made strong—"Worldly Christians" . . . 287

No. XLVII.—To Rev. Mr. H——. Specified wants—The inference—The great exchange—"Was God unfaithful?"—Mr. H——'s statement of his experience—A precise answer to a specific request—Confession delayed—Witnesses of perfect love needed in the ministry . . . . Page 292

No. XLVIII.—To Mr. C——. Impelled to activity by the Word—An enthusiastic doctrine—A nice point—Quietism—Abraham pleading for Sodom—Moses pleading for Israel—Christ in the person of his saints 298

No. XLIX.—To Mrs. ——. Led by a right way—Domestic cares—A mother's trials—Tests of grace should be welcome—Predictions—Trials—Triumphs—Mrs. Susannah Wesley—Daughters of Sarah—The Wesley Family—Influence of American republicanism on American wives—Quotation from Mrs. W——'s biography—Apology 302

No. L.—To Mrs. H——. Wandering thoughts—Satanic resistance—A strong testimony in the midst of temptation—Satan defied—God tempted by questionings—A life of faith—The cost counted—Unwavering reliance—Fruits of faith—A precious gem—Shortness of time—Sudden death contemplated . . . 308

—Obligations vary according to relationships—Abraham's unheard-of path of duty—Remarkable requisition—Satan's subtilties—Just where light meets us—Willing is not doing—The appearance of evil—A questionable practice cripples faith—Crucifixion of the flesh required—David's sacrifice—God will help you—An old habit broken 314

No. LII.—To the Rev. Mr. M——. Can persons who are sincerely pious be deceived?—Satan transforms himself—A visit from a fiend clothed in an angel garb imagined; he quotes Scripture—How Christ received such a one—Satan loves a shining mark—A sure method of finding him out—The Bible the only chart—Satan may answer petitions presented on wrong premises—Gracious assurances may be counterfeited 319

No. LIII.—To Mr. L——. Witness of holiness lost—Unholy class leaders responsible for lowness of piety in the membership—The faithfulness of God proved when the blessing was lost—A light may be extinguished—Gifts derived from God must be diffused—Necessity of coming back—Promises may not be appropriated until the conditions are met—In what a state of holiness consists 325

No. LIV.—To Mrs. J——. Responsibility of parents in regard to the salvation of their children—A memorable struggle—The Spirit's intercession—Prayer answered—Parents should resolve on the salvation of their children—Children under sentence of death—A child born of the Spirit—Young converts may be holy—An interesting disciple—Remarks of a minister . . . 331

No. LV.—To Rev. Mr. U——. Of the act of faith—Humiliating perceptions—Shrinkings from a profession of holiness—The direct path—A ceaseless sacrifice—The key which opens the door—What is the act of faith?—Terms of the covenant—Faith, not works, the ground of acceptance—The blessedness of purity—Why do some receive the blessing sooner than others who are equally sincere?—How example may hinder—How the blessing may be obtained—Tears of desire shed, yet a willingness to be holy not attained 339

FAITH AND ITS EFFECTS;

OR,

FRAGMENTS FROM MY PORTFOLIO.

No. I.—TO MR. M——.

Mr. M—— acknowledges himself unawakened—What is faith?—Interview with a Hicksite friend—Displeasure incurred—Doings and sayings at a class meeting—An unlikely subject of prayer presented—All things possible with God—Mrs. W.'s inquiry—The sinner condemned already—The culprit C——; his agony when under condemnation, the effect of his faith in man—Mr. M—— not a believer in the Bible as the word of God; otherwise not unawakened—Indescribable solicitude—Influential friends cannot save—Mr. M—— under condemnation—Why the word of God has not the same effect as a voice from heaven.

My Dear Mr. M——. You acknowledge yourself unawakened, but in this I think you are in part mistaken. In view of your inquiries after the way of life, I would hardly dare pronounce you wholly unawakened. You would not with so much sincerity desire instruction relative to that faith without which it is impossible to please God, unless you were in a degree aroused to an interest about your spiritual state.

By your inquiry, "What is faith?" I am reminded of an interesting incident in my religious history, which in all its bearings is to my mind signally illustrative of faith and its effects. As you have

Hicksite Friend.

been religiously trained, and are not unused to rehearsals of Christian experience, you will know how to appreciate such intermixtures of my own experience as will be helpful toward illustrating the subject.

Some time since I invited a Hicksite friend to accompany me to meeting. You know of Elias Hicks—of his rejection of the atonement, the only foundation of the Christian's hope, and also of his light estimate of the Scriptures, designating them as the *dead* letter, &c. So you will not be astonished when I say that I could not think of my friend as a follower of Christ. Knowing that she regarded herself as a professor of religion, and that any approach to her which failed to recognize her as such might wound her feelings, I knew not in what form of expression to give vent to my unutterable yearnings for her. At length, after a little suspense, I said,

"Mrs. ——, do you not sometimes feel that you would love to forsake all and follow Christ?"

She gave an evasive answer, and by her manner most clearly indicated that she was displeased. Finding her thus guarded by a religious *profession*, which, if touched, gave displeasure, I ceased to approach her on the subject of her salvation.

About ten months after, in admonishing the members of my class, I said, "Too many mistake the mark, by absorbing themselves in their own experience, whereas the design of God in redeeming us unto himself seems to be this:—That we give ourselves at *once* wholly and for ever away to his service, in order that we may be unto him a peculiar people, zealous of good works, not living to ourselves, as we should do were we ever absorbing ourselves in perplexities about our own experience. Who would not dismiss a servant that was ever saying, 'I have about as much as I can do to serve myself?'" &c. Several members resolved to come up to the point of entire consecration, that is, to serve Christ wholly: we then covenanted together to begin at once to *work for God*. I suggested to them to single out some individual, not the most likely, by way of being religiously influenced, but the most *unlikely*, and to interest themselves, even as for their own souls, in the experience of such, until we should meet again on the coming week.

Pursuant to the advice I had given, I began to think, Who shall I take to labor for so absorbingly during the week? when it was suggested, You had better inquire of God. I did so. To my astonishment, the individual referred to, with whom my former efforts had seemingly been so fruitless, was presented. For a moment, I turned away with dismay. My thoughts ran thus:—Were the most vile, reckless sinner, suggested, or even a *professed* infidel, I might in some way know how to approach

An Unlikely Case.

him with hope of success, but here is one whom I cannot meet with the Bible, for she regards it only as *secondary* authority, neither can I approach her as an acknowledged sinner, for she is wrapped in the cloak of a profession. An "unlikely" case indeed, my heart responded. But this current of thought was arrested by the chidings of the Spirit. The unbelieving lord of Samaria was brought to my remembrance, and I at once said, "Lord, I will not say if thou shouldst open windows in heaven, then might such a thing be, as that this person should be powerfully awakened to a sense of her condition as a sinner. But I will say, 'All things are possible with thee, and all things are possible to him that *believeth.*' Only teach me *how* to approach her, and, 'behold, here am I.'"

It was suggested in return, All you are at present required to do, is to keep her continually before God in prayer. I did so, and most strikingly did God take the work into his own hands. He did not send me to her, but he sent her to me. An account of our interview will answer your question.

With a countenance which bespoke docility such as I had never before witnessed in her, she entered my room one morning, and said,

"Mrs. P——, I have heard you speak of *faith*, and I should like to have you explain it to me."

In return I said,

"I am speaking to you, Mrs. W——, and you

| The Culprit C——. | Efforts of his Friends. |

believe me." She nodded assent. "God hath spoken, and the Bible is his word. Just as truly so, as though you heard him audibly speaking from heaven, in the voice of mighty thunderings, as from Mount Sinai. God hath said, 'The soul that sinneth, it shall die.'" Now, if the sinner should really *believe* God, he would see himself *already condemned*; not to mere temporal death, this were in comparison a light matter, but the condemnation passed upon the sinner extends to soul and body, to all eternity. You remember the culprit C——. He had violated the laws of his country, and in obedience to those laws the sentence of death was passed upon him by a fellow-man.

How awful were his feelings while lying under condemnation! How were the sympathies of the public enlisted in his behalf! How energetic and ceaseless the efforts of his friends for the removal of this condemnation! But what is all the untold agony occasioned by this sentence, compared with what the distress of the sinner would be, if he only had as much faith in the word of God as this culprit had in the word of his fellow-man! He would see himself lying under a sentence which might be executed, not two or three months hence, but at any moment, "in such an hour as he thinks not,"—a sentence which extends not only to the poor perishing body, but to the immortal spirit, which, after thousands on thousands of ages have past, will yet have not one day less to exist, where the worm dieth not, and the fire is not quenched.

I think, my dear Mr. M——, you may now apprehend the kind of faith which the unawakened sinner is required to exercise. You have been in the habit of thinking that you believe the word of God. Should I tell you that you but partially believe it, and that you are in part infidel in principle, you would with abhorrence start from the suggestion, and doubtless would think me unkind. But you say you are *unawakened.* Could you re-remain so, if you verily *believed* that the sentence of *eternal* death had already been passed upon you— a sentence which may be executed even before you lay this paper from your hand?

Other inquiries connected with the awakening of my Hicksite friend were equally interesting and profitable; but my mind at present is so concerned about your perishing condition, that I cannot consent to say more, until you assure me that you are indeed aroused to a conviction of the wrath that abideth upon the sinner. " God out of Christ is a consuming fire." *You* are out of Christ! Do you imagine that your condition may not be so awful, so hazardous, as the foregoing conclusions imply? Ah, my dear Mr. M——, the Bible is the book from which, on examination, you will find these conclusions have been legitimately drawn. You say you believe the Bible. How can you believe

Indescribable Solicitude.

it, and yet regard your condition as one of less peril than the Bible declares it to be?

And now, my dear friend, my feelings for you are those of indescribable solicitude. Shall I apologize for this inexpressible concern? No! As well might the friends of the poor culprit C—— have ceremoniously accosted him thus: "Pardon the interest manifested by us in endeavoring to free you from the sentence which has been passed upon you by the laws of your country; this sentence we know must inevitably and speedily be executed, only as faint hopes are left that the strength of our influence and most energetic efforts may *possibly* prevail." But you will remember that neither the respectability nor most energetic efforts of his friends prevailed in his behalf; they only seemed to increase public indignation. "One with such a training, such associations, &c., ought to have known better," was the response of the popular voice. Just so, I fear with you, dear Mr. M——. If the prayerful sympathies and energetic efforts of your deeply pious friends could have been instrumental in the removal of the awful condemnation which now rests upon you, long since would it have been removed. Will the fact of your advantages for religious improvement stand in mitigation, when at the last it shall be asked, why sentence should not be executed?

O my dear friend, though circumstances forbid

Bible the Voice of God.

my further pleading with you at this time, it relieves my oppressed heart to know that I may go to my closet, and plead with God for the continued influences of that Spirit, which, alas! you have so much grieved by your delays. With yet another word of admonition, which I hope you will now take to your closet, I must leave you for the present. You have said, "The time does not seem to have come for me to begin in earnest to seek the Lord." If God should speak audibly from heaven to you, saying, "*Now* is the accepted time; behold, *now* is the day of salvation:" "*To-day* if ye will hear my voice, harden not your heart"—would you not conclude that the time had indeed come for you to begin in earnest? What is the reason that the voice of God, as sounding through the Bible, has not the same effect which you imagine a voice pealing from the heavens would produce? Is it not because you do not in heart receive the *Bible* as the WORD OF GOD?

From what has been said, I think you now apprehend something more about "faith and its effects."

Yours, with most prayerful solicitude.

Mr. M—— inquires the Way.

No. II.—TO MR. M——.

Mr. M, inquires the way—Inquiries as to the effect of faith—Evidences of the inbeing of faith—Perilous condition acknowledged—Hardness of heart confessed and bemoaned—Heart not impenitent—Not required to save ourselves—Sinful to stay away from the Saviour—A letter to a sincere inquirer—Difficulties in the way of salvation—Repentance known by its fruit; a gift from God, and must be acknowledged.

To Mr. M——. It gives me much satisfaction, my dear friend, to be permitted to address you as one inquiring the way to life. In your letter of inquiry, the effect of your faith in God is indeed most evident.

Though you have not yet exercised that faith, through which the unpardoned sinner is justified, yet you must not yield to the suggestion, that you have *no* faith. Though small in its beginning as a grain of mustard seed, yet let me for your encouragement say, that clearer demonstration could not be asked than that which your inquiries present, of the existence and workings of faith in your heart. You say, "I see my perilous state as a sinner already condemned, but I do not *realize* my undone condition. I hear others cry out from disquietude of soul; yet with an unmoved heart, and with tearless eyes, I am myself brooding over my hardness and impenitence."

Now, my friend, would you be disposed to bemoan your condition thus, were it not that you believe God will verily execute the sentence which he hath pronounced upon you? Here then is the effect of faith thus far: now this is but the first step—the beginning of a life of faith—and if you do not go on you will surely perish. But there are other truths, which are in immediate connection with those which you have already believed. As you have now begun to believe God, O may you, without lingering, take the next step, which I will now endeavor to present to you.

Listen! Your Redeemer and your Saviour is now saying unto you, "Him that cometh unto me I will in nowise cast out." "But," say you, "have I not just been telling you of my hardness and impenitence, and can I expect the Saviour to receive me in such an emotionless condition?" You mistake, in speaking of your heart as impenitent. Impenitence implies absence of contrition, or sorrow for sin. If you are not sorry for sin, why do you so earnestly inquire the way to the Saviour? Why do you want salvation from sin? Is it not because you feel like saying,

"I hate the sins which made thee mourn?"

Then say no more that you are impenitent. It is indeed sinful to have a hard heart; but you are not required to save *yourself* from any of your sins. Christ alone can save you, and he now says, "Come unto me." Will you come now? or will

Sinful to stay from Christ.

you wait till you have made yourself worthy, by a longer continuance in groanings and lamentations?

Do you not perceive that you are by this course endeavoring to *save yourself* in part, *before* coming to Christ? O cease these vain endeavors! Now come to Jesus:

> "If you tarry till you're better,
> You will never come at all."

"Him that cometh unto me I will in nowise cast out." Will you not now comply with the condition, and come to the Saviour *just as you are?* He will not cast you out. The reasons you urge why you may be rejected, are the very reasons why you should come to the Saviour, and why he desires to save you. He came to save you from your sins; and is not this state of feeling, which you urge as a reason why you may not come just now to Christ, *sinful?* Can you be saved from this sin till you trust Christ to save you? It is *sinful* to stay away from the Saviour, and unless you intend to defer coming to him until you are yet more unworthy, you will come believingly now, assured that he will in nowise cast you out.

I have concluded to give you the reading of a letter which was addressed to one whose state of mind was very similar to your own; and may He who hath not said to the seed of Jacob, "Seek ye my face in vain," say to you speedily, "Lo, I am thy salvation."

| Letter. | Fruits of Repentance. |

TO A SINCERE INQUIRER.

MY DEAR FRIEND,—You asked me to remember you in prayer. I have indeed been pleading for you, and am fully assured of the willingness of God to bless you with a knowledge of forgiveness and acceptance. Yet I see difficulties in the way of your receiving the desire of your heart. Not that I do not believe you are most earnestly, and sincerely, seeking salvation; not that you are unwilling to give up the world, and its vanities, and desirous to take upon you the cross of Christ, and come out as a self-denying follower of the Lord Jesus; or that you are not truly *penitent*. These difficulties in the way of your salvation I believe are removed.

But I know you are longing to hear what difficulties I would suggest. Yet I cannot hope to do much good by stating them, unless you consent to promise before God, that wherein you may see your error, you will in the strength of Jesus exercise that holy violence which the kingdom of heaven suffereth, relative to the removal of these difficulties.

1st. You say you cannot feel that you have *repentance*, and you give this as one reason why you cannot *now* come to Christ. What does this turning away from the vanities of the world mean? What this resolute looking Zion-ward? This coming out as a seeker of salvation? &c. Does not

Repentance and its Fruits.

all this show *fruit* meet for repentance? Unless repentance were imparted, could you thus produce its fruits? You can no longer doubt, then, that you *have* repentance, without denying the work of the Spirit; for you could not have had this grace unless the Spirit had wrought it in your heart. Now, unless you acknowledge this to the praise of God, you will add to your former transgressions the sin of ingratitude.

You are called "to the acknowledgment of *every* good thing which is in you by Christ Jesus;" and, unless you are thankful for this gift, God may take away even that which you have. O! bow just now before him who is exalted to be a Prince and a Saviour, to give repentance unto Israel and remission of sin. Thank him that he has given you the gift of repentance, and, through grace, promise no longer to grieve the Spirit by denying that this work hath been wrought in you. Make confession before God of this your error, and then it is your duty to expect that forgiveness will at *once* follow confession. "If we confess our sins he is faithful and just to forgive," &c.

Next you say, "I see other convicted persons manifest much more feeling than myself." But this should not influence your conclusions relative to your state. Difference in constitutional temperament has much to do with the exhibition of the heart's internal movements. There are a diversity of operations, and it is not wise to measure yourself by others, or to mark out a way for God, as though he were to come to a standard which you have raised. Were it for the best, God could give you such a view of yourself out of Christ, as to sink your soul at once into eternal despair. In mercy to you, this view is withheld; but he gives you just such perceptions of your state as are appropriate to the end designed. That is, he gives you such perceptions of your condition as influence you to turn heartily away from the world and its vanities, to loathe sin in every form, and also to beget in you an ardent desire for salvation.

Shall I repeat what the Spirit hath often told you,—

> "All the fitness he requireth
> Is to feel your need of him."

But there are yet other difficulties. You say your heart is hard. Have you a right to expect other than a heart of stone, until you give yourself to the Saviour? He hath promised to take away the heart of stone, and give you a heart of flesh. But you prevent him from doing this for you, because you do not resign yourself to him. You do not imagine that the Saviour needs your help in fitting that heart for his reception. Then why longer withhold, as though you were acting on this principle. He says, "I will take away the heart of stone, and give you a heart of flesh." Do not let

A Tearless Conversion.

him say of you, "Ye will not come unto me that ye may have life."

I knew a person who for hours continued in lamentation, (though *without tears,*) crying out, "O my hard heart—my hard heart!" It was said to her, "Why not give that hard heart to the Saviour? He has promised to give you a new heart—a heart of flesh." Up to this moment, she, instead of looking unto Jesus, had been looking at *herself*— brooding over her hard heart. Consequently, instead of rising, she had been sinking lower, and yet lower, in despair. But she now said, "I will give this heart which will not break to Jesus." At once the Saviour, true to his promise, gave her a new spirit. He took away the stony heart, and gave her, indeed, a heart of flesh. And with tears of joy she now proclaimed his love. Will you not now "go and do likewise?"

As you do not expect that salvation will in any degree come from *within,* cease to look for any good thing from yourself. "Look unto *me* and be ye saved, all ye ends of the earth." Keep steadily looking unto Jesus; if you take your eye off from this one point of attraction you sink. You acknowledge yourself lost. Then you are precisely the character whom Jesus came to save: "For the Son of man came to seek and to save that which was *lost.*" Would you ever have set out to seek him, had he not first sought you? Yes, you are now the sought out of the Lord, and your precious Saviour will not upbraid you if you now rejoicingly sing,—

> "Jesus sought me when a stranger
> Wand'ring from the fold of God,
> He to rescue me from danger
> Interposed his precious blood."

Do I not hear you with gladness of heart saying, Saviour of sinners, thou art *my Saviour?* Yes! Hallelujah to Jesus! "Come and let us exalt his name together."

Your devoted friend.

No. III.—TO MR. M——.

Mr. M—— inquires whether the power to believe may not be withheld—The power to exercise faith never withheld from the truly sincere—Difficulty with one who had been seeking the Lord four years, and how removed—Man possesses the awful power of pronouncing his own blessings and curses—Five individuals converted the same day on which they were awakened—Difficulty with Mr. S.—Of one who thought it was too late.

To my Sin-sick Friend, Mr. M——. "But," you ask, "does not the Lord in his sovereignty at times withhold the power to exercise faith from the seeking soul?" And further, "How is it that some for weeks and months, with so much sincerity and earnestness, go about as mourners in Zion, while others, perhaps, only in a few hours go through the process of awakening and conversion?"

A Four Years' Seeker.

I do not think we have any Scripture ground for the supposition, that God ever withholds the power to exercise faith from the sincere inquirer. It is true that there may be difficulties in the way of exercising faith with some who desire salvation. I once knelt beside a mourner, and said,

"How long since you first began to seek the Lord?"

"Four years."

"Four years!" I exclaimed; "what! seeking the Lord four years, and say that you have not yet found him! Surely this must be a mistake. God hath said, 'And ye shall seek me and find me, *when* ye shall search for me with all your heart.' God cannot be unfaithful, and there must have been some mistake in your manner of seeking him."

I then began to inquire whether there had not been some reservation in her mind, relative to sacrificing all for Christ. "Perhaps," said I, "you may have had your eye upon some worldly minded professor, and thought, 'If I could get religion, and be or do like such a one, how gladly would I enjoy it.' Your mind may have been so enlightened as to see these things inconsistent with an entire surrender, but still you have persevered in endeavoring to bring God to your terms, instead of coming yourself to his."

She frankly acknowledged that this had indeed

Converted in Five Minutes.

been precisely her case. I assured her that she might just as well give up all hope at once of ever being saved, as to continue to seek God with these reservations.

Though you might go on years longer as a professed seeker, you would come no nearer the point. But there is no probability that the Spirit of the Lord would strive with you thus long. What a mercy that your Saviour, grieved and insulted by your offers of half-hearted service, has not ceased to tender you his grace, and left you to utter hardness and impenitence! But you may be now receiving the last urgings of the Spirit; yet let me tell you, if you will now make confession of your sin, in not being willing to give up all for Christ, and will come, renouncing yourself and sin, he will *now* receive you. She made the resolve that she would yield; and the more powerful influences of the Spirit were immediately given to help her infirmities; and in perhaps less than five minutes she was filled with the joys of salvation.

In like manner is the faithfulness of God to the seeker ever exhibited. Though not often so clearly perceivable to the eye of man, as in the case just stated, yet in the eye of Omniscience every case is undoubtedly equally marked. I cannot believe that there is any lingering on the part of God in fulfilling his promises to the seeking soul. When we come to him in the way of his

Five convicted and converted in a Day.

requirements, we are met with his blessing; when unwilling to comply with the conditions upon which salvation is offered, we are rejected. God is not man that he should change, neither is he a respecter of persons. With Israel on Mount Ebal, and on Mount Gerizim, we pronounce our own blessings and curses; for, alike with them, the course which we pursue will draw down just such results as God hath pronounced on the characters we sustain.

But God is love; and it is my desire to encourage you in the assurance, that there will be no delay on his part in meeting you on the ground of the promises. Within a few days I have seen this exemplified in the experience of five persons, in whose awakening and conversion I have been most deeply interested. Neither of the five, I have reason to believe, were really awakened until the day on which I addressed them personally relative to their danger out of Christ. On the same day on which they were convicted they were converted. I believe one had previously attended church occasionally, but the others were habitual neglecters of God's house and worship. They were convinced of the necessity of seeking God with all the heart, if they would find him; and of the uselessness of expecting to find him, unless they came to this decision. I placed this view of the subject prominently before them, when they first promised to seek the Lord. "If you knew

Successful Seeker.   Mr. S.

you were to die before twelve o'clock to-night, you would be very much in earnest, and feel that you had no time to lose," said I to one. "Yes," was the reply. I said, "You would not, in that case, seek God with *more* than all your heart, and unless you seek him just as earnestly now, you will not find; for he has not promised to be found of you until you seek him with all your heart." The same evening on which this conversation occurred she was converted.

I knew an individual who, for years, felt the need of salvation to a degree that imbittered all earthly enjoyments. He was not only willing to come out from the world, but gave most unequivocal demonstration of his unwillingness to be conformed to its Spirit. It was cause of much prayerful concern with me, that one so sincere, and in earnest, should so long remain in this state, and I sent for him to come and spend an evening with me, hoping that the hinderance might, in some way, be ascertained. Nothing seemed to throw light on the subject, until at the close of the interview I said, "Mr. S——, have you never felt it to be your duty to join the church?" With a decision of manner, which told just were his *will* was strongly fixed, he replied, "That I will never do, until I know I have religion; for there are backsliders enough in the church now."

"This," said I, "is just what I believe you will

have to do, *before* you get the witness of your acceptance. Yes, you will have to do it; and then trust the Lord to keep you. To do otherwise implies a distrustfulness which must be displeasing to God," I added.

The next night he came out under circumstances of unusual publicity, and said, "Such and such were my views, but now I have made up my mind to unite with the church." This was on Saturday night, and on Sunday morning, Jesus, the resurrection and the life, raised his soul to the most joyful assurance of renovated nature, even the enjoyment of a life of faith on the Son of God.

A variety of cases might be given, illustrative of the faithfulness of God, and of the effects resulting from faith and obedience; but I must close with the relation of one which, I hope, may be suited to your case:—

An individual, after various expedients in reading, fasting, and praying, at length came to the conclusion that it was too late for him to seek salvation; that he had sinned beyond the limits of mercy. While in heaviness he was thus reflecting upon his sins, the text, "My son, give me thine heart," came to his mind. Can it be, thought he, that God makes such a requisition of me as this? He knows what a heart I have, how hard, how polluted, how unfit for life or for death; and yet he says, "Give me thine heart." What can he

A Heart given to Christ.

want of my heart? He wants to make it good; to create it anew; to wash it in the blood of Jesus, and to make it a temple meet for the residence of his Spirit. "I dropped my flail," said he, (for he was in his barn at work,) "and prostrating myself upon the straw, I said, 'O Lord, if thou canst accept of such a heart as mine, here it is. I give myself to thee just as I am, a poor, vile sinner.'" Instantly he was saved; and so wonderful did the plan of salvation now appear to him—so new, so suited to the condition of the lost—that it seemed as if all his life had been spent in the dark; and he was affected to tears, that no one had ever thus explained to him the way of salvation.

Yours, in Christian love.

No. IV.—TO MR. M——.

Sincerity and earnestness not sufficient to insure salvation—An illustration of how faith is the gift of God—How to show fruit meet for repentance—An error in presenting petitions for awakened persons—Lad on the roof of a building; he is saved—The man near a cataract; not saved by doing *nothing*.

To my Friend Mr. M——.

> "By faith I lay my hand
> On that dear head of thine,
> While like the penitent I stand,
> And there confess my sin."

O that you might thus see all your sins on Jesus laid! It does seem to me, that all you now need

Appropriating Faith.   Illustration.

is the exercise of simple faith; that faith which appropriates the merits of your Saviour to your own case. If sincerity, earnestness, or a willingness to come out and confess Christ before men, were sufficient to bring you into the enjoyment of the favor of God, *without* appropriating faith, such had been your happiness now. Though, without these, your efforts to exercise faith would be unavailing; yet these, though most fully developed, would utterly fail in securing the object *without* faith. But you ask, "Is not faith the gift of God? and can I have it, unless it be given me from above?" No! "Every good and perfect gift cometh down from the Father of lights." But does not God give you the faith now required? He is not a hard Master. The command, "Believe on the Lord Jesus Christ, and thou shalt be saved," would be unreasonable, unless the power to be obedient were given with the command.

Imagine that you were embarrassed with pecuniary liabilities, hopelessly beyond your resources. Now suppose you have a friend of unbounded reputation and wealth. His name commands universal confidence; his uniform bearing toward you has been that of benevolence and love; he hears of your distress, and writes you word, "I have taken your liabilities upon myself. I knew of your inability to pay; I have therefore paid the debts contracted: and now I am not merely willing that you should reckon yourself free, but it is my pleasure that you should do so *now*. My name has already gone forth in promise to relieve *all* those alike distressed with yourself, who may apply to me, and the honor of my name requires that your acknowledgment of my faithfulness in fulfilling my word be at once made before the world."

I need not make the application; you cannot dishonor your Saviour more, than by doubting whether he will fulfill his promises. His name is FAITHFUL and TRUE. O how sinful must a distrustfulness, whether he will *now* fulfill his promises, appear in his sight, when he hath said, "Now is the accepted time; behold, *now* is the day of salvation. For all the promises of God in him are yea, and amen, unto the glory of God." The Saviour is now looking upon you with an eye of infinite love, longing to fulfill his promises to you; but he cannot bless you in your unbelief. It is inconsistent with the principles upon which the government of his kingdom is established; unbelief is a sin, and you must renounce it; for the Saviour came to save you from your sins, not *in* your sins.

The best way to show fruits meet for repentance, is to pursue a course directly opposed to that which is now lamented. I have known persons to mourn over the sin of unbelief most piteously for months, and even years, and yet not renounce it.

Error in Prayer.   A Fall.

Does this exhibit to the eye of God fruit meet for repentance? To the eye of man, this course may indicate repentance, and his petitions to God in behalf of the suppliant may be drawn from conclusions thus begotten. Thus it is that we not unfrequently hear petitions, framed in words which imply that the delay is on the part of God, as though the sinner were all ready for the reception of the blessing, and only waiting for God to become willing to bestow it. Approaching God thus in behalf of the awakened sinner, I conceive to be an error of great magnitude; its effect on the mind of that sinner is necessarily disastrous, inasmuch as it removes the cause of delay from himself, and casts it upon God: and how insulting is such a petition to that God who ever stands, with extended arms, calling upon the sinner, saying, "Come, for all things are now ready!"

I remember, my dear Mr. M——, once to have met an illustration of faith, which I think may be helpful to you. The relater gives it thus:—"I once saw a lad on the roof of a very high building, where several men were at work. He was gazing about with apparent unconcern, when suddenly his foot slipped, and he fell. In falling he caught by a rope, and hung suspended in mid air, where he could neither get up nor down, and where it was evident he could sustain himself but a short time. He perfectly knew his situation, and expected in a few minutes to be dashed on the rocks below. At this moment a kind and powerful man rushed out of the house, and, standing beneath him with extended arms, called out, 'Let go of the rope; I will receive you. I can do it. Let go of the rope, and I promise you shall escape unharmed.' The boy hesitated for a moment, and then, quitting his hold, dropped easily and safely into the arms of his deliverer." Here is an illustration of faith; here is a simple *act of faith.* The poor boy knew his danger; he saw his deliverer, and heard his voice. He *believed* in him—*trusted* him—and, letting go every other dependence and hope, he dropped into his arms.

Do you feel that you have done all you can? Let me take the language of another, and say, "Just stop *doing,* and begin to *trust Christ to do all for you,* and you are safe. A man is rowing a boat on a river, just above a dreadful cataract; the current begins to bear him downward; the spectators give him up for lost. 'He is gone,' they exclaim; but in another moment a rope is thrown toward the wretched man—it strikes the water near the boat: *now* how does the case stand? Do all the spectators call upon him to *row?* to *try harder* to reach the shore, when with every stroke of his arm the boat is evidently nearing the falls? O no! the eager and united cry is, 'Drop your oars! give up your desperate

Seize the Rope.

attempt! *take hold of the rope!*' But he chooses to row, and in a few moments he disappears, and perishes. All his hope lay, not in rowing, but in laying hold of the rope; for while he was rowing he could not grasp the rope. So the sinner's hope lies not in struggling to save himself, but in *ceasing* to struggle; for while he expects to accomplish the work of salvation himself, he will not look to Christ to do it for him."

But some abuse this doctrine of unmerited grace, and say, "If all I have to do is to cease from attempting to save myself, and to be willing that Christ should do the work of my salvation, why urge me to become a Christian, or to do *anything?* why not let me sit still, and wait till Christ shall come and pardon me?"

And what if the man in the boat had dropped his oars, and then folded his hands, and waited for the rope to save him? He might as well have died rowing as sitting still; and would as *certainly* have died in the latter as in the former case. But he must *grasp the rope.* So the sinner must *lay hold* of the *hope set before him;* not by waiting till he is better, but by first concluding that he never shall be any better in the way he is going on, and then *looking to Christ.* May I not believe that you are now trusting your all in the hands of your Saviour? I do not say that I hope you *were* doing it a few moments since, but that you are *now* doing it. O that this may be the work of every succeeding moment, until I hear from you.

> "Venture *on him*, venture freely,
>   Let no other trust intrude ;
> None but Jesus
>   Can do helpless sinners good."

Your much interested friend.

No. V.—TO MR. M——.

A matter of surprise with Mr. M——Reasons for delay wholly with the creature—Singular case of a lady where conviction followed conversion—Late Rev. S. M. relates a similar case—God ever meets us on the ground of his word—How to keep a new heart—Progression required—The Bible ; its excellence—The scheme of salvation conditional.

TO MY HAPPY BROTHER IN CHRIST, MR. M——.
"Why did I not before venture on the Saviour?" you exclaim. Just so hundreds have with amazement asked before you. But the unrenewed mind cannot form proper perceptions of the power of faith. In reference to every stage of experience it may be said, "If any man will do his will he shall know of the doctrine." In complying with the condition, "*Believe* on the Lord Jesus Christ, and thou shalt be saved," you have been brought to a blessed knowledge of the doctrine of justification by faith. Such effects must of necessity follow such acts of obedience and faith. I say must of *necessity* follow, because the principles by which the kingdom of grace is governed are unchangeable.

Christ always ready.   Remarkable Instance.

The reason why you were not before blessed, you now perceive, was not because God was unwilling to meet you, but wholly from delay on your part in complying with the conditions upon which you were to be received. The *moment* you complied with these, you found the Lord. Thus it is that the Saviour ever stands waiting to save the sinner, and from no cause will he ever withhold salvation one moment after the sinner has complied with the conditions of salvation.

I have known some instances peculiarly illustrative of the fact, that God ever meets us thus, on the ground of his word. One is that of a lady whose solidity of Christian character is well known and appreciated. For one whose birth had been in a Christian land, she was surprisingly ignorant of her accountability to God. She had not been in the habit of reading the Bible, nor attending public worship; neither had she mingled with pious associates; and thus all her early years were spent, having no hope, and without God in the world. She fell in the way of a devoted Christian, who told her of the claims of her Redeemer. Her heart seemed at once won, with a view of his great love in dying to save her, and she quickly renounced the world, and gave her heart to God. Immediately she was made happy in the enjoyment of the Saviour's love. This sudden transition astonished her friends, as they had heard so little about her

Painful View of Sin after Conversion.

convictions for sin. But the fruits of conversion were so evident, that the most skeptical could not doubt the reality of the change.

In relating her experience some time afterward, she informed me, that she in reality had few of those deeply distressing perceptions of guilt spoken of by many *previous* to her conversion. She felt, indeed, that she needed a Saviour, and was told that Jesus received sinners. In accordance with what was told her, she verily believed that all the Lord required of her was to give up herself, as a sinner, into his hands. She at once believed, and according to her faith it was done unto her. Afterward, as she became better able to bear the view, the guilt of her former life, with powerful convictions of the exceeding sinfulness of sin, and of the wrath awaiting her, had not the Saviour, "his own self, borne her sins in his own body on the tree," so appeared to her, that nature could scarce endure the sight. How this view endeared the Saviour to her, you can now form some conception.

Another case was related to me by that eminent minister, the late Rev. S. Merwin. It occurred where he was laboring, and I think under his own eye. The brothers of a certain young lady had been converted, but she as yet had resisted the influences of the Holy Spirit. One evening she accompanied some of her gay friends to a singing school, and on her return stopped at a meeting

A Young Lady suddenly converted.

then in progress. Several kneeling penitents were at the altar, and presently she saw one, newly entered upon the joys of salvation, praising the Lord. "The same happiness is for you, if you will only renounce your sins, and give your heart to the Lord," was suggested. She counted the cost, and then deliberately decided on the surrender. The first intimation which her pious brothers had of her change, was conveyed in her joyful acclamations of praise for salvation through Christ. They had only thought of her as of one resisting the Holy Spirit, and now to witness her sudden triumph filled them with amazement, and for a moment they thought, "Has our sister become a scoffer? has she in her opposition come to ridicule the subject of religion?" But they were soon undeceived, and by her life were assured that she was truly converted.

My object in giving these narrations is to exhibit the faithfulness of God in meeting us at any moment on the ground of his word; and if you had come to the act of surrender and reliance on Christ, the first moment you saw yourself to be a condemned sinner, pardon and acceptance would at once have followed. Only think how soon the jailer and his household were converted.

But now, my dear friend, you have only entered upon the heavenly way of a life of faith on the Son of God. In order to be sustained in this state, ceaseless reliance on your part, and the continued agency of the Holy Spirit, will be needful. You are required to work out your salvation with fear and trembling, for it is God that worketh in you. Though you are required to keep yourself in the love of God, yet you can be kept only through the power of the Holy Ghost, in answer to the ceaseless intercessions of Christ.

"You obtained a new heart, by giving it away to Jesus," said I to a very youthful disciple, "and the only way you can retain it is—" She caught the words from my lips, and said, "By giving it away, and giving it *all the time.*" It is only by this *act* of ceaseless surrender that you can retain the ground gained. But while you retain, you must not think you are not gaining, for you cannot abide in Christ without becoming hourly more assimilated to his likeness.

As you have received Christ Jesus the Lord, so *walk* in him. This, as you will observe, implies ceaseless progression—"*walk.*" Settle it in your mind now, at the commencement of your heavenward pilgrimage, that there is no standing still in religion. The Saviour says, "He that gathereth not with me, scattereth abroad; he that is not with me, is against me." Much that passes for religion is nothing more than an empty profession. Though you may often be much benefited in looking at the example of devoted Christians, for Christ says of such, "Ye are the light of the world," yet it is not safe to have your mind too much absorbed, even in the contemplation of this. At best they shine but in borrowed rays; and it is possible to have your vision so filled with these lesser lights, as to draw the attention from those believing views of Christ which are ever transforming. And then there is danger here. The best human beings are, at least, liable to err; and if your eye is on them, instead of being fixed on the Sun of righteousness, most disastrous consequences might ensue.

Good books are often very helpful; but let the Bible be the book of books with you. Try to have one ever about your person, so that at any moment you may turn to it, as the man of your counsel. In this way you may often save moments for communing with God, and with David hide his word in your heart, so that you may not offend. The eminent Wesley, when he had nearly finished his earthly pilgrimage, in speaking of the Bible, says, "O give me that book! At any price give me the book of God! I have it: here is knowledge enough for me. Let me be a man of one book." How unlike all other books is the Bible! Here the appetite never satiates. Here you may feast with increasing relish, until with unutterable longings the spirit cries, "Lord, evermore give me this bread."

But this is a subject on which I know not where to pause. My heart gathers inspiration whenever

Faith in the Bible. Justification.

I speak of the excellence of the Scriptures. Would that my lips or pen were empowered to give utterance to the sentiments which possess my soul, in reference to this wonderful book. O, it is in verity the WORD OF THE LORD! If the whole Christian world indeed believed this, then all perplexities about faith would be at an end. "God hath said it, and I believe it," would be the ready response from the lips of thousands, who are now groping their way in darkness, because of their unbelief; and the effect of faith would be most gloriously manifested in the lives of professors, by their entire renewal in the image of God.

I have much more that I wish to say on this, and on many other points. I greatly desire that you may know the full power of saving grace, and not stop short of any state made possible for you through the death and present intercession of the Saviour. Fix your aim here; to apprehend that for which you have been apprehended of Christ. You have attained a state of justification before God. This is indeed a state of great blessedness; and when, in view of higher attainments, I have heard it spoken of disparagingly, I have been often greatly pained. But in order that you retain this state, there are duties which come in, link after link, forming one continuous chain of gospel privilege. The entire scheme of our salvation is conditional. "Now, therefore, if ye will obey my

The Conditional Promise. Inconsistency.

voice indeed, and keep my covenant, then ye shall be a peculiar treasure unto me," meets us at every point. Would you remain in this glorious state of justification? the condition at once meets you: "If ye will obey my voice indeed," &c. I am sure you will much desire to know more of the conditions upon which you may remain in this state, and of the obedience required; but I must defer what I would say on this point till my next.   Yours as ever.

No. VI.—TO MR. M——.

Condemned and justified at the same moment impossible—Case of a young lady who mistook a state of condemnation for one of justification; she was not intentionally hypocritical—How the mistake may almost imperceptibly be made—Condition upon which a state of justification is retained—How soon may perfection be attained?

To my Friend in Jesus, Mr. M——. I said in my last, that there are conditions upon which a state of justification is retained. From the views of some persons, one might imagine that there is such a thing as being justified and condemned at the same moment. I once met a young professor, whose general lightness of character and frequent inadvertencies gave painful indication that she was a Christian only in name. I expostulated with her upon the hurtful tendency of a matter she had just been prosecuting. This, with her habitual

The Self-deceived Professor.

course as a professor, was too questionable to admit of an attempt at justification, and she did not propose it. But my heart was yearning over the wounded cause of God, and I really wished to remove the foundations of a profession which so dishonored it. In view of this, I asked whether she did not think her course at variance with the requirements of Scripture. She admitted it to be so. I said, "Do you feel, then, that you can stand justified before God, in view of such conduct?"

"Yes."

"Why, the word of God *condemns* you, and this you acknowledge; how then can you stand *justified?* You surely cannot be justified and condemned at the same time!"

Now, I would not say that this person was hypocritical in her profession; no, she was only following in a path which hundreds of young professors pursue. At the commencement of her Christian career, she had doubtless joyfully said, "There is therefore now no condemnation to them which are in Christ Jesus, who walk not after the flesh, but after the Spirit." But unmindful at length of the character to whom it is said, "There is no condemnation," she perhaps, almost at unawares, began to walk after the flesh. Now, by walking after the flesh you will readily perceive she ceased to sustain the character to which the apostle says "there is no condemnation," &c.; and a state of

| Wrong Name. | No standing still. |

justification was of course lost. These derelictions continued, would soon end in the loss of adoption also, and the soul be cast off as a withered branch.

I would not accuse such of intentional insincerity; but surely this mistake of calling a blessing by a name which the state of the individual professing it contradicts, tells disastrously upon the interests of experimental piety in the church.

You will now see that the condition upon which a state of justification is retained, is, that you "walk after the Spirit." Walking implies going forward. By your surrender to God the foundation of your Christian character has been laid. The principles of the doctrine of Christ have now been learned. But do you stop here? No! As well might the child who has learned his alphabet say, "I have finished my education." It is true that many, very many, do stop at this point; and here was the error of our young friend, whose erratic course told so grievously on the cause of God: and more or less so will be the course of all who do not steadily purpose to "leave the principles of the doctrine of Christ, and go on unto perfection."

Do not imagine that you can retain the state in which you now stand, unless you "*go on*." O may this, by the power of the Spirit, ever stand before your mind, in the form of living truth! Would that you could witness the fervor of my desires for you on this point. God *commands* it;

Progress urged. .Question.

and can I urge its importance more than by reminding you of this? You abhor a backslidden state, yet with all your abhorrence you will inevitably backslide, unless you obey the command, "Go on to perfection." There is no standing still in religion; and now, at the commencement of your Christian career, let me say, Deem that day *worse* than lost which is not in some way marked by religious progress.

But you may say, "If I keep going steadily on, how long before I may expect to arrive at a state of perfection? And if I arrive at this point, will not the summit of Christian attainment on earth be reached, and the command, '*Go on*,' no more be needed?

Your inquiries are indeed most important, and did opportunity now permit, I would at once endeavor to answer. The Lord willing, you shall soon hear from me again.

In yet more tender Christian regards, yours.

No End to Christian Progress.

No. VII.—TO MR. M——.

The summit of Christian attainment may never be reached in time—Paul not perfect in attainment—He professes perfection, and in what sense—A state of perfection requiring progression urged—Christian, not Adamic perfection, the object—It already belongs to man as soon as the conditions upon which it is offered are met.

My Dear Christian Brother,—In view of the admonition, "Go on unto perfection," you inquire, "Should I go steadily onward, how soon may I expect to arrive at a state of perfection? And when I arrive at this point, will not the summit of Christian attainment be reached?" Permit me to answer your latter inquiry first, and it will enable me more readily to meet the former.

The summit of Christian attainment reached? No, not in eternity itself, with receptive powers still growing, while immortality endures, will the attainments in love, knowledge, light, and power, which have been made possible through the atonement, be grasped. Paul says, "Not as though I had already attained, either were already perfect: but I follow after, if that I may apprehend that for which also I am apprehended of Christ Jesus. Brethren, I count not myself to have apprehended: but this one thing I do: forgetting those things which are behind, and reaching forth unto those things which are before, I press toward the mark for the prize of the high calling of God in Christ Jesus."

Christian Perfection requires Progress.

It is evident, as you perceive, on Scriptural authority, that a state of perfection which will not admit higher degrees is not to be expected. But that a *state* of *perfection* is attainable is most evident, and is proven upon the same premises. The apostle, in continuation of what I have already quoted, goes on to say, "Let us therefore, *as many as be perfect*, be thus minded;" including, as you observe, both himself and a part of those addressed as being in a state of perfection. I am the more particular in speaking of this subject, because it is not uncommon for those who oppose the doctrine of Christian perfection to refer to this passage.

Just the state of perfection aimed at in these passages (Phil. iii, 8–15) is what I would now urge upon you: that is, a state of perfection which *requires* progression—a state which could not even be retained, without obedience to "this one thing—forgetting those things which are behind and reaching forth unto those things which are before." The perfection to which your attention is urged, does not imply perfection in knowledge or light, but a state of supreme love to God, where all the powers of body and mind are perfectly subject to love's control, and ceaselessly offered up to God *through* Christ. This is Christian perfection; not angelic perfection, neither Adamic perfection, but Christian perfection. To think disparagingly of Christian perfection, implies, to my mind, thinking lightly of the atonement. To undervalue the efficacy of the blood of Christ to cleanse is sinful. And it would be sinful to doubt whether the offering presented to God, *through* Christ, is holy and acceptable.

What you need, in order to bring you into this state, is an offering up of yourself through this purifying medium. Now do you still ask, How *soon* may I expect to arrive at this state of perfection? Just so soon as you come believingly, and make the required sacrifice, it will be done unto you *according to your faith*. Christ came to take away our sin, to destroy the works of the devil, and to purge us from all iniquity. The purpose of man's redemption is not accomplished until he is presented perfect in Christ Jesus. When the Saviour said, "It is finished!" then this full salvation was wrought out for you. All that remains is for you to come complying with the conditions, and claim it. As it has been purchased for you, it is *already* yours. If you do not now receive it, the delay will not be on the part of God, but wholly with yourself.

Yours, truly.

Privilege of the Young Convert.

No. VIII.—TO MR. M——.

Inquiries relative to the length of time intervening between a state of justification and entire sanctification—Mr. Wesley's views on the subject—How backslidings might be less frequent—Another inquiry from my Hicksite friend—Unreasonable not to be holy—How unholy professors encourage skepticism—The case of a young man whose friends were professing Christians—Salvation from all sin may be obtained now—*How a housekeeper obtained it.*

DEAR BROTHER M——. "But do not persons generally wait months, and even years, after justification, before they are brought into this state of entire sanctification?" Mr. Wesley, in speaking on this subject, says, "This we know: but we know likewise, that God may, with man's good leave, 'cut short his work' in whatever degree he pleases, and do the work of many years in a moment. He does so in many instances."

If believers from the hour of their justification, with all the ardor of early unquenched love, should *walk after the Spirit,* how soon would they be ushered into the highway of holiness! Would that this duty were simplified, and urged with point and power upon young professors! Then would backslidings in heart and life be far less frequent. If the way is so plain, that wayfaring men, though fools, shall not err therein, young converts surely may be brought to understand it. The truth is, the difficulties are not attributable to the intricacies of the subject, but to the want of simplicity. We do not need great powers of mind to reach it, but deep humility of spirit to come down to it.

I am again reminded of my Hicksite friend. In continuation of the conversation referred to when I first wrote you, she asked another question, almost as important in bearing as her first inquiry, which will illustrate what I would say on the momentous subject before us. As soon as I had answered her first question, "What is faith?" she said, "I have heard you speak of sanctification, and now I should love to have you explain that to me." My mind for a moment recoiled, and I thought, She does not yet understand the principles of the doctrine of Christ, and now, how can she be brought to understand the deeper things of God? I looked to the Lord to help me to simplify the matter, and then said,

"If you should purchase an article from me, you would expect to have it whole, entire, just as you bought it, would you not?" "Yes."

"If I should keep back any part, it would be unreasonable, would it not?" "Yes."

"Well, the Bible says, 'Ye are not your own, ye are *bought* with a price, therefore glorify God in your body and spirit, which are God's.' Now, when we acknowledge the claim which God has upon us by the right of redemption, and set ourselves wholly apart for his service, he sets the seal

Infidelity promoted by Professors.

upon us which proclaims us his, and we are *sanctified*—set apart for God."

While I was thus endeavoring to simplify the subject to her, it was suggested, What will she think of those professors whom she has heard from week to week say, "I know I am not *wholly* given up to God: I know there are things in my heart contrary to his will?" Will she not regard the *unreasonableness* of such professors in a light which will make their course inexplicable to her, and will not their evident inconsistency destroy her confidence in all religious professions?

And just so inexplicable doubtless is a half-hearted service in the eye of the world. O the harm thus inflicted on the cause of Christ! It is only to the degree that God's people are a *peculiar* people, *zealous* of good works, that the interests of the Redeemer's kingdom can be promoted, through their instrumentality. I have but little doubt that unawakened persons often cherish the idea that professors do not *really* believe what they profess to believe. I had been urging the necessity of an immediate turning to the Lord, and setting forth the *danger* of a moment's delay, upon a sinner. I told him, as you will remember I once told you, that the sinner is condemned already, and that the sentence might be executed at any moment, with other truths equally startling. He was much moved, and seemed about to yield

Unfaithful Relatives.   Sympathy with Christ.

to the force of truth, when, as if he had just thought of something to strengthen his unbelief, he said, "I have a brother who is a minister, also sisters who are members of the church, and they have never talked to me in this way; and I am sure if they thought my state so dangerous as you say it is, they would tell me of it, for if I thought that either of them were in such a state, I could not rest day nor night without warning them." Satan succeeded apparently with this well-circumstanced temptation in rendering his mind yet more impervious to the awakening influences of the Spirit, and, for aught I know, he is already doomed to everlasting burnings. At whose hand may God require his blood?

Let me still urge you, dear brother M——, in view of the perishing around you—your relatives and friends—who are fast passing away, to seek with earnestness to know what it is to have a perfect sympathy with the heart of Christ, in that love which induced him to die for a lost world. "Let that mind be in you which was in Christ." *This is* HOLINESS. If you have that mind which was in your Saviour, it will induce you to feel and to act just as your Redeemer would have felt and acted were he placed in circumstances similar to your own. You need this conformity to the divine image at the present hour, if you would be clear of the blood of all men. Perhaps the next hour

A Wife and Mother amid her Cares.

may witness you in the society of some poor sinner who is already condemned, and unless you are all given up to Christ and have the power of his Spirit resting upon you, you may fail in giving him such a warning as his condition requires, and another hour may witness either his sentence executed, or you called to give an account of your stewardship.

But you may have this full salvation now—just now. Let me give you the experience of a friend who received it under less favorable circumstances than those by which you are surrounded. I had spent the evening previous in company with her and other friends, and had especially urged upon her the duty of a present and entire reliance on Christ for salvation. But though she had commenced the evening with large expectations, she was still unwilling to make the venture just now. The next morning she waked later than usual. She was both a mother and a housekeeper, and everything seemed to shape toward a commotion. Husband's breakfast must be ready at an early hour—children both crying at once—no help, &c. "How well it was that you did not get the blessing last night, for if you had, you surely would have lost it amid these commotions this morning," suggested the enemy. Before being aware of the current her thoughts were taking, she began to congratulate herself rather than otherwise that such had not been the case, when this current was suddenly arrested by the chidings of the Holy Spirit. "You need the blessing of holiness this morning to keep you; for if you yield to this influence which is now brought to bear upon you, you will *sin*—and will you *sin* against God?" The idea of thus knowingly grieving her Saviour was most abhorrent to her heart, and she said; "No, I will not sin; I will this moment trust in Christ to save me from sin!" That moment she trusted, and felt that she was *saved!* She continued to trust, moment after moment, and continued to feel the power of Christ to save, and greatly did her heart rejoice in the knowledge of salvation. How sweetly was her heart now assured of the words, "Thou wilt keep him in perfect peace whose mind is staid on thee, *because he trusteth in thee!*" "Domestic duties never seemed so light and pleasant as they did that morning," she remarked; and she longed to get where she might pour out her soul alone in praises to God for salvation from all sin.

And now, my beloved brother M——, may you speedily be brought to an experimental knowledge of Christ, as your "Redeemer from all sin." My heart is inexpressibly desirous that you should fix your aim on knowing the full power of saving grace. May you now, in the strength of the Lord Jehovah, deliberately purpose that every motive of earthly ambition shall know no higher point than that of standing perfect and complete in all the will of God. "*This is the will of God, even your sanctification.*" What can be more explicit, or more clearly exhibit your privilege, or more forcibly present your *duty*, than this declaration! Yes, it is not only your privilege, but your solemn duty, to be holy. God commands, "Be ye holy." Surely it is not optional with my dear brother whether he will obey this command or not. My great solicitude for your rapid progress in the divine life has induced me to gather from my portfolio several communications, which I hope may be helpful toward elucidating the principles, experience, and practice of holiness. Universal, symmetrical holiness, should be the first and absorbing aim of all who name the name of Christ; and that the papers which I now submit to your perusal may throw some light upon the heavenward way of my brother in Christ, shall be the prayer of

   Your ever devoted sister in the Lord.

No. IX.—TO MRS. W——.

An apology—Fruits of holiness partially enjoyed—Work of the Spirit, and tenderness of conscience at an early age—Regret—Difficulties—The cost counted—Activity required—Intense breathings—A wrong standard of experience—A darling object—Great things anticipated.

Dear Mrs. W——. You will be surprised on receiving a communication so long after my promise, and I question whether I shall be able to furnish such an apology as will render my long silence excusable. Scarcely a day passed, for a month or two after my return from B——, but my thoughts recurred to the pleasure I enjoyed in your society, and the remembrance of my unfulfilled promise as often caused me much uneasiness.

When I tell you the reason of my delay, I trust you will rather rejoice with me than accuse me of remissness. There has been a great improvement in my religious experience, as the result of a decision made at that time, that my undivided purpose should be the attainment of the witness of entire holiness.

Previous to this I had, in a degree, partaken of the fruits of holiness: my mind reverts to some sweet assurances that I was not without a measure of its blessed enjoyment while on the road to Baltimore and Washington. I am not sure but

Early Reminiscences.

that the love which casteth out all fear then had possession of my heart. Yes, I think I was then enabled to "reckon myself dead indeed unto sin, and alive unto God, through Jesus Christ our Lord." But I did not, at that time, habitually enjoy that abiding, lively consciousness of the seal of consecration on all my powers, which for some months past I have enjoyed in the rich plenitude of its blessedness.

O how I love to exhibit to the lovers of my adorable Jesus the riches of his grace, as manifested toward me, without money or price! I am sure, if you but knew how unworthy I have been, how disobedient in former time to the heavenly vision, you would wonder, even to amazement, at the riches of grace. That this may be the favorable result—yes, to furnish yourself and your beloved husband with new motives for adoring gratitude—I will proceed to present the more prominent portions of my experience in the things of God from my infancy; for from that early period I trace his hand leading me to himself.

My parents, prior to my being intrusted to them, were rather devotedly pious. I was therefore early instructed in experimental religion. Of the necessity of its affecting my life, and even in minute things inducing a change of conduct, I was in the morning of my existence aware. I shall never forget the intense anguish I suffered in

Scrupulousness.   Regeneration.

consequence of telling an untruth, when but about three and a half years old.

This extreme sensitiveness, as to moral and religious obligation, grew up with me; so much so, that I was sometimes smiled at for my well-intentioned scrupulousness, and at other times almost censured for carrying it to a troublesome excess. I then regarded refuge in God as the safe sanctuary for the recital of the little grievances incident to childhood. Thanks be to God that the maturer knowledge of later years has never erased the principles thus early cherished by the operation of the Holy Spirit, and pious parental solicitude.

Would that from these early drawings of the Father it had been my ceaseless endeavor to follow the Lord fully; how much more gloriously had I, ere this, been led on by the Spirit of holiness toward the attainment of that fullness of stature in Christ Jesus, for which my soul now eagerly waits! But Jesus forgives; yes, he forgives freely! Hallelujah to his excellent name!

But, to proceed. It has been my opinion, from the survey of subsequent experience, that I, from this early age, enjoyed a low measure of regenerating grace, though, for much of the time, not precisely conscious of my state before God. How often have I labored to bring myself into a state of extreme anguish before God, and wept because of the failure! imagining if I could only bring myself to feel the burden of sin upon my conscience, to the degree which I have heard others express, that I could then easily come to God, with the expectation of obtaining the witness of justification.

The state of my mind for years, as nearly as I can express it, was this:—I had rather a belief that I was a child of God; yet I had not enough of the spirit of adoption to cry with unwavering confidence, "Abba, Father." O how often did I feel a longing thirst for holiness, conscious that nothing less could supply my need! Yet this seemingly impassable barrier was ever present, to stay my onward progress, "You are not yet clear in justification." In the strength of faith I many times endeavored to surmount this difficulty, by looking at the reasonableness of the requirement of holiness, believing that Christ had purchased full salvation for me, and as it was already my purchased inheritance, the sooner I entered into the enjoyment of it, the more I should glorify the Purchaser, by being made a witness of his power to save unto the uttermost. And thus at times my faith became almost victorious; and doubtless would soon have triumphed, had I only held fast the beginning of my confidence steadfast unto the end; yet my proneness to reason, and also the unwise propensity I had of measuring my experience by what I imagined the experience of others,

Little Progress.   A Resolve.   Activity required.

gave the enemy advantage over me; so, as frequently as I arose in the majesty of faith to go forward, he threw me again on my former ground.

Thus I continued to rise and fall, and consequently made but little progress in the way to heaven, until the early part of last June, when, in the strength of Omnipotence, I resolutely determined that I would set myself apart wholly for God, fully purposed that my ceaseless aim should thenceforth be the entire devotion of all my powers to the service of my Redeemer. This, through grace, I then more deliberately decided upon than at any former period. I calmly counted the cost, which I felt would be the surrender of my own will in all things. I then took, as the motto for my future guidance, and the sole principle of every subsequent effort, *entire devotion of my heart and life to God.* To this one object, I resolved that every earthly consideration should be subservient, fully purposed that all ordinary pursuits should cease to be absorbing, till the witness was obtained, that the offering was accepted and sealed.

You are aware that I have been accustomed to devote a portion of my time to writing, but I now felt that I could proceed no further in any ordinary pursuit. I apprehended in yet clearer light, that God required activity in his service, and an intense desire was imparted to glorify his name;

but such a deep, piercing sense of my helplessness prevailed, that it seemed as though I could not go forward until endued with power from on high. Yet, notwithstanding this, hope gathered strength, while the whisperings of the Spirit seemed to say, "Stand still and see the salvation of the Lord." Yet these convictions were not accompanied with those high-wrought feelings, or that distress of spirit, which I had heard some speak of, as given preparatory to receiving purity, and which I had thought indispensable; few, perhaps, may more emphatically say, that they were led by a way they knew not.

From the time I made the resolve to be wholly devoted to the service of Christ, I began to feel momentarily that I was being built up and established in grace: humility, faith, and love, and all the fruits of the Spirit, seemed hourly maturing: such was the ardor of my spirit, and the living intensity of its fervor, that in the night season, though my body partook of repose sufficient for the refreshment of nature, my spirit seemed continually awake in communings with God, and in breathings after his fullness.

Perhaps I should have said, that, previous to these exercises, I had resolved on taking the word of God, and simply trying myself by its tests of a new creature, determined to abide by its decisions, without regard to my particular emotions; assured that there is no positive standard for *feeling*, in the Scriptures. Yet, upon reviewing my slow progress, I cannot but regard the fault of taking the feelings and experience of others as a standard for my own, in place of going to the word of the Lord, as having been my greatest hinderance. I now took this portion of divine truth: "As many as are led by the Spirit of God, they are the sons of God." I soon found, by the light of the Spirit, that I had conclusive evidence of my adoption. As I had resolved that I would abide by the decisions of Scripture, the Holy Spirit did not leave himself without a witness in my heart. Quietness and assurance now took possession of my breast, and an undisturbed resting on the promises became my heritage.

After this resolve on entire devotion of heart and life to God, my breathings for divine conformity became more satisfactory. The appeal to my understanding seemed to say, "God is all in all;" yet my heart did not fully attest the witness. One exercise which I then commenced, and have since continued with increasing benefit, I will mention:—It was that of making *daily*, in form and in the most solemn manner, a dedication of all the powers of body and soul, time, talents, and influence, to God.

Thus I continued to enjoy increasing happiness in God, but not yet perfectly satisfied as to the

> A Beloved Object. Surrender contemplated.

witness—the indubitable seal of consecration. I was kept in constant expectation of the blessing.

July 26. On the morning of this day, while with most grateful emotions remembering the way by which my heavenly Father had led me, my thoughts rested more especially upon the beloved one whom God had given to be the partner of my life. How truly a gift from God, and how essentially connected with my spiritual, as also my temporal happiness, is this one dear object! I exclaimed.

Scarcely had these suggestions passed, when with keenness these inquiries were suggested: "Have you not professedly given up all for Christ? If he who now so truly absorbs your affections were required, would you not shrink from the demand?" I need not say that this one dear object, though often in name surrendered, was not in reality given up. My precious little ones, whom God had taken to himself, were then brought to my recollection, as if to admonish me relative to making the sacrifice. I thought how fondly I had idolized them. He who had said, "I the Lord your God am a jealous God," saw the idolatry of my heart, and took them to himself. The remembrance of how decidedly I had, by these repeated bereavements, been assured that He whose right it is to reign, would be the sole sovereign of my heart, assisted me in the resolve, that neither should this, the yet dearer object, be withheld.

Difficulties surmounted.   Great Expectations.

The remainder of the day, until toward evening, was unexpectedly spent from home. The evening I had resolved to spend in supplication. So intense was my desire for the seal of the Spirit, that I made up my mind I would not cease to plead until it were given. Thoughts were presented as to risk of health, &c.; but my spirit surmounted every discouraging insinuation. Thus fixed in purpose, I, in the firmness of faith, entered as a suppliant into the presence of the Lord. As if preparatory to a long exercise, I thought, Let me begin just right; and though I have heretofore entered into covenant with God, let me now particularize, and enter into an *everlasting* covenant, which shall in all things be well ordered and sure. I imagined some extraordinary exercise, such as an unusual struggle, or a desperate venture of faith, &c., preparatory to the realization of my desire, saying in my heart, though hardly aware of it, that some great thing must surely be wrought. But how God works in order to hide pride from man, I will endeavor to show you in my next.

Yours in the bonds of love.

Eternal Obligation.   Retrospection.

No. X.—TO MRS. W——.

A sacrifice contemplated—The surrender is made—The seal of consecration enstamped—Apprehends a state of holiness—Exults in the knowledge of the sanctification of body, soul, and spirit—Scruples removed—Christ all in all.

My Dear Mrs. W——. I left you in my last endeavoring to lay hold on the terms of the covenant,—fixed in purpose,—surrendering myself in the bonds of an everlasting obligation to God.

I began to particularize. The thoughts and exercises of the morning occurred again with yet greater power. Can God be about to take from me this one dear object, for which life is principally desirable? thought I. Looking into the future, I said, "What a blank!" Never before had I realized, that the very fibres of my existence were so closely interwoven with his. My impression was, that the Lord was about to take my precious husband from me. The inquiry with me was, whether it were possible that my heavenly Father could require me to make the surrender, when he had authorized my love, by making it my duty to be of one heart and soul with him. But grace interposed; and from more mature consideration, I was led to regard it as extraordinary condescension in God thus to apprise me of his designs, by way of preparing my heart for the surrender.

With Abraham I said, "I have lifted my hand

Obligations not apprehended.   Set apart.

to the Lord." In word, I had again and again made the sacrifice before, and said, "My husband and child I surrender to thee." I had not been insincere, but I now saw that I had not in fact done that which, in word, had often been named. Far, indeed, had I been from realizing the depth of obligation which, in word, I had taken upon myself.

Truth in the inward part I now in verity apprehended as God's requirement. Grace triumphed. In full view of the nature of the sacrifice, I said,

"Take life or friends away."

I could just as readily have said, "Take *life*," as I could have said, "Take friends;" for that which was just as dear, if not dearer, than life, had been required. And when I said, "Take him who is the supreme object of my earthly affections," I, from that moment, felt that I was fully set apart for God, and began to say, "Every tie that has bound me to earth is severed." I could now as easily have doubted of my existence as to have doubted that God was the supreme object of my affections. The language of my heart, and, as far as memory serves, the expressions of my lips, were, I live but to glorify thee. Let my spirit from henceforth ceaselessly return to the God that gave it. Let this body be actuated by the Spirit, as an instrument in thy hand for the performance of thy pleasure in all things. I am thine —wholly thine. Thou dost now reign in my heart

Holiness.   Sanctification.   Purity.

unrivaled. Glory! Glory be to the Father, Son, and Holy Ghost, for ever!

While thus glorying in being enabled to feel and know that I was now altogether the Lord's, the question, accompanied with light, power, and unquestionable assurance, came to my mind, "What is this but the state of holiness which you have so long been seeking?" It was enough! I now felt that the seal of consecration had in verity been set. God, by the testimony of his Spirit, had proclaimed me wholly his! I said, and also felt, in such a peculiar sense as my spirit still most delightfully appreciates, "Henceforth I am not of earth; the prince of this world, though he may come, yet hath nothing in me. The Lord, my Redeemer, hath raised up a standard against him; *I am set apart for ever for thy service!*"

While thus exulting, the voice of the Spirit again appealingly applied to my understanding, "Is not this sanctification?" I could no longer hesitate; reason as well as grace forbade; and I rejoiced in the assurance that I was wholly sanctified—throughout *body*, *soul*, and *spirit*.

O with what triumph did my soul expatiate on the infinitude of the atonement! I saw its unbounded efficacy, as sufficient to cleanse a world of sinners, and present them faultless before the throne. I felt that I was enabled to plunge, and lose myself, in this ocean of purity—yes,

Language inadequate.   Former Scruples.

"Plunged in the Godhead's deepest sea,
And lost in love's immensity."

It was enough! My spirit returned consciously to its Source, and rested in the embrace of God. From my inmost soul I said, "Lord, it is enough!" I pause at the exclamation; for I hesitate what language to use, or what expression to make of my views of the condescension of my covenant-keeping God, relative to this eventful period of my Christian history. Ah! I have no doubt but, even after innumerable ages of eternity have past, the amazing condescension thus manifested for the establishment of one so fearful and unbelieving, will be by me exultingly rehearsed to a listening multitude of rejoicing angels, and cause a renewed burst of holy triumph from the adoring throng.

Every shade of objection, or thought of scruple, was thus by Omnipotence himself rebuked, or rather utterly silenced. What I mean by scruples should be mentioned. It is this:—Though I have ever been a firm believer in the doctrine of Christian holiness, embracing the entire sanctification of body, soul, and spirit, as taught from the Scriptures by the apostolic Wesleys, and their cotemporaries; yet the terms made use of, in speaking of this attainment, were objectionable to my mind, in a manner which I cannot now take time to explain. Though from early life I had felt that I needed just the blessing comprehended, yet the terms made use of I seldom used. Now there seemed such a glorious propriety in the words "HOLINESS," "SANCTIFICATION," that I thought nothing less than infinite Wisdom could have devised words so infinitely proper.

What more reasonable, thought I, now that I have been enabled through grace to resolve on being wholly the Lord's, than that he should set the seal which proclaims me his; and still further, now that I have set myself apart exclusively for his service, that he should take cognizance of the act, and by the seal of the Spirit ratify the engagement? So clear was the work, and so apart from anything like extravagance in feeling or otherwise, that though I had fixed my calculations on the performance of some great thing, such as an amazing struggle—a desperate venture of faith—I was now ready to exclaim, "How simple and rational! and how precisely as might have been expected as the result of such exercises. It is all here; I, through the Spirit's influence, have given all for Christ, and now he hath revealed himself, and given himself to me, and become my all in ALL.

Your sister in Christ.

A Blissful Hour. A Holy Compact.

No. XI—TO MRS. W——.

The bliss of dwelling in God—Blessings are received for the good of others—Confession contemplated—What had been a hinderance for years—Hearty submission to the order of God.

To my Sister in the Lord, Mrs. W——. I could almost wish that the barrier preventing thought from mingling identically with thought, might for this once be passed. It is thus only permission might be gained to lay open to you fully the deep exercises of that devoted hour to which I referred in my last. O that blissful hour! when the spirit, redeemed by the blood of the covenant, was permitted to pass through the veil of outward things, and return to its Source, with all its tide of affections. Nothing but the veil of mortality, which now seemed almost drawn aside, appeared to prevent the enraptured, blood-washed spirit, coming into the full blaze of the presence of the eternal Trinity.

Such was my sense of dwelling in God, and being surrounded by his presence and glory, that it seemed as if my spirit mingled in worship with the heavenly company. The exercises through which I passed I regarded as nothing less than a holy compact, entered into between the Triune God and the spirit which came forth from him; and as such have I ever since felt the power and weight of the engagement.

Cost counted.   Confession.   Inquiry.

Not as the least of the privileges of this period do I regard that of being permitted to count the cost so fully. I foresaw, that, if I would perfect holiness in the fear of the Lord, I must not lean to my own understanding, or exercise independently my own will. Also, that the blessing I had received was not imparted for my own enjoyment exclusively; but that, in accordance with the requirement of Him, who, by the offering up of himself, made this great salvation possible for me, I had been constituted a *witness* of it, for the good of others.

I was convinced that for years I had been hindered from rising in holiness, by a neglect to comply with the order of God, implied in the passage, "With the heart man believeth unto righteousness, and with the mouth confession is made unto salvation;" and though the deep quiet of my soul seemed to present a natural obstacle to anything like personal publicity, yet I was inspired with the resolve that, through grace, Satan should never again triumph over me in this matter.

The requisition seemed to be (whether temptation, or otherwise, time must determine) to the acknowledgment of what God had done for me, before hundreds and thousands. "Can you, will you, do it?" was the inquiry proposed. "Yes, Lord Jesus, even before an assembled universe, if this be thy will," was the response of my now perfectly subdued heart. Now, though I well know that this blessing is the gift of God, through our Lord Jesus Christ; yet I fully believe, if I had not yielded to these convictions relative to confession, I could not have retained it.

I then felt, and time continues to confirm the conviction, that if I should cease to comply with the terms implied in being *set apart* for God, as a vessel dedicated to holy-service, it would be at the forfeiture of sanctification itself. Yet need I state conclusions so evidently inferable from such premises? Here the distinct idea of *symmetrical holiness* first impressed me.

By symmetrical holiness I mean that result of entire devotion to God, which is achieved in the *perfect consistency and agreement between the various elements of the character possessing it*. Never in heart-felt realization did I before so apprehend the great goodness of God in issuing to polluted mortals the command, "BE YE HOLY," and for such a reason, "For I the Lord your God am holy." O, well may angels desire to look into such a scheme!

Yours, in the fellowship of the gospel.

A Firm Resolve.   Eventful Evening.

No. XII.—TO MRS. W——.

The adversary foiled—Unbroken quiet—Tempted in a dream—Sweet repose—Encouragement given during sleep—Peace, the heritage of the believer.

To my Dear Mrs. W——. With my natural propensity to reason, it was suggested that it would require a miracle of grace to sustain me in this state of salvation. The example of those who were apparently possessed of much more spiritual firmness, and yet had failed in retaining it, was presented to weaken my faith; especially the experience of the sainted Fletcher, who, at three or four different periods, let go his confidence, was presented to induce despair. But the adversary was foiled. In the strength of Omnipotence I was enabled to count the cost of living a life of *faith*, and firmly did I resolve rather to die than to doubt. I gained beyond calculation, by the determination that I would not *reason* with the enemy; assured if I ventured even to parley, as in the case of the first transgression, his suggestions would soon assume the appearance of plausibility.

O can I ever, my dear sister W——, cease to retain in lively remembrance this eventful evening! I began it, intending to devote it in prayerful waiting before God. I was prevented from continuing long, by some friends calling in; but the deep quiet of my spirit was not in the least dis-

Manifestation expected.

turbed by the visitors. After they had retired, I spoke of the sweet rest upon which my soul had entered to my dear sister Sarah, and then went to my chamber.

Previous to retiring to sleep, my reflections ran thus:—As I have not been favored with extraordinary emotion, such as I have heard many express, may I not expect something especially confirming during the night? I had been enjoying sweet and hallowing communion with God during the night season for some time previous to this, and now, thought I, may I not expect some extraordinary manifestation during these hours of repose? Whether this should be given, or otherwise, I felt that I was resting consciously in the arms of everlasting love; and the breathings of my passive spirit were, Lord, it is enough! thou art my soul-satisfying portion! The assurance had been imparted, that just the portion of ecstasy best fitted to enable me to glorify God would be given. Already unutterable peace, fresh from the throne, was flowing into my soul, and thus I resigned myself to repose.

But I was made painfully aware that I was not yet out of the reach of the enemy, even while asleep. After the above reflections, imagine my surprise on awaking in a frightful dream. Yes, Satan himself, transformed into an angel of light, was permitted to assault me. But the wrath of

Frightful Dream.

our enemy may be made to praise the Lord. Thus it was now. I think the narration calculated to be useful, and, therefore, will give it in part.

I imagined myself standing in the back parlor. All the circumstances of the evening, embracing the precious experience I had gained, were still vividly before me. Presently I was aroused by a loud knock at the door. Knowing that all about the house had, by the lateness of the hour, been quieted, and all the inlets secured, I was assured that something was wrong: but remembering that I was already in the power of the intruder, and resistance in vain, I, with firmness, said, "Come in;" when, lo! a personage, altogether unlike any I had before conceived of, entered. Added to a countenance fiendish in the extreme, was a costume of the Highland order, with a covering of thin white, and black underneath; the black, in many places, projecting below the white. He harshly demanded, "Is the doctor in?" "He is in the front parlor, on the sofa," I replied. As he passed me, I ran and screamed for assistance, and was awakened by the effort. Quick as thought the suggestion came, "Where is the expected manifestation? Is not this enough to call in question the exercises of the evening?" I remembered how sweet had been my communion for several preceding nights, and now to be thus assaulted by the fiend of darkness was, for a moment,

| Trial. | Victory. | An Angel. |

a trial. But, blessed be the Lord my strength, I was kept by the Angel of the covenant from yielding to the temptation. Yet there was so much seeming reality in the assault, that my nervous system suffered, much the same as though it had been an actual occurrence; but it was thus far only that the adversary was permitted to exert his power. The tranquillity of my spirit was not disturbed. All was a silent heaven of love. Soon I again sunk sweetly to repose, as under the shadow of the Almighty.

In about an hour and a half after this I was again aroused by these words: "Behold, I, an angel, beseech you that ye walk worthy the vocation wherewith ye are called." An angel? an angel? inquired I, as if conscious of its not being the exact phraseology of Scripture. With the exclamation I again awoke, filled with glory and with God, sweetly assured that God had sent his angel to strengthen me. I arose, and returned thanks to God. Soon after this, my beloved husband came in, who had been absent on professional business since quite early the preceding evening, and was, therefore, unapprised of the glorious assurance of hope I had received.

I told him how the Lord had blessed me. Of the assault from Satan, and how the Lord had just sent his angel to strengthen me. He seemed overjoyed, and regarded the condescension of God as so surprisingly glorious, that I wondered at him, for I felt it was only what might have been expected. Through the power of the Spirit I had first endured temptation, and then that a ministering spirit should be permitted to visit a fellow-heir of glory, appeared altogether natural; for my mind had become so spiritualized, that I seemed to apprehend, in most happy realization, that I had, through the blood of sprinkling, come not only to Jesus, the Mediator of the new covenant, but even "unto Mount Sion, and unto the city of the living God, the heavenly Jerusalem, and to an innumerable company of angels."

Again my sheet admonishes me that I must close; but I shall take an early opportunity to tell you how I have since been borne onward by the might of the Spirit. I find a firm, abiding peace, the heritage of the believer after having entered the rest of perfect love. I daily feel that God requires I should be holy, in order that I may be more useful, and, consequently, more happy. I am ever enabled to endure, *as seeing* the Invisible. Having entered through the blood of the everlasting covenant into the holiest, I realize daily that I cast anchor deeper within the veil.

Yours, in the blessing of perfect love.

Temptation.   Resolve.   Effects.

No. XIII.—TO MRS. W——.

Temptation relative to retaining the blessing—Mental conflict—Peace—Confession—Desires to know the precise foundation of faith—A statement of the way in which prayer was answered—The consequences of turning out of the way apprehended.

To my Dear Sister, Mrs. W——. I am happy to avail myself of an opportunity which offers to continue the recital of the way by which the Lord hath brought me thus far on my Christian pilgrimage.

You may remember the temptation that I mentioned before relative to the improbability of my retaining the blessing, and the resolve which I made thereupon, that I would sooner die than relinquish my claim. I have since felt that this resolution was entirely of the Spirit's influence; and as often as my mind has referred to it, it has been cause of intense gratitude to God. Had it not been for this decision the enemy might have triumphed over me in many of the struggles to which my faith has since been subjected.

I felt the binding nature of the obligation to profess the blessing, yet whenever opportunity offered, there seemed to be an increased effort on the part of the adversary to darken my evidence. Though he could not induce me to surrender, his continued suggestion was, that I believed because

Intense Struggle. Victory.

I would believe. In answer to this, in the resoluteness of faith, I replied,

> "Be it I myself deceive,
> Yet I must, I *will* believe."

I had said, I will die in the conflict rather than unloose my grasp. On the third day after I received the blessing, the mental conflict was so great, under the power of temptation, as to have reached apparently my utmost power of endurance. I had no sensible communication whatever, and nothing but the shield of faith to defend me. The contest lasted, I think, more than an hour, during which my physical nature was so affected by the struggles of my spirit, that my whole frame was in feverish excitement. The conflict continued till I was both physically and mentally prostrated, and then, on resting my cause wholly with Christ, I proved the truth of the words, "I will subdue all thine enemies."

It was night, and on resigning myself thus, wearied nature sunk to repose. The next morning I awoke at an early hour, with peace reigning in all my borders, and with a soul unutterably filled with God.

Still greater confirmation followed this severe conflict. Much of the time my mind was kept calmly staid upon God, exulting in the blessedness of the rest upon which I had entered. On the afternoon of the sixth day (it being Tuesday,

Wrestling.   A Reason sought.

an opportunity of which many witnesses of full salvation avail themselves at our house, to bear testimony) I felt it my duty to declare explicitly the salvation wrought out for me, when I was again most powerfully assailed with the temptation, that I believed merely because I would believe. During the evening I wrestled importunately with God that these distressing temptations might cease, and that I might have clear, enlightened views of the *precise* ground upon which I obtained, and might retain, this blessing.

In the simplicity of my heart I expressed my desires as nearly as I can remember thus: "Let me have the blessing in some such tangible form, that the enemy may never be successful in the insinuation, that I believe merely because I will believe, without a reasonable foundation for my faith to rest upon." What I wanted was a certain knowledge, which would always be available, by which I might be enabled at any moment to come at the precise ground of my belief.

My prayer was answered; and such clear views were given in answer to my petition, that the adversary was completely vanquished. The Holy Spirit took of the things of God and revealed them unto me, by opening to my understanding Rom. xii, 1: "I beseech you, brethren, by the mercies of God that ye present your bodies a living sacrifice, holy, acceptable unto God, which is your reasonable service." Abiding views by which I have ever since been enabled to give a reason of the hope within me, were then imparted.

I saw that nothing less than the omnipotence of grace could have enabled me thus to present my whole being to God. That the power to do so was of itself a miracle. That while I was thus empowered to present every faculty of soul and body a *living*, or, as Dr. Clarke says, a *continual*, sacrifice, it was an express declaration—a truth to be *believed*, and therefore not to be doubted without sin, that the blood of Jesus *cleanseth* the offering thus presented from all unrighteousness.

This, I was given to see, was in verity placing all upon that altar which sanctifieth the gift. So long as my heart assured me that I offered all, I saw it was not only my privilege, but my solemn *duty*, to believe that the blood of Jesus *cleanseth*, at the present and each succeeding moment, so long as the offering be presented. Thus I learned the imperative necessity of living by the moment. I learned, that in order to maintain a constant witness of present purification, the sacrifice to God must be ceaselessly made. Should I discontinue the entire abandonment of every power and faculty to God, by shrinking from some duty because the flesh is not willing, it would be at the forfeiture of a state of holiness.

A direct path, marked with light, hath from this

period been before me. I see the inevitable consequence of turning either to the right hand or to the left. I realize that holiness to the Lord consists in being set apart for his service—not doing my own will, or leaning to my own understanding. But, in acting upon these principles, I am wholly the Lord's: not an hour of my future existence is at my own disposal: I have willed myself over to God, and made an absolute surrender of time, talents, and influence, to his reasonable service: by the power of his Spirit he hath enstamped the seal, which proclaims me his: henceforth it is not for me to confer with flesh and blood; the warfare upon which I have entered is not at my own charge: God requires that I should be holy, in order that I may be more useful, and consequently more happy.

In my next I will endeavor to tell you something more of my establishment in these blessed principles. In the mean time, praying that you and I, with all the household of God, may be rooted, grounded, and built up, in our most holy faith. I remain,

Yours, in the love and faith of the gospel.

Advantages of Personal Holiness.

No. XIV.—TO MRS. W——.

Heaven begun below—Holiness the believer's strength—"If I get it I cannot keep it"—Remark of Dr. B—— Mysticism—Consecration a simple act—Holiness maintained by constant faith—The Scriptures a medium of communion with God—The way of the cross—A new existence—The command, "Be ye holy"—Effect on the world of universal holiness in the church.

DEAR MRS. W——. You will remember the promise in my last, relative to the continuance of my narrative. Through grace I can say my heart is daily becoming more rooted and grounded in those blessed truths. My experience continually attests the truth of the assertion, that the life of the believer is a heaven below. The divine tranquillity; the deepened communion with the Father, Son, and Holy Spirit; and the accompanying increase of love, faith, light, and humility; make it such: while the quickened power of perception in discerning the subtilty of the tempter, together with the increased power it gives in contending with him, make this state not only the high privilege, but the imperious necessity, of the believer. Can a reasonable, holy, acceptable service, be rendered without it?

A present and full salvation would not have been made available unless it were needed, in order to glorify God. Yet, my dear Mrs. W——, we need the experience of this salvation in order to know its excellency—its entire adaptation to every

Holiness will keep you.   Mysticism.

want. O the fallacy of the observation, "If I get the blessing I am sure I shall never be able to keep it!" It is precisely what is needed in order to produce that stability of soul which renders us less liable to vacillate in our Christian course; or, in the language of an eminent minister now living—in answer to the objection of a trembling heart, "I fear I could not keep it"—"Brother, nothing but holiness will *keep you.*"

Do you not think, dear Mrs. W——, that there is too much mysticism thrown around this blessing? I have thought so, and this I believe to be the principal hinderance with many whom I approach on this subject. With the eye of carnal wisdom they seem to be looking at something quite beyond their present reach. Thus they overlook its simplicity. Now, for a soul all athirst for God, what is more easy than to come with a purpose fixed in the strength of the Lord Jehovah, to be his—irrevocably his—whether living or dying: and then, relying on eternal veracity for the acceptance of the gift, to leave there the offering upon the altar? Is not this being set apart for God? And, in its immediate effect, is it not the sanctification which God demands?* The strength required in bringing the offering to the altar is wholly of God; and would he impart the power to do it, without fulfilling his gracious design in inducing the sacrifice?

* "The altar sanctifieth the gift." Matt. xxiii, 19.

No! If God-dishonoring unbelief does not bind the hands of Omnipotence, a mighty work will at once be accomplished.

But the declaration must be believed: "The blood of Jesus *cleanseth*." Mark! it is in the present tense. It is a *living* sacrifice that is required. I now, this moment, offer the sacrifice, and it *is cleansed*—I continue in the same act, the succeeding moment, and continue to feel that the blood of Jesus *cleanseth*. To the soul that thus continues to live in the spirit of sacrifice the veracity of the immutable Jehovah is pledged. It is thus that the blessing is obtained, and also retained, by *faith* in the sufficiency of the atonement, and a firm reliance on the indubitable WORD OF GOD.

With most grateful reflections do I look back upon the way by which I have been brought in reference to the Scriptures. Blessed be the Lord Jehovah for this chart, by which my way has been so luminously marked out! Would that I could convey to your mind an idea of my hallowing, delightful communings with the God of all grace, through this precious medium, while by most unequivocal assurances he has made himself known to me, and I have joyously exclaimed, "It is the Lord!"

I shall also ever with most grateful emotions retrace the way of the cross. In reference to some of its most painful peculiarities, I have been led to

Crucifixion of Nature.   *Witness.*

exult in its blessedness, and exclaim, "O the depth of the riches both of the wisdom and knowledge of God!" There have been some demands to which my nature could not have submitted unless there had been an entire crucifixion of it. But I do not remember to have made one sacrifice, however unaccountable the nature of it at the time may have been, without proving by subsequent experience that my spiritual advancement required the surrender.

To the praise of Almighty grace, I ought to acknowledge that he has caused me to become so established in the assurance that I know nothing aright, only as taught by the Spirit, that it is my most earnest endeavor to know the mind of the Spirit, and after being once convinced of the will of God concerning me, I have never dared, nor even wished, to hesitate in the performance of it.

Never, previous to receiving the witness of holiness, did I realize that I had received the sentence of death in myself; that I should not trust in myself, but in Him who raiseth the dead. So conscious have I since been, that all my sufficiency is of God, that for worlds I would not live one day without the *witness* that I have returned all my redeemed powers to him. Momentarily do I *know*, yes, deeply realize, that the seal of consecration is set.

On my first entering into this blessed state, a

constant effort seemed necessary in order to retain it. I have thought my views and feelings at the time, in a manner, comparable with one who had just entered upon a new existence, without being precisely aware of the principles upon which that existence is to be sustained. He inhales the life-sustaining air joyously, yet with a degree of tremulousness; queries whether he can again, and yet again, be sustained in a like effort: until the principles by which he is held in existence are gradually apprehended, and he breathes more and more freely, till at length, without even a careful thought, he revels in new existence. Thus at first I was continually asking myself, Do I now present all? Do I now believe? This slight degree of restlessness has since graduated into the blessedness of unquestionable certainty, that I *do present all; I do believe.*

This assurance, that all my powers are consecrated to holy service, gives me to feel the imperative necessity of being a laborer in the vineyard of the Lord; and this knowledge of consecration brings with it the inspiring persuasion that my labor is not in vain. " Forasmuch as ye *know* that your labor is not in vain in the Lord." O, my dear sister W——, it would be impossible, even though time and space might permit, to describe to you how comprehensive in bearing this blessing has been upon all my experience since its reception.

Holiness a Command.   Not optional.

The light of eternity alone can reveal the superior blessedness of that soul, who, through the blood of the everlasting covenant, has entered into, and abides in, a state of holiness.

And now I cannot longer view it as *optional* with any redeemed child of Adam whether he will rise to this state or not. No! within the lids of the Bible a more authoritative command cannot be found, than, "BE YE HOLY." And would the command be given, and yet the power to obey it withheld? And if empowered, by the might of the Spirit, to live in this state of entire consecration, surely it would be to the praise of God, that the clear, decided witness, be given, in order that his witnesses may declare it to the glory of his grace.

O that every master in Israel might teach, from experimental knowledge, the necessity of this great salvation! Pray fervently for this, my dear friend. When this object is gained, how soon shall we see the armies of our Israel coming up to the help of the Lord against the mighty, and by the power of personal holiness hastening the time when the kingdoms of this world shall become the kingdoms of our God and of his Christ!

Yours, in the bonds of perfect love.

No. XV.—TO MRS. R——.

Questions—Unreasonable not to be holy—Danger of slighting convictions—Sad remembrances—A fearful state—Count the cost—Decision—Self-sacrifice—The martyrs—The offense of the cross not ceased—Self-distrust—The way opened to the holiest—Temptations.

DEAR SISTER IN CHRIST,—And now, dear sister R——, how does your soul prosper? Has the consecration of all your powers yet been made? and is the sacrifice accepted? Or are you still halting between two opinions? Your *Redeemer* demands your *entire* service. O that this may be the hour when you may fully acknowledge his claim, and render back your whole existence to him!

I know I need not say that this is but a *reasonable* service. Your would-be-devoted heart already assures you of the reasonableness of your Redeemer's demand. O yes! you know that it is *unreasonable* not to be holy. Will you not *act* this moment upon your conviction of duty? The delay of one hour may witness a great abatement in the fervor of your desires. The very conviction of your need of holiness, and these restless aspirations after it, are talents for which you will be held responsible when you give an account of your stewardship. Yes, these are, indeed, gracious gifts from God. It is GOD that worketh in you.

| Fearful State. | Calculation. | Claim settled. |

Should you now, by delay, refuse to be a *worker* together with him, and thereby grieve the Spirit, and cause the withdrawment of its operations, how fearful would be your case! Ah! I have witnessed such cases, and my heart is agonized at the remembrance. Could rivers of tears purchase the return of these gracious influences, or any sacrifice, however costly, it were less fearful to trifle with, or to treat as of secondary importance, these God-wrought exercises. It is a solemn truth, that the light which is in us may become darkness; and then, O how *great* is that darkness! The light may shine afterward, but the *darkness comprehendeth it not.* What a fearful state!

Now is God's time! Will you choose any future period? If so, you take your *own* time. And is not this exceedingly perilous? Do you say, "It is but meet that I should count the cost?" Well, dear sister, begin just now to make the calculation, and let it be with the decision fixed irrevocably, that you will abide by the reckoning. I entreat you, in the name of the Lord Jesus, to pause, and now bring this matter to an issue. Do you find aught but what *already* belongs to God? Ah! the obligation, implied in the demand of your Redeemer, *settles* the claim with unquestionable certainty: "*Ye are not your own, for ye are bought with a price; therefore glorify God in your body and spirit, which are God's.*"

A Point which must be gained.

Will you not now begin to render back your *whole* existence to God? I appeal to you in the name of the Lord of hosts—and in the presence of those angel spirits that encamp around about them that fear him. Will you not now begin to count *all* things loss for the excellency of the knowledge of Christ Jesus? There must be a point in your experience when this is done, if you are ever numbered with that blood-washed company, of whom it is said, "These are they that have come up out of *great tribulation*, having washed their robes, and made them white in the blood of the Lamb." Does not this imply that a self-sacrificing spirit is *necessary?* Of this I am assured, that no *less devotion* than that which carried the martyrs through the flames, will carry us, unpolluted, through this present world. The idea that the state of the world is now such as to make but little sacrifice of public opinion necessary, in order to be a traveler in the King's highway, is unauthorized, either from Scripture, or *Scriptural* experience. "The servant is not above his master. In the world ye *shall* have tribulation. If ye were of the world, the world would love its own; but ye *are not* of the world, therefore it hateth you."

O, dear sister, fix your eye on a BIBLE *experience*, and this will lead you at once to HOLINESS!

And now, will you not begin to carry out with entire decision those views of privilege and respon-

Self-distrust.   Why delay?   Suggestions.

sibility which were, through the Holy Spirit's influence, apprehended by you at the time we met?

You, doubtless, feel as if you would fain with full purpose commence. But you are distrustful of yourself. And should you not be distrustful of *self?* God grant that you may ever feel that you have received the sentence of *death* in yourself, that you may not trust in yourself, but in *Him* that raiseth the dead. But, unworthy as you are, Christ is your Saviour. He has paid your debt, and purchased your *entire* freedom from sin. Why not this moment, then, begin to reckon yourself *dead* indeed unto sin and *alive* unto God, *through our Lord Jesus Christ?* Behold your *present privilege—*your *duty!* The way into the holiest is open. The Spirit and the Bride say, Come! come! for all things are ready. When Jesus bowed his head upon the cross, and said, "It is finished!" the veil of the temple was rent, and the way into the holiest made accessible for all, through the blood of the everlasting covenant. Why, then, should you delay to enter? O arise with a holy boldness! "The kingdom of heaven suffereth violence, and the violent take it by force." You may be assured that Satan will take every possible way to hinder you. He will tell you that "you are *not yet ready* for the reception of the blessing." When you begin to venture, he will tell you that it is "*presumptuous;* you have not *feeling* enough; 'tis too much the work of imagination to be *real;* perhaps you have not yet given up *all;*" with nameless other suggestions. But, in the *name* of the Lord, *you* may say, with David, "I can run through a troop."

Your affectionate friend.

No. XVI.—TO MRS. R——.

Power of faith—Terms of the covenant—Unsanctified resting in creature-good—Self-denial—A Jewish offerer—The Christian's altar; where?—It is Christ; it is here—The sacrifice to be offered—The altar sanctifieth the gift—Sinfulness of doubting it—The altar greater than the gift—Self-sacrifice reasonable; our duty; its benefits—The offering must *touch* the altar—The will must be resigned.

My Dear Sister,—This is just the state of salvation you need. Without this establishing grace you will ever be wavering in your purposes; and is it not possible that you may have it even before you lay this communication aside? Dear sister, all things are possible with God, and all things are possible to him that *believeth!* Do you observe that this implies a *present* act—not something in the future? "He that *believeth* on me, though he were *dead,* yet shall he live! O the omnipotence of *faith!* the want of it may even stay the hand of the Almighty. You will remember that it was said of the blessed Jesus, "He could not do many

Sanctification conditionally received.

mighty works, because of their unbelief." He cannot work where unbelief prevails, consistently with the order of his government, a principle of which is explicitly stated,—" He that believeth not is condemned already." John iii, 18.

And now, dear sister, let me again say, " Come, for all things are ready." A redemption from all iniquity has *already* been wrought out for you, and all that remains to be done is, that you accept it, on the conditions specified in the word of God. One condition, which may be readily apprehended by an individual who is seeking to be wholly sanctified, is recorded in 2 Cor. vi, 17: " Come out from among them, and be ye separate; touch not the unclean thing, and I will receive you." Here are the conditions on the part of God, and also on the part of the creature. Take this in connection with the first verse of the succeeding chapter, and you will find a thorough exposition of the process by which the soul is *sanctified*.

Are you willing to comply with the conditions? Ah! I fear your mind is resting on this and the other beloved object. Your heart may be saying, in view of some cherished idol, " Am I indeed called to sacrifice this object, which surpasses all others in desirableness?" Why *this*, probably, is precisely the object which God intends to dethrone. You know he is a jealous God, and will have no other gods before him. But perhaps you

| Obedience. | Self-denial. | Covetous Jew. |

may say, "It is not an idol—it is but one of the precious gifts of God; and can he now require that I should resign it?" Why, dear sister, if it is indeed a gift from God, is not this a conclusive reason why you should give it up, at the bidding of the giver? Abraham did not know why he was called to sacrifice his beloved Isaac; but he conferred not with flesh and blood, and without questioning the right of God, immediately obeyed.

Job said, "The Lord gave, and the Lord hath taken away; and *blessed* be the name of the Lord." Can you not say the same? Perhaps nature still shrinks, notwithstanding all your efforts to induce a willingness to make the sacrifice. Well, be it so. You know that every onward step for the disciple of the Lord Jesus Christ is marked with self-denial. "If any man will be my disciple, let him *deny* himself." "As ye have received Christ Jesus the Lord, so *walk* ye in him." By this you are assured that every successive step must be thus marked. An illustration is suggested to my mind, which I think will help you:—Imagine a Jew in ancient time, fully aware of the requirements of the law demanding the choice of his flock; for a moment he hesitates while covetousness, murmurs in his heart, as he gazes with increasing interest on the valuable sacrifice, until aroused by the consideration of what indulgence in the unhallowed

How we are sanctified.   Christ present.

propensity will lead to, he, with decisive step, hastens at once with his offering to the hallowed altar. The sacrifice is presented; and the very moment it touches that "*altar* most holy" it is sanctified. The sanctification of the gift did not depend on any inherent good in the offerer, but upon the sanctity of the altar upon which it was laid. The ALTAR *sanctifieth the gift*.

And now I presume that you are saying, "Would that I could find the altar! gladly would I hasten to it! but where, O where, is the *Christian's* altar? Has God indeed provided an 'altar most holy,' whereunto the believer in Christ may come, and upon which he may lay his offering? Had I a thousand miles to journey, gladly would I this moment leave all and hasten to it; and my *all* should at once, and for ever, be laid upon the Sanctifier."

Listen to God, dear sister:—"*We have an altar, whereof they have no right to eat who serve the tabernacle.*" The fact is settled beyond controversy. Is your spirit asking whether it is an "altar most holy?" sufficient to warrant the expectation that the altar will sanctify the gift which you lay upon it? Let the Holy Spirit answer: "We are sanctified through the offering of the body of Christ, once for all." Heb. x, 10. The ancient altar was sanctified by modes of purification prescribed by the law; and now, "if the blood of bulls and goats, and the ashes of an

| The Altar. | The Sacrifice. | The Offerer. |

heifer, sprinkling the unclean, sanctifieth to the purifying of the flesh, how much more shall the blood of Christ, who, through the eternal Spirit, offered himself without spot to God, purge your conscience from dead works, to serve the living God?" Christ speaks: "For their sakes I sanctify *myself*, that they may be *sanctified* through the truth." John, xvii, 19.

And now, what more, dear sister? Is your heart saying, "I cannot apprehend the altar as *near?*" In the name and strength of the Lord, banish the thought. "It is nigh thee." Say not in thy heart, Who shall ascend into heaven to bring Christ down? or who shall descend into the deep, to bring him up? He is as near you this moment as you are to yourself. And now, what is wanting but that you, as a worker together with him, perform the work assigned you? You may have forgotten that you are of God's royal *priesthood;* and that it is *now your* duty to offer up continually spiritual sacrifices. The *offering* to be presented is as near to you as is the *altar* upon which it is to be laid. The description of sacrifice required is thus given: "I beseech you, therefore, brethren, by the mercies of God, that ye present your *bodies* a living sacrifice, holy, acceptable unto God, which is your reasonable service." Rom. xii, 1.

If the scribes and Pharisees were reproved for thinking more of the gift than of the altar which sanctifieth the gift, who can portray the guilt of that unbelief which prompts the offerer at the Christian's altar to doubt whether, when he lays his offering upon the altar, it will be sanctified? And yet another course, if possible, even more dishonoring to God, is pursued by many: it is that of thinking more of the gift than of the altar itself. Did the temple service require sacrifices? How much more commanding are the claims of Christ our Redeemer! His cause requires a whole burnt-sacrifice. The entire service of body, soul, and spirit, is not only a *reasonable*, but a required service. Christ has purchased all unto himself. How unreasonable, then, not to live ceaselessly in the act of returning to him all these redeemed powers! O it is but meet that it should be a *living* sacrifice! And is it not blessed to know that we may thus be unto God a sweet savor of Christ?

Abiding here, you will *realize in verity* what it is to have your life hid with Christ in God. How can it be otherwise, than that the soul abiding thus in humble confidence on the Lamb slain from the foundation of the world, should realize momentarily the purifying efficacy of the atonement? Living in this state, must necessarily induce the enlistment of all our powers in his holy service. Reposing thus on the heart of infinite Love, the pulsations of his heart all beat in unison with the Saviour's.

Our interests being all identified with the interests of the Redeemer's kingdom, how can it be otherwise than that all our sympathies should be thrown out upon a perishing world? And is the design of redemption answered in any lower state of grace than this? If you live in the enjoyment of this salvation, you will then be constrained to acknowledge yourself but an unprofitable servant, rendering no more than is His due. You will have cause for deepest abasement before God, that you have ever neglected thus to acknowledge the claim of your Redeemer.

If you delay presenting the sacrifice, from any cause whatever, you make food for repentance. God demands *present* holiness. Every earthly consideration should dwindle into insignificance in comparison with this. Resolve, sister, from this moment, that this demand of your God shall be met. Say to every minor object, "Let the dead bury their dead."

Remember, the offering must *touch* the altar before it can be sanctified. This is God's unalterable decree. With him there is neither variableness nor shadow of turning. The act, on your part, must necessarily induce the promised result on the part of God. But do not forget that all is not laid upon the altar, until that will that requires signs and wonders preparatory to believing is also resigned. This seems to be the last point about which the heart lingers. What you are aiming at is *holiness*, not feeling. Trust the matter with God, and he will give you just the amount and kind of emotion that will best fit you to glorify his exalted name; and this is all that you are now to live for. Your God is now saying unto you, "Bring *all* the tithes into my store-house, and prove me herewith."

Do it, dear sister, and you will at once know, most assuredly, that if any man will do His will, he shall know of the doctrine. Not to-morrow, but NOW.

Your faithful friend.

No. XVII.—TO MR. K——.

An impression confirmed—Religious joy—Temptation succeeds—Unwise inference—Holiness a state of character, not of emotion—The disciple with Jesus in the wilderness, and on the mount—The disciples on Tabor—The unwise request—The disciple as his Master—The crown coveted; not the cross.

DEAR SIR,—Your letter confirms what I said to Dr. P., on the evening after I parted with you. "Brother K—— has, I believe, received the blessing of holiness, for my prayer has been turned to praise in his behalf." So I said to my husband, and this persuasion your letter verifies. You observe, "During that night, I awoke with a sweet, heavenly feeling, that I was the Lord's. I felt a *perfect* assurance that I was wholly his, and my

Emptiness.   The Disciple with his Master.

joy truly was unspeakable. I arose, and gave God thanks for his great mercy to me. After an hour or two, I fell asleep again; but, in the morning, these feelings had left me." Had your faith been wholly founded on the faithfulness of God, and not dependent on your feelings, you would not in any way have lost anchorage, as a consequence of this destitution of emotion.

But it was when on your homeward journey, at a time to which you had looked forward as a season favorable for special communion, "when alone in the car," that you were called to endure the trial of your faith more fully. It was now, you say, that you "experienced a strange feeling of emptiness, or a destitution of holiness." Why say "a *destitution of holiness*," unless you had consciously taken your offering from off the hallowed altar? If you still had power to keep all there—to continue in the same act of presenting all *through* Christ—you were just as truly in a state of holiness then, as when filled with joy unspeakable and full of glory. Holiness is a state in which all the redeemed powers are given up to God through Christ.

The follower of Jesus may as truly be with the Captain of his salvation, realizing close and holy fellowship when in communion with him, as the Man of sorrows, and permitted to know a fellowship with his sufferings; or, if possible, when driven

The Disciples on the Mount.

with him into the wilderness to be tempted of Satan; or in any other conceivable state, where the disciple may in this world be as his Master: "Ye are they that have been with me in my temptations." In either of the states glanced at, may the lowly disciple be as truly conformed to the will and also to the image of his Saviour, as if permitted the enjoyment of holy fellowship with him on the mount of transfiguration, with every impulse or *feeling* of the heart saying, "Lord, it is good for us to be here."

If *feeling* were the principle commanding religious action, instead of calm, deliberate, steady faith, how often should we be led astray, even when in our most pious moods! Think of the disciples, who, from the impulse of exuberant, pious feeling, desired to have three tabernacles reared, in order that they might ever abide on the mount, alone with the Saviour and his heavenly visitants; unmindful that the work of the Redeemer in saving the world was not yet accomplished, neither the work to which they, as his disciples, were called, in establishing his kingdom. Imagine that the pious feelings with which they were at this time favored had formed the principle of action, what would have been the fate of a lost world?

A destitution of joyous emotion, then, is not a destitution of holiness. On receiving an increase of faith, or of any other grace, we ought always to

Trials succeed Joy.

expect the trial of this faith, or whatever grace we may have received, to succeed. Jesus was driven by the Spirit into the wilderness to be tempted of Satan, immediately after being favored with special tokens of the approval of his heavenly Father. And ought not we, who have purposed to follow the Lamb whithersoever he goeth, to expect to be carried through a process somewhat similar, after having received special tokens of divine approval? Thus it was with you, dear brother; and there are reasons, of which we shall know more when knowledge is made perfect, why it is that God permits Satan to assault so powerfully his chosen ones. It is blessed to know that the veracity of our covenant-keeping God is pledged that we shall not be tempted above that we are able. And it is enough for the servant that he be as his Lord. The violent assault of which you speak, which so quickly succeeded the strong consolation consequent on your faith, was not of forty days' continuance.

Consider the Apostle and High Priest of your profession, "forty days in the wilderness, and with the wild beasts." Did you *suffer*, being tempted? Think of him: "For in that he himself hath suffered, being tempted, he is able to succor them that are tempted." I am delighted with some remarks of an old writer, which have just met my eye. They are so precisely suited to your case,

Theophylact.   The Cross and the Crown.

that I might have substituted them in place of my own remarks, had I seen them sooner. Theophylact observes: "One grand end of our Saviour's temptation might be to teach us that when we have consecrated ourselves to God's service, and have been favored with peculiar marks of divine acceptance, and the consolations of his Spirit, we must *expect* temptations; and to teach us, by our Lord's example, how we may best and most effectually resist them, even by an *unshaken* faith, 1 Pet. v, 9; and by the sword of the Spirit, which is the word of God. Eph. vi, 17."—*Benson's Comment.*

"We count them happy which endure." O may this happiness ever be yours! I do not mean to express a wish that you may be ever enduring the fires of temptation, but that you may endure as seeing the Invisible through whatever trials you may be called to pass, remembering that you "are *appointed* thereunto," and that the same afflictions are accomplished in your brethren. It is true, that but few covet the blessedness of that man that endureth temptation; though many eagerly aspire after the crown, which the Lord, the righteous Judge, hath promised to give unto such.

Yours, in Christian love.

Struggle. Resolve. Faith.

No. XVIII.—TO MR. K——.

Mr. K——'s statement of his case—Questions—Mr. K——'s resolution—Comparison—Inconsistency of Mr. K——'s position—May the sanctification of the soul be achieved gradually? &c.—"God's word its own evidence"—Correspondence between faith and confession—"Have I lost my will?"—Answer—Illustrations—The obedient child—Abraham—The Saviour—Family government—Ruling by love—Daily intercession—Household dedication—Restraint—Abraham's family—Joshua—Eli.

Dear Sir,—After the violent assault of Satan, referred to in my last, you say : " Not being conscious of having offended, I was alarmed, and renewed my struggle ; sometimes endeavoring to consecrate myself to God, and sometimes believing that the consecration had been made; until I finally concluded that I must and would believe I had given up all, and trust his blessed promise, and live a life of faith. From that time to this, I have endeavored so to live, and yet I am not able to say that the blessing is mine." I have quoted thus largely, in order that you may review your position. You finally concluded that you must and would live a life of faith.

Do you mean a life of faith on the Son of God? Have you indeed consecrated yourself wholly to him? And is your all now being presented to God, *through* Christ, the Lamb of God, which taketh away the sin of the world ; and yet you cannot say that your sins are taken away ; that you

The Gift and the Altar.

are cleansed from all unrighteousness—wholly sanctified? Surely you are not willing to assume the position, that a living sacrifice, presented to God through Christ, is not holy and acceptable? I know you would not intentionally undervalue the precious blood of the atoning Lamb, and yet your position assumes it.

Your final conclusion was, to live a life of faith on the Son of God; that is, a life of entire dependence upon his merits, trusting in him to purge your conscience from dead works, to serve the living God. Far be it from you to say that you have trusted, without fully proving the faithfulness of God. With far less guilt might one in ancient times say, "I have laid all upon the hallowed altar, the altar that sanctifieth the gift, but cannot say that it is sanctified." Under these circumstances, both the word of God would be doubted and also the inherent virtues of that altar which God hath declared to be an altar most holy. This is the sin which is aimed at when Christ says, "Ye fools, and blind! for whether is greater, the gift, or the altar which sanctifieth the gift?"

You come to the Christian's altar. "We have an altar." Your final conclusion is that you have consecrated all upon this altar, which is Christ. In view of his sacrificial sufferings and death, should I ask whether there is virtue sufficient here to cleanse from all unrighteousness; to sanctify wholly; what would you say? I know you would tell me that the virtues of this most holy altar are amply sufficient for the cleansing of a world of polluted mortals. Allow me to remind you of your final conclusion; that is, to live a life of faith on the Son of God: if so, then it is upon this hallowed altar that you are now resting.

And now, my dear brother K——, if you will resolve to let your faith depend on the word of God, and not upon your uncertain feelings, your difficulties will all be at an end. This, I believe, will from this time be your experience. Shall I henceforth hear it said of brother K——, "He staggered not at the promise of God through unbelief, but was strong in faith, giving glory to God?"

You ask my opinion relative to the evidence of the blessing being received slowly, or perhaps at intervals. We can conceive of one, who, on being informed of a matter of great importance, at first but partially relies upon the word of his informant; until accumulated evidence of the veracity of his friend puts it beyond doubt, and he becomes established in assurance that the word of his friend is *evidence* sufficient. He then proceeds to inform others of the fact: and if asked what evidence he has of its being so, he gives the name of his friend, and exclaims, "This is authority sufficient; I have his word, and the *word* of such a friend is its own evidence."

"I will believe." Confession.

"God's word is its own evidence," said an excellent minister, who loves to live by faith on the Son of God. Here let me again remind brother K—— of his final conclusion, of which this forms a part, "I *must* and *will* believe that I have given up all, and trust in God's promise, and live a life of faith." Do you believe God's promise constitutes reliable ground for your faith? *Is his word evidence* sufficient to rest your faith upon? If you have come to the point to rely upon it fully as the foundation of your hope, you will not hesitate in making confession with your mouth. If you are not willing to do this, it proves that your faith is yet defective; for you will speak with a confidence precisely proportionate with what you deem to be the authority and faithfulness of Him upon whose word you rely.

But do not forget that believing with the heart, and confessing with the mouth, stand closely connected, and "what God hath joined together, let not man put asunder." To the degree you rely on the faithfulness of God, O hasten to make confession with the mouth of this your confidence; and to the degree you honor God, by reposing on his faithfulness, will God honor you, by conferring upon you the graces of his Holy Spirit in their rich plenitude. My dear brother, let me urge you to be instant in season and out of season, in the performance of this duty: if we meet no more in time, may we hail each other in the city of our God, and there joy to find our names enrolled among those who have been foremost among Christ's holy confessors on earth.

But I observe a clause of your letter, not before noticed, of which I would say a word. You say, "I fear I have a will of my own;" but of this you do not seem entirely confident. I am glad to observe your carefulness on this point. O may your conscience ever be

"Quick as the apple of an eye!"

But while endeavoring to ascertain the truth of this matter, do not forget that you have an enemy who day and night accuseth the saints before God. Would you indeed be willing to have your own will done, instead of the will of your heavenly Father? Imagine that the ruling of your destiny were, in any degree, taken out of the hand of God and placed at your own disposal, would you not be afraid to be intrusted with it, in any degree? If you would at once refer it all back to God, then the conclusion is evident; you have not a will of your own. But we may have *natural* shrinkings from certain forms of duty; yet if we do not yield to nature, it is still evident that the will of God predominates over our own will, and all is yet in obedience to Christ.

If a judicious parent require a child to do that to which his nature is strongly disinclined, and the

"Thine only Son."   "As thou wilt."

child, fearful of grieving his father, yields, though nature still strongly shrinks, to what he knows to be the superior judgment of the father, the child is even more worthy of commendation, than if the requisition had not been painful to his nature. The love, obedience, and confidence of the child, have all by the act been tested, and exhibited in a manner calculated to move the heart of the father, quite beyond what it would have been had no such test been instituted.

If Abraham had been required to offer up Ishmael, instead of Isaac, would his faith and his obedience have been as thoroughly tested as they were? God said, "Take thy son, thine *only* son, whom thou lovest." When the Lord said this, doubtless all the tender yearnings of the father for his only son were roused even to an unusual degree. God did not forget this, when he said, "Now I know that thou fearest me, seeing thou hast not withheld thy son, thine only son, from me."

The Saviour also, who possessed as truly the human as the divine nature, had a will which shrunk from suffering: "If it be possible let this cup pass from me. Nevertheless, not as *I will*, but as thou wilt." His will was obedient to the will of his Father. If, in our brother K——, the human will is subject to the divine will, then he may thank God and take courage.

Ruling in Love. Early Intercessions.

You inquire relative to our management with our little family; but, as you perceive, the size of my sheet forbids my saying much on this subject in the present communication. We have deemed it important

"Never to take the harsher way,
When love may do the deed."

And we have endeavored to cherish in their young hearts that love and confidence which you observe. It is certainly far more desirable to rule by love than by fear, if such a thing may be. And it is my opinion that this may be done to a degree quite beyond what many parents imagine. God is love; and it is our earnest prayer that the atmosphere in which our children live and move may be that of love. We have dedicated our house to God, and believe that he hears our prayer when we ask that his presence may abide with us, so that every one that enters our dwelling may feel the hallowing influence of the Spirit of holiness.

Before the routine of domestic duty for the day commences, I feel it a blessed privilege to present each member of our household individually before God. After having presented myself, with all my interests, temporal and spiritual, afresh to him through Christ, I daily plead the promise, "I will pour out my Spirit upon thy seed, and my blessing upon thy offspring." I try to claim the fulfillment of this promise, and believe myself successful.

Restraint.   Abraham's Family.

We have dedicated our children to God with an intention of devoting them in some special manner to his service, and are endeavoring to have their moral and religious training all directed to this point—usefulness in the church of Christ. You may infer from this that it is needful that their natural inclinations should at times be crossed to meet this point. In reference to gay society, or conformity to the world in dress, and other respects, we should think it proper to exercise parental authority if there were occasion for it. We are looking for wisdom to train them in the way in which they should go, and not in a way from which it would be needful that they should depart, on becoming themselves self-denying followers of the Saviour.

"Fathers, provoke not your children to anger, lest they be discouraged," is an admonition most important in family government. But I imagine that the sin of Eli is far more prevalent than that of undue family restraint. God said of faithful Abraham, "I know him, that he will command his children, and his household after him, and they shall keep the way of the Lord, to do justice and judgment; that the Lord may bring upon Abraham that which he hath spoken." We observe by this, that the parental and household government of Abraham stood closely connected with the fulfillment of God's promises to him.

Firmness and love equally blended are most essential in family discipline. Courageous Joshua says, "I and my house will serve the Lord." I have feared that some professors rather prefer that the cause of Christ should be wounded, than the feelings of their children and other members of their household. Thus was it with Eli. If expostulation and entreaty had been the only thing required, he does not seem to have been particularly deficient. Doubtless his sin was, that he did not, with faithful Abraham, *command* his children. You inquire about the religious state of our two younger children—whether they are Christians. I am not prepared to answer this question directly, and you see I have now almost filled another sheet.

In love, farewell.

No. XIX.—TO MR. K——.

Remarkable visit of the Spirit—A new heart given to a little child—"I want to pray more"—An accusation of the tempter—Little W—— Infantile anticipation—Propriety.

DEAR SIR,—Were you not praying for us as a family the evening I parted with you? Soon after my return home, while at supper, an unusual sense of the divine presence came upon me, and a heaven of love and sweetness seemed to fill the house. Being later than usual for supper, all the members of my family, with the exception of my two young-

A Little Girl with a New Heart.

est children, (who had retired for the night,) had gone to meeting. As I left the parlor and went up to my room, about eight o'clock, to my surprise I found our daughter still awake, and, at her earnest call, I went to her room. Her eyes looked as though she had for some time been weeping bitterly, but she was now smiling amid her tears. "O ma!" she exclaimed, "I have been asking God for a new heart, and he has given it to me." I questioned her, but could see no reason to doubt that the Lord had indeed visited her with his salvation. Among other things, she said, "But Satan told me something very naughty." She hesitated for a moment as though it were something that she hardly dared repeat, and then observed, "He said that I should never go to heaven; but I asked the Lord, and he told me if I loved and served him I should." She seemed very happy in the love of the Saviour, and as I observed before, the whole house seemed filled with a heaven of love.

Little W—— then called me to his room, and a divine influence seemed to be resting upon him also. "O ma!" said he, "I want to pray more than my own prayers." I remained some time instructing him in answer to his many inquiries, some of which surprised me much, inquiries which I knew must have been prompted by the direct influences of the Holy Spirit on his heart.

In consequence of not being home as early as

"What is it to give my Heart to God?"

usual, I had not conversed with these little ones as I generally do, especially on sabbath evenings. It was clear to my mind, therefore, that the feelings of my dear children had not been produced by any external influence.

The accuser had been suggesting, that in not being with them when they retired, I had neglected an obvious duty, for that which was questionable; but on finding them so unexpectedly receiving the gracious teachings of the Spirit, the Holy Comforter said to my heart,

> "Fix on God's work thy steadfast eye,
> So shall thy work be done."

I should not like to answer your question, that is, Are these children Christians? unhesitatingly. But I will say, that from their *earliest* existence we have given them up to God. We believe that the Lord in some special manner recognizes the surrender, and gives the more direct influences of the Holy Spirit as a consequence of their being set apart for his service.

They love to talk about spiritual things, and from the dawn of reason have manifested much interest, and sometimes deep emotions, while I conversed with them. A few months since, little W—— asked this question, "What is it to give my heart to God?" Bishop H—— was with us, and he took the child on his knee, and with most heavenly sweetness told him in a manner suited to his capa-

"I mean to be a Minister."

city *just* what it was to give his heart to God. After which, W——, in a solemn and impressive manner, said, "I give my heart to Jesus Christ." This was a memorable period, and he since says that he has given his heart to God, and I would not dare say he has not done so. When he is asked, as is often the case with such little creatures, What do you intend to be? His almost invariable reply, whether to worldlings or others, is, " I mean to be a minister, *if God will make me one.*"

We have set him apart for that work, with the prayerful desire that he may be called of God, as was Aaron. "The harvest is great, but the laborers are few." In view of the need of faithful laborers it seems most reasonable, and not unauthorized by the spirit of the word, that pious parents should thus set their children apart, not with an idea that they are to decide the matter, but to order their entire moral and religious training in such a manner as may best fit them for the service of the sanctuary; and then, if the thus consecrated one is not sure in after life that he is "moved by the Holy Ghost to preach the gospel," he will, by pious culture, have been fitted for other work in the vineyard of the Lord.

But if a case should occur in which a person thus dedicated to the ministry should not be called, it would be unlike any case I have yet met with. In reference to little W——, we cannot help treasuring up in our hearts these indications that he has received something like a baptism into the Spirit, of what may be his work, and we take courage. This morning he said, "I wish I was in '*Exico*,' (Mexico;) they fight there!" I felt troubled at his saying what seemed so unlike himself; and chidingly said, "Why, W——, they are wicked there because they fight, and if they do not take care they will soon all go to the bad place together:" "I thought I might go and tell them that it is *wicked to fight*," he replied. On sabbath morning a boy was crying "Sunday Morning News" past the door. W—— came to me with a saddened countenance and said, "Do you not think I had better run and tell him that it is wicked to sell papers on Sunday? it may be he does not know how wicked it is." This is but a specimen of the way in which he often talks. I think you will with us conclude, that God is not unmindful of the consecration which we have made of our children to his service. And it is because we think this a most important matter that I have so much at length answered your inquiries.

Yours, &c.

An Undivided Saviour.

No. XX.—TO MR. K——.

Faith receives Christ in all his offices—Distrustfulness—Illustration—A specific kind of unbelief pointed out—The Bible the voice of God to man—Reference to 2 Pet. i, 21—Profession on the authority of the WORD urged—Waverings in faith sinful—Triumphs of Satan—Loss to the church—Slight notions of the sin of unbelief lamented.

DEAR SIR,—I had hoped that my dear brother K—— had counted the cost of living a life of faith on the Son of God; yes, of faith on the Son of God, and of faith on him in all his relations to you. He is your Prophet, Priest, and King. Remember, brother, Christ is not divided. If he is received at all, he must be received in all his offices. You cannot be saved by receiving him as your atoning Priest, while you reject him as your reigning Sovereign or your Prophet—your Teacher. You have faith in the efficacy of his atonement as Priest. You, doubtless, consent to his control as your King. But, brother, may the Spirit mightily convince you of the necessity of an unwavering trust in all his teachings! His "words are Spirit, and they are life."

I imagine you say, "Sister P—— has mistaken my position. It is not the *word* of God I distrust. It is *myself*. The language of my heart ever is,

'Lord, I believe thy every word,
Thy every promise, true.'"

And yet, brother, I think, on careful examination,

you may find yourself in some degree given to distrustfulness. To the degree you are so, you dishonor God. If Christ, robed in human flesh, were now standing before you, repeating words of living truth in your ear, and should a distrustful look cloud your brow, or words betokening a hesitating faith fall upon the ear of the listening multitude, would not the Saviour's heart be pained, and his name be dishonored before the whole assembly?

But you may desire to know whether I can direct to one point where your faith in *God* is defective. Perhaps I may discover to you more than one, if, through the Holy Spirit's influence, I be successful in placing before you what I think I perceive. You say, "Were I only *sure I had given up all*, I could at once believe, irrespective of frames and feelings. The promise, 'I will receive you,' I could at once claim as my own, and thus, in obedience to God, I should be empowered to cleanse myself from all filthiness of the flesh and spirit." One point, marking the defectiveness of your faith, is here. You labor prayerfully to be sincere, and then, just as well as you know how, you give yourself wholly up to God through Christ. After making this surrender, you ask if anything is kept back, that it may be clearly discovered. But, in answer to these intercessions, nothing further is revealed. Just here a promise

"*The Just shall live by Hearing.*"

meets you: "If in anything ye be otherwise minded, God shall reveal even this unto you." Now, why do you not believe the word of the Lord? It is just the promise which you need at this point in your experience. God is now saying this to you, and you are doubting him, and by this he is dishonored. Yes, *unbelief is a sin.* If you conceived the *word* of God a sufficient foundation for your faith, and were not looking for some evidence apart from this, you would believe. "But is it not through the direct agency of the Holy Ghost that I must believe?" Yes; but holy men of God spake as they were moved by the Holy Ghost; and you will, indeed, prove these words are spirit and life, as soon as you fully rely upon them. Yes, you will realize that the Holy Ghost hath given them a life-giving energy,—

> "To him that in thy name believes,
> Eternal life with thee is given;
> Into himself he all receives,
> Pardon, and holiness, and heaven."

The Bible is the voice of God speaking to man. If holy men spake as they were moved by the Holy Ghost, the words thus uttered are in verity the words of God, as though they were *heard* sounding forth from the highest heavens. If they were heard, faith were no longer requisite. If this were the order of God, it would have been written, The just shall live by *hearing,* or something

Faith better than Sight.

answerable thereunto. Or, if this were the better way for man in his present state, God had ordained it. But the holy apostle Peter, who had both *heard* this voice which came from heaven, and was also an eye-witness of his majesty, does not pronounce the indulgence of these senses the *surest* way for establishing the heart: "We have also a more *sure* word of prophecy, whereunto ye do well to take heed, as unto a light that shineth in a dark place, until the day dawn, and the day-star arise in your hearts, knowing this—*first*, that no prophecy of the Scripture is of any private interpretation, for prophecy came not in old time by the will of man: but holy men of God spake as they were moved by the Holy Ghost."

I note this most important passage, with the hope that you may, as in the presence of God, mark, learn, and inwardly digest; and from this time believe, when you comply with the conditions upon which the blessings which you need are promised, that they are *already* yours. The word is nigh thee, *in thy mouth and in thy heart*. I will return to the point which I may seem to have left, but which, in truth, I have aimed at in the foregoing remarks. Now, should you believe, when you ask God to discover to you anything which may be unrevealed, that he fulfills his word to you; in your confessions before God and man, you would say, "Through the power of the Holy Spirit, I am

Confession on the Authority of the Word.

now wholly given up to God. I have laid *all* upon the altar." Were an inquirer to ask, "What authority have you for speaking so confidently of your state?" you would reply, "I have the authority of God's word. Upon this alone my confidence rests. I, in sincerity, have given myself wholly to him. I *have* the promise that he will receive me when I make the surrender; and I cannot now believe otherwise than that he *does* receive me, unless I doubt his word, and this were in itself *sinful*." "But, perhaps, there may be something undiscovered, which may mar your sacrifice, and render it unworthy the acceptance of God." "I am bound to believe that the Faithful and True *fulfills* his word to me; he cannot deny himself. I have asked, if there be anything withheld, or if in anything I be otherwise minded, that God will reveal even this unto me; and now it were, indeed, most dishonoring to God, for me to doubt his faithfulness in this respect." Just in proportion to your confidence in the *faithfulness* of God would be the strength of your testimony in your confessions of what he had done for you.

O if these doubtings and waverings were only regarded among professed believers as *sinful*, as they are in reality before God, what a different state of experience would the church present! Satan, surely, is peculiarly successful in blinding the minds of multitudes who believe in the attainableness of the rest of faith, relative to the enormity of this sin. When one who has been brought out of the bondage of spiritual Egypt arrives at the borders of the promised land; if an enemy, perchance his last unvanquished foe, prevent his leaping over, even though but within one step of his long-sought rest, what a victory is gained! Shall an enemy, capable of detaining his victim for days, months, and even years, at this point, be thought of as an enemy of small moment? Shall a foe, possessed of power sufficient to keep hundreds among the ministry, who are sincerely endeavoring to gain the rest of faith, and thousands also among the laity, who, for years, have been uttering strong desires for its attainment, O shall such an enemy be regarded as a slight foe? But, alas! too well does Satan succeed in keeping the understanding of multitudes in comparative darkness, relative to the aggregate loss of the church in the holiness of her membership, through this form of unbelief.

Why do you not enter into the enjoyment of full salvation? asks the inquirer of one who would be a sincerely devoted follower of Christ. "I cannot say why," says the latter, "unless it be my unbelief. I have for a long time been seeking, and I know of nothing that I would not be willing to sacrifice for its attainment; and I conclude, that it can be only my unbelief which keeps me from the enjoyment of this my promised inheritance. I know that the kingdom of heaven suffereth violence, and also that God hath made it my duty to believe, and frequently I have almost made the venture, but again I waver!" So says the doubting one: as if it were comparatively a small matter to indulge in these vacillations of faith; and this, too, when it is the word of the unchangeable Jehovah which we claim the privilege of crediting or rejecting at our pleasure.

I have not yet finished what I would communicate on this subject, for my heart is indeed full; but circumstances render it inexpedient that I should write more at present. I will give you my thoughts more fully, soon.

Yours, &c.

No XXI.—TO MR. K——.

"*Only* unbelief"—Ancient Israel—Borders of the promised land reached—Met and vanquished by an enemy—Who was it?—God dishonored by unbelief.

DEAR SIR,—O how infinite in importance is the point which the arch deceiver gains by the little words "ONLY unbelief!" Here is just where for months past the enemy has gained a signal victory over my dear brother K——. Not only over yourself has he triumphed, but, according to your own acknowledgment, the precious cause of Christ has suffered loss, by your not being in the enjoyment of this blessing. You say, "I feel that if I had the blessing, the circumstances in which I am placed would be peculiarly favorable to my usefulness." How many might have believed through your testimony, had your unbelief been given up, when you gave up every other sin? Why was this exception persisted in? Surely, brother, you did not consider how derogatory to the character of God it is to doubt his word. Relative to the enormity of this sin, well may God complain of you and many others, as of ancient Israel, "My people doth not consider."

Let us, dear brother K——, for a moment glance at the nature and consequences of this sin. Think of Israel. God, with a high hand, and an outstretched arm, had brought them up out of the house of bondage. The Red Sea was safely passed by a miraculous interposition, and Israel looked on and beheld the destruction of his enemies, as they were overthrown by the power of the Highest. Gently, as a nurse cherisheth her children, were they led forth through the wilderness. One obstacle after another, most formidable in prospect, had been overcome by the power of God, until they had become fully instructed relative to the almightiness of his hand to deliver, when they arrive at the borders of the promised land. They have escaped their Egyptian task-masters. They

| A Terrible Foe | Dreadful Doom. |

have passed the Red Sea. The parched and howling wilderness, too, has been traversed, and the hosts of Israel stand at Kadesh Barnea ready to enter in triumph upon their long-sought rest.

Just here, they are met by a foe more formidable than the hosts of Pharaoh, more terrible than the sea or the desert. That foe subdued them and drove them back into that terrible wilderness, where they wandered till the bones of that whole generation were strown bleaching on the sands. Who was that mighty foe of Israel? Paul tells us. " They entered not in because of unbelief "—" ONLY UNBELIEF."

Ah! when Israel discovered the consequence of this one act of unbelief; when they saw that they had thereby so greatly displeased God, that they were for ever debarred the privilege of entering that land, in prospect of which their journeyings had been commenced, and continued down to that point of time, when God sware that they should not enter into his rest; O, think you, that they were disposed to speak of unbelief as a light matter? As their doom was being accomplished, and they were, one after another, fast falling in the wilderness, do you imagine that they were prone to look back and say, O, it was *only* unbelief?

Now, if Satan succeed in blinding our minds to the formidableness of this enemy, O is not this indeed a mighty achievement? I need not say that the honor of God is as truly concerned in us his spiritual Israel; "being delivered out of the hand of our enemies that we might serve him without fear, in holiness and righteousness before him, all the days of our life;" as it was in the deliverance of his ancient people. How greatly was the name of God dishonored by the sin of Israel in their refusing to enter; and O how greatly is our heavenly Joshua, the Captain of our salvation, who hath undertaken to bring his redeemed people into this Canaan of rest, dishonored, when we by our unbelief refuse to enter!

Dear brother K——, be no more of a doubtful mind. Give up your waverings: "For he that wavereth is as a wave of the sea, driven with the wind and tossed; for let not that man think that he shall receive anything of the Lord." "This is the command of God, that ye believe." Is it left optional with yourself whether you will obey this command? How presumptuous to doubt God! Resolve that you will do so no more. Be without variableness or shadow of turning in your purposes. To the degree you are otherwise, instability in experience will be your portion. "If ye will not believe, *surely* ye shall not be established."

In Christian love, yours.

Roll away the Stone.   Valley of Decision.

No. XXII.—TO MR. P——.

Difficulties in the distance—Humility and decision—Divine protection—Daniel—Workers together with God—Witness of the Spirit—Distinction between faith and sight—Abraham; his *patient* faith—The wavering one.

DEAR SIR,—On looking at difficulties in the distance, how oft have travelers in the heavenly way exclaimed, "Who shall roll us away the stone?" when, on coming up to the dreaded point, they have found the stone already removed, and a risen Saviour ready to meet them with his comforting smile. Thus, my dear brother P., you found it relative to the long-dreaded difficulty, which was matter of such serious forebodings in your last.

"The day of the Lord is near in the valley of decision." You, dear brother, are being led by the Spirit low into the valley of humility, and doubtless this is only permitted, that God may in due time exalt you. His word is pledged, that if any man will do his will, he shall know of the doctrine. You, my brother, have decided at every sacrifice to *know*, in order that you may *do*, the whole will of God. Through the energies of the Holy Spirit, which have been momentarily imparted, through the intercessions of Christ, you have, day and night, sleeping or waking, been sustained in the absorbing desire to stand perfect and complete in all the will of God.

A Miracle.   Satan restrained.   Daniel.

To be thus kept amid so many opposing influences, is of itself a miracle. Imagine that the decree should pass the throne of Heaven, that you for five minutes should be left to the will of your enemies. An entire destitution of every gracious intention, or desire, would in a moment succeed. Desolation of body, mind, and estate, exceeding the desolations of Job, would be the immediate consequence. Limits, as you will remember, were, by the fiat of the Almighty, set to the power of Satan, when Job endured the trial of his faith. But for the present and continuous intercessions of your Saviour, inconceivable power would at once be given to Satan over body, mind, and estate. Yes, brother, you are " kept by the power of God, through faith, unto salvation;" and every moment you are thus kept, you may exultingly sing,

<blockquote>" I'm a miracle of grace!"</blockquote>

How do you suppose Daniel felt when he stood among the lions? He well knew that if his God had not sent his angel to shut the mouths of the devourers, his doom had been inevitable. Do you not think he ever afterward regarded himself as a peculiar monument of the saving grace of God? But he was not in reality more so than you are; for the roaring lion, who seeketh whom he may devour, is ever prowling about your path, and every moment you are preserved, it is by the miraculous intervention of divine power.

God at Work.   Faith and Sight.

Your letter was encouraging to my faith in your behalf. Yes, my brother, it is God that worketh in you. Even now, while you are reading this communication, our God, who hath said, "I am the Lord which doth sanctify you," is carrying on the sanctifying process in your heart. "But when shall I be enabled to testify, that I have the direct witness of the Spirit, that I am wholly sanctified? This I believe to be my privilege." Yes, brother, this I also believe to be your privilege, and this I am sure you will have the moment you *unwaveringly* rely on the promises of your faithful God; for the Spirit bears testimony to the truth of the word, when with perfect confidence we rest upon it. It is true, that you may not have any *sensible* manifestation, by way of assuring you of the acceptance of your offering, as the *immediate* consequence of your faith. To the degree manifestations addressed to the senses are given, the necessity of faith is precluded; but it is written, "The just shall *live by faith*," not by *sight*.

When the father of the faithful *saw* the heavenly fire descend, and with his natural eyes was beholding the consuming process, as the flame steadily ascended heavenward, was faith in any way necessary, by way of assuring him of the acceptance of his offering? Surely not; for open vision precluded that necessity. But this sensible

Abraham's Patient Faith.

assurance would not have been given, had not a continuous act of steady faith *preceded* it. Had he, after laying his offering upon the altar, removed it again from that hallowed shrine; had he, forgetful that he had need of patience, yielded to weariness, from watching the consecrated offering, and then began to indulge in questioning why the Lord should so long delay the expected token of acceptance; and then, turning his mind off from the faithfulness of God, indulged in various conjectures, expressive of unsteady faith; would Abraham, amid these waverings, have received anything from the hand of the Lord? Surely the appellation of the "father of the faithful" had not been given him; for in reference to the wavering one, our God hath said, "Let not that man think that he shall receive anything of the Lord."

O that my dear brother P—— may be an example to believers, in *faith* and purity, as well as in doctrine! Yours truly.

P. S.—I perceive that I have not fully answered your letter. Your numerous inquiries demand much more time than I can command at present; but I will write from time to time, as circumstances may permit.

No. XXIII.—TO MR. P——.

Premature application of the promises—Not willing to be holy—Paul's concise statement of the way to holiness—Distinction between consecration and sanctification—Obedience must precede appropriating faith—Wickedness of removing a sacrifice from the altar—Thomas—The will; its language—Of one who gave up his will.

DEAR SIR,—I think many err by urging the promises upon those who have no right to them. It was only this morning that a friend observed to me, "I asked brother L—— how his mind stood, in relation to the subject of holiness. He acknowledged his need of the blessing, and said that he desired it.

"'Can you conceive of any reason why you do not receive it?'

"'I do not know, unless it is my *unbelief.*'"

This friend then began to urge the promises upon him; but she soon found that he rather needed the threatenings which are denounced against those who are unwilling to be holy, as he soon afterward frankly intimated (and as though it were a light matter) that he was not willing to consecrate all to God. This brother, then, according to his own concession, was not willing to be holy. How unsuccessful would have been the solicitude of his anxious friend, though she had continued hours longer in endeavoring to overcome his unbelief, by urging the promises upon him! It is my

Labor lost. Consecration. Promise. Cleansing.

opinion, that a large amount of well-intended labor, in urging persons to lay hold upon the promises, is lost precisely in that way.

Paul, in his Second Epistle to the Corinthians, chap. vi, 17, 18, and chap. vii, 1, presents the way by which holiness may be attained, in the clearest and most concise manner. The question, "Is consecration entire sanctification?" is here also fully met. First in order stand the terms of the covenant, "Come out from among them, and be ye separate, and touch not the unclean thing." Next come the promises, "I will receive you, and will be a Father unto you, and ye shall be my sons and daughters, saith the Lord Almighty." Here, then, is entire consecration, and immediately follow the promises, which, the moment the conditions are met, are given to the seeker, (and not one moment prior to this compliance,) and yet the apostle addresses the thus consecrated one, as not *yet* cleansed from all filthiness of the flesh and spirit! But he admonishes the humble aspirant, as already in possession of the means by which he is to cleanse *himself*—not as though he were to accomplish this work unaided by the power of God. No. *Having* these promises, which the Lord Jehovah *gave* him the moment he made an entire consecration of himself, he is at once directed to the next step in order, which is to appropriate the promises; and from that point he goes on perfecting holiness in

Premature Attempts to believe.

the fear of God. It is thus that the words of the Saviour, "Sanctify them through thy truth, thy word is truth," are illustrated in the experience of the disciple.

Thus we see how obedience to the primary injunctions of the word must precede the act of appropriating faith. As has been before premised, the difficulty which most persons find in endeavoring to exercise that faith which appropriates the blessing, comes through the effort to believe, *before* the steps which should precede it are taken. Suppose Abraham had tried to believe that his offering was "truly acceptable," *before* he had laid it upon the hallowed altar. How inconsistent! Imagine that he had even brought it within reach of the altar, and yet had not laid it upon that "most holy" place, would it have been sanctified? But, after it was once laid there, was it any more at the option of the offerer? No. It was no more at his disposal, than if it had been borne away by Gabriel, and laid upon the throne of the Eternal, the moment it touched that altar, by the virtue of which it was sanctified to God. If God saw fit, for the trial of his faith and patience, (and shall we say his honesty also?) that it should for a season remain, in order that these various graces might be tried, it was not for him to dictate. Had Abraham yielded to impatience, and again resumed the offering and appropriated it to his own use, it

Sacrilege.   "I will not believe."   Great Mistake.

would have been a most sacrilegious act; for the offering was no more his own—no more in any possible way at his own disposal. Had he thought of it as otherwise than wholly sanctified, he would have greatly dishonored God by his want of faith in his word: "*He that believeth not, maketh God a liar!*"

But does an offerer at the Christian's altar really give up all, until he gives up his *unbelief?* There are many who imagine that they have given up all, who still retain their own *will,* especially on this point—except they see signs and wonders they will not believe. With unbelieving Thomas they say, "Except I shall see"—thus and thus, according to some preconceived plan—"I *will* not believe." And thus it is, though willing, perhaps, to surrender everything else, they hold on to this point, "*I will not believe,* except—." The real position of such persons seems to be expressible as follows: Unless the high and holy One shall come down to meet my *will,* and give me the witness of this salvation, in a way to meet my own views, as to the manner of its reception, "*I will not believe.*" What an egregious mistake is here! If it had been said, "If any man will do *his own* will, he shall know of the doctrine," then there were some hope of the will of such being met. But since Jesus hath said, "If any man *will do* HIS *will,* he shall know of the doctrine," no hope remains for the

A Man without a Will.   *Belief without a Sign.*

entire sanctification of such, until the will be surrendered.

This surrender of the will may, to some, seem a small matter; but to me it appears tremendously great. If a man resigns his will to another, the identity of that man is, in every important sense, lost. His words and actions are all expressive of the mind and will of the other, not of himself. Thus, when the will is wholly given up to God, that person will, in all the minutiæ of life, in word and action, present a transcript of the mind and will of God.

An interesting case, corroborative of the sentiments just expressed, occurred at our house some time since. A lovely young brother, now in heaven, had said in the Tuesday afternoon meeting, "I do not obtain the blessing, and yet it seems to me I am willing to consecrate all." After the meeting had closed, I addressed him thus:—

"If I should tell what you have not given up, would you endeavor *now*, in the strength of the Lord, to make the surrender?" "I will."

"It is here. You, doubtless, give up all but your will, which requires something *besides* the word of God as a foundation for your faith: 'Except ye see signs and wonders, ye will not believe.' But God says, No other *sign* shall be given you, than that which has already been given; that is, the WORD OF GOD. Are you now willing to rely

Just the Difficulty. Unconscious Faith. Intellectual Faith.

upon that alone, and trust God to give whatever emotion he may judge best as the fruit of your faith?" He saw just where the difficulty had been—made the surrender of his will, and received the end of his faith, even the full salvation of his soul, and the witness of that salvation.

I cannot precisely see how one can believe, and yet not *know* it. If this be a truth, I need further instruction on this point. I prefer the good old Scripture doctrine, "He that *believeth* hath the witness in himself." Yours, &c., in love.

No. XXIV.—TO MR. P——.

Temptation as to the genuineness of faith—"Man-work"—Faith without works—"Workers together with God"—Queries about self-sanctification—Answers—Scriptural test—Exhortation.

DEAR SIR,—You seem to be afraid that there may be too much of your own works and doings in this way of receiving the blessing. Satan tempts you that your faith is a mere intellectual effort, and not that faith which is through the operation of the Spirit. If your faith produces such works as prove the leadings of the Holy Spirit, you need nothing more to settle your mind on this point. The effect of righteousness is quietness and assurance. Perhaps if the faith of believers in general were more intellectual, it might be more efficient in its operations. I do not desire to believe anything in such

A Bible Reason. Man-work and Spirit-work. Faith without Works.

a way that I may not give a *reason* for my hope from the Bible. I hope you may have come to about the point in your heavenward journeyings where "wisdom and knowledge shall be the stability of thy times and strength of salvation."

"But is there not danger of being too much absorbed with man-work? I want to have the work of my salvation all Spirit-work, so that I may never in any degree walk by sparks of my own kindling." This then makes it all important that you should have a purely Scriptural experience, and not one merely conformable to what you witness in those who are alike fallible with yourself. Man stands intimately connected as a worker together with God in the work of his salvation.

Is not the more general fault of professors that of seeking to be justified by faith, without such works as God hath ordained, as the necessary prerequisites to an appropriating faith? I think by far the greater number of difficult cases that I meet with are of this description. "How can ye believe which receive honor one of another, and seek not the honor that cometh from God only?" When Paul said, "I beseech you, therefore, brethren, by the mercies of God, that ye present your bodies a living sacrifice, holy, acceptable unto God, which is your reasonable service," did he not mean that they, through the power of the Spirit, should bring the sacrifice, and lay it upon the altar? Would God have commanded this without giving power with the command for the performance of it? God will never do our part of the work, neither does he require that we should do his. It is God that worketh in us, but we must work out our own salvation with fear and trembling.

"Was not Abraham, our father, justified by works, when he had offered Isaac, his son, upon the altar? Seest thou how faith wrought with his works, and by works was faith made perfect, and the scripture was fulfilled which saith, Abraham believed God, and it was imputed to him for righteousness: and he was called the friend of God." "But does not this savor too much of sanctifying ourselves, instead of recognizing the Holy Spirit as the sanctifier? I want to know, most assuredly, that I am sanctified *through* the Spirit."

Let me ask, brother, how were the first movings in your heart, prompting you to seek a state of holiness, induced? Was it not by the power of the *Spirit* that you were incited to take the first step toward the attainment of this grace? And now, that you have for weeks past been sustained in a state of progression toward it, have you been enabled to go forward in your own might, or have you been empowered by the might of the Spirit for every progressive step? And when you were gradually brought to submit to what you felt to

The Spirit's Leadings and Testimony.

be an entire crucifixion of the flesh, I need not ask how you were brought to this point, for I am sure you will acknowledge the direct agency of the Holy Spirit. What abundant cause have you, my dear brother, to thank God and take courage.

In your last you acknowledged that you had been testing yourself in order to ascertain whether you were in truth led by the Spirit, and the result was, that you were enabled to settle the point incontrovertibly by the Scriptures, that you were indeed thus led, and consequently a child of God, and if a son, then an heir of God, and joint heir with Jesus Christ. In order that you may be brought into the enjoyment of all those high and holy privileges, which are already yours by the right of inheritance, the Holy Spirit has undertaken to teach and instruct you in the way in which you should go. Through the operations of the Spirit you are now brought to Jesus, the Mediator of the new covenant, and to the blood of sprinkling. O that you may now yield implicit obedience to the voice of the Spirit, while he may not testify of himself, but take of the things of the Father and of the Son, and reveal them unto you. Jesus, through his merits, now waits to present you to the Father, without spot or wrinkle, or any such thing. Do you doubt? Behold him, as he

> "Points to his side, and lifts his hands,
> And shows that you are graven there."

Patient Waiting.   Danger of drawing back.

I must now close; but permit me first to say, that "we are bound to give thanks always to God for you, brother, beloved of the Lord, because God hath from the beginning chosen you to salvation, through sanctification of the Spirit and belief of the truth." Adieu.   Yours, &c.

No. XXV.—TO MR. P——

Baptism of the Spirit—The just shall live by faith—Witness of the Spirit—Answer delayed—Need of patience—My sister—Interview with Rev. T. Merritt—Confession—Steadfastness—Zeal.

DEAR SIR,—I learn by your letter, that you have not yet received the full baptism of the Holy Ghost. O that you, by the Spirit, may be sustained in a patient waiting! "For yet a little while, and He that shall come, will come, and will not tarry." "Now the just shall *live by faith;* but if any man draw back, my soul shall have no pleasure in him." O, my beloved brother, may you not be of those that *draw back!* Did time permit, I could refer you to cases where individuals, after having been brought to the point where you now stand, have, through the tremendous assaults which Satan hath here made upon their faith, *drawn back* fearfully. May the Lord save you from the painful experience I have witnessed in others who have thus cast away their confidence!

Yet, though I would urge you to wait pa-

Expect the Witness.   Something gained by the Delay.

tiently, and with the resolve never to remove the offering from off the hallowed altar, I would also press the importance of looking momentarily, and with earnest wrestlings, for the witness of the Holy Spirit. It is your privilege to be filled with the Spirit, and with all the fruits of righteousness. We may conceive something of the *feelings* of him whose faith we are admonished to follow, while he continued expecting and longing for the descent of the hallowed fire. The poet doubtless gives some idea of the state of his feelings when he says,—

"Restless, resign'd, for this I wait."

But Abraham did not wait long; neither will you, if you remain steadfast in the faith. Yet you must not imagine that you are not gaining anything by this delay: "Knowing this, that the trial of your faith worketh patience; but let patience have her perfect work, that ye may be perfect and entire, wanting nothing." Even while lingering here, you may be strong in faith, giving glory to God.

You ask if I ever knew any one so long detained at this point as you have been. Yes; I have known some who have been eminent examples in faith, in purity, and in doctrine, who, in like manner with yourself, have been called to endure the trial of their faith. One of these is my sister in the flesh, who in the enjoyment of this

My Sister.   The Reckoning.   Rev. T. Merritt.

blessing was in Christ before me, and whose example and prayers have been very helpful in all my heavenward way. Her experience has been written, from which I will quote briefly.

After she had most solemnly and irrevocably resolved, in obedience to God, to "reckon herself dead indeed unto sin, but alive unto God, through Jesus Christ our Lord," she waited about one week before she received any *sensible* assurance of the fact, (to use your expressions,) "that she was thus dead, and thus alive." But she had counted the cost of living a life of *faith*, and was not to be moved from her steadfastness. While thus lingering with intense longings, the Spirit, through the medium of the written word, encouraged her faith greatly, by the continuous application of these words: "Blessed is she that believeth; for there shall be a performance of those things which were told her from the Lord." She continued, though buffeted and variously tempted, steadfast and unmovable, until one day, occasion requiring that she should call on the Rev. T. Merritt, she said something expressive of her interest on the subject of holiness. "You enjoy that blessing, do you not, sister?" said Mr. M. She was startled at the inquiry, for she had not yet thought of confessing it, and soon replied, "I have dared to reckon myself dead indeed unto sin, and alive unto God, through our Lord Jesus

| Presumption. | Confession, | Joy. | Efforts. |

Christ; but I do not know but that it may be presumption." "Why, sister, presumption lies in doubting God, not in believing him," he returned. She had now joined confession to her faith; it was not enough that with her heart she had believed, the order of God not being fully met, until she had made confession with her mouth; and now she was filled with joy unspeakable, and full of glory. Throughout body, soul, and spirit, she felt the holy fire of divine love penetrating, as it were, her entire being. So great was the weight of glory which rested upon her for several days and nights in succession, that her mortal frame could not have long borne up under it, had not the Lord in a measure staid his hand. Ever since, her faith has been steady and active, inclining to ceaseless and well-directed efforts in promoting the cause of the Redeemer, rather than those fitful, and often misguided endeavors, which the habits of those present, whose efforts and faith are graduated by the state of their emotions. May our faith lead us to "go and do likewise."

Yours affectionately.

Faith without Joy.   Inquiry.

No. XXVI.—TO MR. P——.

Mr. P.'s singular statement of his case—Conclusions questioned—Illustration—The effect of my faith in Mr. P—— Witness of the Spirit—"The Spirit speaketh expressly"—The Bible the voice of the Spirit—The blessing apprehended in the promise—Faith in a dark hour—Resignation.

DEAR SIR,—I am hardly disposed to say that you can really and fully *believe*, and yet not be in possession of "either joy, peace, or even satisfaction." Either your statement of your case does not convey to my mind a correct view of your mental state, or your faith must be in some manner deficient. You say that you now "reckon yourself dead indeed unto sin, but alive unto God, through Jesus Christ our Lord." If you do thus reckon yourself dead unto sin, and alive unto God, then you in reality now *know* that you *are* dead unto sin, and alive unto God. Can you be assured of this fact, and in verity rest in the knowledge that you are even now free from the law of sin and death, and at this moment one with Christ your living Head, and yet not even feel satisfaction in this blessed state?

There may be such a thing as to *think* we believe, or to hope we do so, and yet not in reality give the hearty and entire assent of the mind. To believe God, and yet not to *know* that we believe, is morally impossible. It cannot be otherwise than

Fruits of Faith in Man.		Illustration.

that "he that *believeth* hath the witness in himself." Let me give an illustration. Brother P—— has a father who is a minister of the gospel. You write me word that your father deceased yesterday morning at five o'clock, in the triumphs of faith. You add, "Please have this inserted in the Advocate." I believe your word as heartily as though your living voice had sounded in my ear, and the *fruit* of my faith is at once manifest. My heart is touched, and in my eyes gather the sympathetic tears. My husband enters, and, in haste to enlist yet another sharer in your sorrow, I say, "Brother P——'s father is dead; he died thus," &c. He now wishes you to make an announcement of the fact in the Advocate. He believes, without a thought of doing otherwise, in consequence of the confession I have made of my faith in you, and perhaps, without even looking at your letter, goes to the Advocate office, showing the effect of his faith in you, even though his knowledge of your word has reached him through a second person.

Here are faith and its fruits, inducing a confession which is to tell upon the hearts of hundreds; for the wide-spread circulation of a public journal will bear it to the hearts of multitudes to whom he has ministered, producing, perhaps, corresponding effects on each, and all this is the result of my faith in your *written* word.

Had I not had an internal conviction that what

The Witness of the Spirit. "The Spirit speaketh expressly."

you had written was in verity so, that is, the witness in myself that I believed you, would I have taken such a responsibility upon myself as to have authorized this announcement? Yet in all this I have not been in anywise unmindful of the fact that *"the Spirit itself beareth witness with our spirit,"* testifying to the truth of the word. This must ever be the case. It would involve strange and irreconcilable contradictions, such as would greatly dishonor the God of the Bible, to say otherwise. But *is not the entire voice of the Scriptures the voice of the Holy Spirit?* Never was there a more incontrovertible truth uttered than this. In the presence of God, angels, men, and devils, I would fearlessly utter it. Myriads of men in all ages have, in reliance on this fact, been sanctified through the "*belief* of the truth," and are now enjoying the fruit of their faith in that world of glory of which the Spirit speaks through the Scriptures. Devils also rely on facts revealed in the Bible as the voice of the Spirit, and their faith also produces effects, for they believe and *tremble.* To me it seems wonderful that this fact, namely, that the Scriptures are *expressly* the voice of the Spirit, should be so little felt, though so generally acknowledged. Paul, referring Timothy to some Scriptural assertions, says, "The Spirit *speaketh* expressly on this wise," &c. Yet if one is admonished to rely upon the *written* WORD as in

Faith always brings Power.   A Mountain of Gold

verity the voice of God, the answer may be with surprise returned, "What, believe without any *other* evidence than the *word* of God!" O when will the truth fully obtain among professors, that "prophecy came not of old time by the will of man, but holy men of old spake as they were *moved by the Holy Ghost!*"

Let me tell you, my dear brother, to the praise of the God of the Bible, that in my experience I find *faith always brings power.* I apprehend the lively oracles as the words of the living God, and to me the Bible is not a "*dead* letter," but spirit and life. When I kneel in my devotions before the Lord of heaven and earth, I spread out before me that WORD, by which he hath said I am to be judged at the last day; and conscious that it is only the Spirit which indited the Scriptures that can give them life-giving energy, I wait only on God, humbly believing that

> "God is his own interpreter,
> And he will make it plain."

Every promise of God, as one hath said, is worth more than a mountain of gold. I search as for hidden treasure, to know what promises are suited to my condition, knowing that such are *given* to me, because Christ hath purchased them for me, and all the promises of God in him *are* yea and amen. The designs of God are frustrated, and his name dishonored, if I refuse to call them mine, and to claim the proffered benefits, after being by the Spirit brought to sustain this character, in answer to the intercessions of Jesus.

I am endeavoring to trust in the Lord at all times, and under all circumstances. To the glory of his name I will say, that I believe I have been enabled to confide as unwaveringly, under dark dispensations, as under those more light and joyous. If all were light, then there had been no tests of faith. But it has not been so. I thank the Lord that some of the most instructive lessons I ever received have been painfully acquired. I do not remember to have been brought through one trial, however contradictory circumstances may have appeared, but that I have been enabled to rest in the assurance, that "all things work together for good to them that love God." I fully believe that my covenant-keeping God will keep that which I have committed to him unto the perfect day. But I would not dare choose the way in which I am to be kept; this I leave to God, with a sure trust and confidence that he will lead me through just such "Trials, in number, measure, weight," as will best show forth his praise, by exhibiting his power to sustain. Even so, Lord Jesus. Amen.

At the end of life's journey may I, with the spirits of the just made perfect, meet my dear brother P——. Though we have never seen each other in the flesh, yet, doubtless, there we shall meet as kindred spirits—ay, even as children of one Father, in our Father's house. Yours, as ever.

No. XXVII.—TO BISHOP AND MRS. H——.

Separated friends—The day of my espousals—Judge W——, and Judge R—— Happiness without holiness—A forty years' seeker obtains the blessing in a few hours—An evening on the camp ground—Struggles of a minister for holiness; his confession—The morning; doubt; profession; the witness—A member of his flock—Conversation—Full salvation in five minutes—Brother and sister B—— "This *now* salvation"—A youth—Proposition—Decision—Self-denial—Sweet peace.

DEAR BROTHER AND SISTER H——. You say, "Direct your next to Cincinnati." How fast and how far you are receding from us! The thought is painful. At times I have almost wished that I did not love you so well; but in reality I am not sorry.

> "Jesus, the corner-stone,
> Did first our hearts unite;
> And still he keeps our spirits one,
> Who walk with him in white."

Ten years ago, on the 26th of July, Jesus became the all-absorbing object of my heart's adoration. September 28, 1827, was a memorable day. I am sure I shall thank the Lord throughout time and eternity that I ever saw it: but far, O how far more memorable, is the 26th of July, 1837, when Jesus became the Bridegroom of my soul, and condescended to enter into the bonds of an everlasting covenant with me! "Surely goodness and mercy have followed me all my days." "The lines are fallen to me in pleasant places, and I have a goodly heritage." "Come and let us exalt the name of our God together."

Sister H—— says she is staying with Judge W——, of D——: the mention of it reminded me of Judge R——, of M——, whose family I visited some time since. Judge R. was also a class-leader and a prominent member of the church at M——. He did not profess the enjoyment of the blessing of holiness. One day, after I had been urging the subject with earnestness, he replied: "O, sister P——, I am happy." For a moment I felt hurt, and, looking imploringly upon him, said, "Why, brother R., imagine you had a child, to whom you had given a command, the observance of which was most important for his welfare and also for your honor as a parent. The child, though fully aware of your command, still goes on in disobedience. You remonstrate. He replies, 'O, I am happy.' Would you not wish your child were not quite so happy?" I shall never forget his looks; they spoke of shame-facedness before his heavenly Father; he had not a word to say in reply. Soon afterward he received the blessing of holiness. I have once or twice mentioned this, of late, at meetings where the people seemed contented to enjoy happiness without holiness.

At the Eastham camp meeting, I heard an in-

Law's Call.   "Speak of Holiness."

teresting item in the experience of a minister who has enjoyed the blessing of holiness forty years past. Before receiving the blessing, he had often thought how much he wanted it. One day, on taking up "Law's Call to a Holy Life," his eye rested on these words: "Men are not holy, because they never really purpose to be holy." He thought, "Surely here is my case. I have never really brought the matter to a point, with a fixed purpose to be holy." He then made the resolve, and, if I remember right, in a few hours afterward was made a happy witness of full salvation.

I was at N—— camp meeting when I last wrote you. The evening of that day was interestingly spent. I was in quite a large and crowded tent, where the exercises were of a general character. As most present seemed to be professors, it was suggested, "Speak of holiness." I was not well, and an unusual prostration of body and mind had come over me, of which the enemy endeavored to take advantage, by causing an uncommon shrinking, perhaps I may say, of both flesh and spirit; but I thought of Mr. Wesley's Scriptural admonition, "Casting aside that enthusiastic doctrine, that we are not to do good unless our hearts are free to it." I promised the Lord, if he would help me to a word in season, that I would ever look back and say, "Is the hand of the Lord shortened?"

Struggles of a Minister.   "God has humbled me."

I spoke, and the power of the Lord was present. One, in an especial manner, was wrought upon, and cried out with a loud voice. When the people were called to the stand, this brother remained with several others, who seemed as though they could not leave the place. To my surprise, I found that the individual, who had been so signally brought out, was the minister of the people with whom I had been worshiping. He continued to struggle during the services from the stand, most of the time on his knees, and obtained a little light just toward the close. He was then taken to another tent, where it was somewhat more retired; but his people followed him. Here he disclosed the secret of the matter.

Amid many sighs and tears, he said, as nearly as I can remember, "O, my people, God has *humbled* me before you. I have, as you know, now and then tried to preach holiness to you; conscious that I did not enjoy it myself, but fully purposed that you should not know it, I had hoped to get it in the privacy of my chamber. To-day I had serious thoughts of returning home, to plead with God in secret for it: but God would not let me do this; he has brought me out, and *humbled me before you.* I must, I will be holy." While he was kneeling during the exercises from the stand, so unyielding had been the character of his unbelief, that I had, perhaps almost reprovingly, said, "You are a minister, and as a leader of your flock you ought to be an example in faith, as well as in doctrine ; and God doubtless means to bring you out as such." Alluding to this before his people, he observed, "The sister said I was a minister. Ah! this was the worst of all; but I deserved it." This was, I think, one of the most affecting scenes I ever witnessed, and it was made the means of awakening a deep and absorbing interest on the theme of holiness in the minds of his people.

I was obliged to leave the ground before the meeting closed, as I slept at a house a little distance from the encampment. On the morrow I returned at an early hour, as a love-feast was about being held. I had asked the Lord to direct my feet, and amid the multitude, at the entrance of a tent door, I met this minister, who, until the evening before, had been a stranger to me. I found him prepared to say that he *knew* he had laid all upon the altar, but was not sure that he was wholly sanctified.

"How would it have been," said I, "with one in ancient time who had laid all upon the altar, in view of the divine declarations, 'The altar sanctifieth the gift,' 'Whatsoever *toucheth* the altar shall be holy?' A friend meets this offerer on his return from the hallowed altar, after having, according to the best of his ability, presented such sacrifices as the law required, and inquires, 'Is your gift sanctified? or is your offering holy, acceptable?' Imagine that the offerer had said, 'My offering is laid upon the holy altar, I know; but that it is wholly sanctified, I dare not say.' 'How dare you say otherwise?' replies the questioner. 'If God hath said, "The *altar* sanctifieth the gift," it surely is not left optional with yourself whether you will believe or not; it is presumptuous to doubt. You cannot dishonor God more than by doubting his word.'"

The brother at once saw that it would be a sin which would bring down the displeasure of God upon him, should he longer indulge a doubt, and resolved, on the authority of God's word, to make confession with the mouth. He hastened to the stand. Love-feast exercises had already commenced. As soon as opportunity presented, he came out most clearly in the confession, that he was wholly sanctified, throughout body, soul, and spirit. Great peace, quietness, and assurance, took possession of his heart, and he bids fair to be a very zealous, clear-minded professor of the great salvation.

On the afternoon of the same day I asked a member of his flock, whether she was enjoying the blessing of holiness. The following conversation, as nearly as I can remember, ensued. She replied, "No." "When do you think God will be willing to give it to you?" "He would be willing to give

A Seeker of Holiness questioned.   The Venture.

it to me now, I think, if I were only willing to give up my unbelief." "Do you think unbelief to be sinful?" "Yes." "Do you expect to save yourself from this sin, or do you expect Christ to save you?" "O, Christ alone can save me." "Do you believe that Christ is willing to save you now, from this and from all your sins, and that he will do it if you will only now trust him for present salvation?" With much fervor, she answered, "Yes." "And will you now trust him to save you this moment from all sin? I do not ask what you will do to-morrow, or five minutes hence, for the future is in eternity, and at the expiration of that time you may be there also; all you want is *present* salvation, which can only be received by a present act on your part of entire reliance on Christ, for it, and which will be continued just so long as this act of entire reliance on your part is persevered in. If you do not expect to save yourself in any degree, every moment you do not thus fully rely on Christ as a whole Saviour, you only make yourself more unworthy by the delay, for in not venturing wholly you grieve his Spirit."

"O I *will* venture," she said. "That is not it. *Do* you *now* venture? Does Christ *now save you* from all your sins?" She fell on her knees, and cried out, "I am saved! Christ saves me *now!* 'My Redeemer from all sin, I will praise thee, I will praise thee.'" I left her rejoicing with a joy unspeakable and full of glory. I do not think more than five minutes were occupied in this conversation, and when I arrested the sister, I think she was concerned with some domestic arrangements in the tent. I mention this to say, How truly it is not according to the tears shed, nor the length of time spent in the pursuit, nor according to anything else, other than, "according to our faith it is done unto us!"

That evening God also gave me another signal victory of faith. A dear brother and sister B——, who seemed to take pleasure in showing us every kindness in their power, (we had not our own tent on the ground,) were neither of them in the enjoyment of full salvation. It seemed as if my gracious Lord said, "Ask what thou wilt, and it shall be done unto thee." Thou hast condescended to say, that "even a cup of cold water given to a disciple, in the name of a disciple, shall not lose its reward;" and now, I ask that this dear brother and sister may be abundantly rewarded, and let it be by their receiving the blessing of entire sanctification this night. It seemed too much, and human probabilities considered, intimations did not seem to favor my expectations, especially on the part of brother B——; but

> "Faith, mighty faith, the *promise* sees,
> And looks to that alone ;
> Laughs at impossibilities,
> And cries, It shall be done."

"This now Salvation."   Three saved.

I do not think more than half an hour intervened before God gave me the desire of my heart relative to brother B——. He laid hold while I presented the simple way in which brother J——, of P——, received the blessing while I was conversing with him in the cars, which you may perhaps remember. After I had repeated just how brother J—— stepped over the bar of unbelief, brother B—— cried out, "*Jesus saves me now!*" Praise the Lord. O, it seemed as if he could never cease talking about "this *now* salvation," as he called it. A clearer or more joyful witness of full salvation through faith I scarcely remember to have seen. His wife also, with another dear friend, for whom I was much interested, and greatly longed for, entered into the rest of faith before the close of the interview.

And now, what a recital of doings I have given my dear brother and sister H——, and yet I have scarcely commenced to say the many things of similar description I have witnessed within a few weeks past. I would stop, but there is one thing with which you will be so interested, that I am sure you would scarcely forgive me should I not add it to the list. Dear sister A—— is also rejoicing in possession of the peace of God. O, I am sure you will say, Praise the Lord. The degree of quietness and assurance attained was brought about so noiselessly, and was also so characteristic of herself, that I must give you a glance at this also.

In speaking of the conformity of professors to the world, a few weeks since, she expressed her regret that there should be so much of it, especially in the church where she worshiped. "And A——, dear, why do you not set them an example on this point?" said I. "If I were a professor of religion, I should then feel it my duty to do so," she replied. "If you think it would be your duty then, it is your duty now; and I do not believe, if such are your views, that you will ever get into the enjoyment of religion till you do." "Well, it would be no cross for me," she observed. "You had better try it," said I. I had long believed that A—— knew something of the transforming power of religion on the heart, and that she only needed something to bring her out, by way of confession; but I little conjectured that this was to be the means. I had thought she possessed so much independence of mind, that the matter of dress was a small concern with her.

She said nothing more, and I remembered no more of it, until two or three weeks after, when, on observing her little gayeties laid aside, I inquired the cause. She replied, "When you mentioned the matter to me I thought it would be no cross, and resolved on trying it. But twice, on going out, I heard persons behind me remarking,

"What a pity!"   Sweet Peace.

'What a fool she makes herself!' 'What a pity!' and things to that effect, and I have indeed found that it was a cross. But I have had *sweet peace.*" Her decision, in other respects, is marked. Though we may not glory in the creature, yet it seems to me that we may have another S——, than whom a more decided follower of the Saviour I never knew.

And now, do you not think it quite time for me to close? How little I thought of such a letter when I commenced writing. I question whether I shall let Dr. P—— see it. Do you not think he ought to chide both for your sake and mine?

Yours, in the love and faith of the gospel.

No. XXVIII.—TO REV. T. M——.

The "Third Monday evening meetings"—Rev. Mr. C,—— Our calling—Mrs. —— The testimony of a maid in Israel—Searching the Scriptures—"It is all here"—A pious visit—Interrogations—An object of great desire—Withstood by Satan—The vow—The assurance—"Let it be now"—Suggestion—The word—The victory—Delay—Trial—A hearty profession of full salvation.

YOUR very interesting letter of December 31st was received. It is with much pleasure I respond to the inquiries of our father in Christ. You have so long, and so ardently, devoted your life to the special promotion of holiness, that I do not wonder you now, standing, as you do, on the borders of your heavenly inheritance, feel like inquiring earnestly how the battle goes.

You desire to know how those meetings, which you established when in our city, are prospering. Let me tell you that I think the "Third Monday evening meetings promise more than to equal your most sanguine anticipations. Monday of last week was the time for our last regular meeting. The power of the Lord was present. A good number of clear-minded witnesses testified of the enjoyment of present salvation from all sin. The Rev. Mr. C., who had been unusually desirous of the blessing for two or three weeks previous, was at this meeting enlightened to discern his privileges in Christ Jesus more fully, and, with a heart flaming with fervor, he left the place. The next day, about noon, he began to venture on Christ, and at once felt the power of saving grace. On the evening of that day, at love-feast, he gave in a cheering testimony of the power of Christ to save. O it would indeed have been another drop which would have told most sweetly in our cup of bliss, had our dear father M. been permitted to witness the desire of his heart granted relative to these meetings! We sat together under the shadow of the Almighty, in heavenly places; while, as under the more immediate eye of Omniscience, with the Spirit of holiness brooding over us, one witness after another, in quick succession, and

A Design of God.   Utility of Testimony.

with holy delight, praised the beauty of holiness. The "Third Monday evening meeting" previous to this was held at the Forsyth-street Church: it was quite as satisfactory as the one just noted. Though you so dearly love the people of your early choice, and greatly desire their establishment in this grace, yet I know it is your belief that it was the design of the Head of the church, in raising us up as a people, that we should be as a light in a dark place, relative to the attainment of holiness in the present life; and when you hear that God has not been wholly unmindful of us in this our calling, I know it gives you abundant joy. And now let me give you matter for special thanksgiving, by referring to one of the witnesses, who gave in a delightful testimony of the power of our Lord and Saviour to "wash and keep us clean." She is the wife of Prof. ——, and for several months has been enjoying the witness, that the blood of Jesus cleanseth. She informs me that she takes the "Guide," and as she hails from your way, I have thought your pages might be enriched by her pen, as her experience is remarkably clear and instructive. It furnishes further assurance of the utility of meetings for testimony on the subject of holiness. This lady, as she has since told me, found herself under rather unlooked-for circumstances at a Methodist meeting, and, from a little maid in Israel, heard an unsophisticated tes-

A Witness. Truth unfettered. A Persevering Inquirer.

timony of the power of Christ to save from all sin. The testimony was from one who could say, "We speak that we do know, and testify that we have seen." Had the learned disquisitions of a theologian been brought to bear thus unexpectedly upon her mind, however truthful his position had been, Mrs. ——, not unacquainted with theological warfare, might have been better prepared for resistance; but *truth*, unfettered by adornment, with the sharpness of the two-edged sword, penetrated her heart, and she left the place deeply conscious that a further work must be wrought in her heart before she could stand perfect and complete in all the will of God.

Conceiving that what she had heard was Bible truth, she set herself, as far as circumstances would permit, to searching the Scriptures, in order to assure her heart before God whether she might indeed expect salvation from all sin in this life; not for a moment doubting but that, if such were her privilege, the Lord would make it known to her through his word and bring her into the enjoyment of that state. For weeks she continued in this employ; while clearer light with every day shone upon the word, leading her to the Lamb of God which taketh away the sins of the world. While passing through this process, her husband often pleasantly inquired, "Well, wife, how comes on Christian perfection now?" and as her confidence from her Biblical investigations gathered strength, she daily expressed her belief, her increasing belief, in the doctrine, until, with a full heart, and with her eye upon the word of God, she exclaimed, "O, husband, IT IS ALL HERE." As intimated, it was only for her to be assured that the Scriptures presented it as her privilege to be saved from all sin in this life, in order to enter upon the enjoyment of this blessed state. I think she said to me that she never thought of doubting the faithfulness of God in fulfilling his promises at once to her, so soon as her faith was settled scripturally, as a preparation on her own part for this reliance. According to her faith it was done unto her. She no sooner found the doctrine in the Bible than she at once received the blessing in her heart.

But this is not all : I have something to relate relative to her distinguished husband, which will raise the note of praise yet higher. Ever since Mrs. ——'s mind became interested on the subject of holiness, he had been in an inquiring state. On the 24th of December, Mrs. —— came to the Tuesday meeting, which she very much enjoyed. She afterward expressed a wish that her husband might be permitted to attend, during his visit to this city, which was of course acceded to. On the intervening Thursday, Prof. and Mrs. ——, with some other Christian friends, supped at sister L——'s. It was truly a pious visit; and the interview I shall never forget. During the evening the Professor asked very many questions, involving some nice points, most evidently with the single aim to elicit light on the doctrine and experience of holiness. The enlightening and hallowing influences of the Holy Spirit seemed to be very present, both with the questioner and the questioned; and when, at the close of the lengthy interview, he was called upon to pray, in defiance of former prejudices in reference to females exercising before men, he called upon the female friend whom he had questioned during the evening to pray. She had heard of his views on this point, and the cross was heavy; but she saw that, in order to carry out the principles of holiness, no other way remained, and she led in prayer.

After her return home, until about midnight, she continued to plead for him with groanings unutterable. Her mind seemed to take within its comprehensive range how the entire sanctification of such mental energies as the Lord had bestowed upon him might promote the cause of holiness, when wholly enlisted. And she well knew that it was not possible for any one to live in the enjoyment of the blessing of sanctification, without feeling it as a consuming fire shut up in the bones, enlisting all the powers of body and mind in its promotion and with desires inexpressibly intense; did she long that an understanding acknowledged to

Wrestling with Principalities and Powers.   A Vow.

be so clear in philosophical truth, might concentrate its energies in presenting to the world the principles of holiness; for well did she know that the more closely it was examined, the brighter it would shine. If time would permit I should love to tell you how Satan tried to withstand her, for it was a season of wrestling with principalities and powers, never to be forgotten; but I may not extend my communication on this point, further than to record a most solemn vow, which was uttered in this hour of extremity. "If thou wilt do this," said she, in her importunity, "I will, through thy grace, be more truly 'instant in season and out of season,' in urging the subject of holiness on persons of this description, and will henceforth regard the granting of this, my desire, as a *special* subject of praise through time and eternity." The high and holy One at that moment condescended to assure her heart, that her prayer had in truth come up in remembrance before him. Had a voice from the highest heavens fallen upon her ear, saying, "Thy prayer has been heard, and thy vow shall be in perpetual remembrance before God, the desire of thy heart shall be granted;" she could not have been more confirmed in the persuasion that she should have the thing she had desired of God. Yet, though so fully assured that it should be granted, the bestowment was in prospective, and she retired to her couch so burdened for the bring-

Strugglings for Deliverance. "Laid hold and *kept* hold."

ing forth of her desire, that the whole night was spent in strugglings for deliverance; even when the bodily powers had yielded to broken slumbers, the spirit remained conscious in its unutterable groanings. Before morning dawned she was again in the attitude of a suppliant, and in her earnest implorings she said, "Let it be *now*, that he may have such perceptions of the way of faith, of its simplicity and power, as he never before had any conception of." It was suggested, "He is probably asleep, and it is inconsistent to ask that he may be so signally blessed *just now*, when his mind may not be in a state to receive the blessing." The response of her heart was, that whether he was now waking or sleeping, his spirit was doubtless in a state of preparation; for the power of the Holy Ghost, which had been operating on her heart, as if it were almost apart from herself, must have influenced his heart simultaneously, and still she cried, "Let it be *just now*." As ever, her heart fled to the blessed WORD for a foundation upon which to rest her faith, when yet again, as in former emergencies, she was enabled to say, "And this is the confidence that I have in thee, that if I ask anything according to thy will thou hearest me, and if I know that thou hearest me, whatsoever I ask, I know that I *have* the petition that I desire of thee." She laid hold, and *kept* steadfast hold on the promise implied in this wonderful portion of the word, and

Venturesome.   The Delay.   Terrible Struggle.

now began to say, "I *have* the petition I desired of thee," and prayer was turned to thanksgivings to God for the reception of the thing desired. Many temptations had she during that day to give up a faith which the enemy suggested was so venturesome. Hour after hour she waited the expected arrival of Professor —— to announce the victory of faith, and as the moments succeeded each other, without bringing any *sensible* assurance of the effect of her faith in his behalf, the trial became more severe. She well knew that the blessing could not be enjoyed without exerting upon the mind a pervading and all-controlling influence, and "if you had not believed in vain," said the deceiver, "the object of your faith and prayers would have been moved to hasten to you with the confession of how great things the Lord had done for him." But the whole of that day passed, and it was not until near the close of another that she again saw Professor ——. The struggle which was endured in holding fast her confidence, two or three hours previous to seeing him, can never be forgotten. It was, indeed, terrible, but grace empowered her to endure. On seeing her the professor said, "At about such an hour yesterday morning I received such clear views of faith, of its simplicity and power, as I never before had a conception of. It was the *full assurance of faith.*"

The hour named was precisely the time the sister

had claimed the blessing for him, and he also stated, that, during the hours of the night preceding this transition, his spirit had been under an unusual influence, and in wakefulness had been progressing toward that point of light and power upon which it had now entered. "O," said he, with intense ardor, "*faith hath power in it.*" He since delights in calling the state of blessedness upon which he has entered, "HOLINESS." Since his return home we have received a letter from him filled with assurances of his identity with the blessed theme of full salvation. He says, "On this point, namely, whether I love God fully, entirely, I can say, with the devoted Mrs. Rogers, Satan has ceased to tempt me and my soul is entirely at rest. If I am not mistaken, (and how can I be mistaken, when I have a consciousness of it as deep and as distinct as of my own existence?) my soul has panted after God until it has found him, and has entered into the inner sanctuary of the divine love." Relative to promoting the cause of holiness, he observes, "I feel as if I had nothing else to live for. I consider myself consecrated and pledged for ever." I have thought that some profitable communications for the "Guide" might be expected from either Professor —— or his gifted lady. Such talents, consecrated and pledged to the promotion of holiness, may surely be expected, through the blessing of God, to tell advantageously on the cause; but I

"Not by Might."   Miss L.'s Letters.

well know that brother M—— truly feels that it is "not by might, nor by power, but by my Spirit, saith the Lord." I have far exceeded the intended bounds of my letter, and were it not for the preciousness of my theme might fear I had wearied you. May your most enlarged desires for the sanctification of the church be granted, and may our dear father in Christ ever feel that the Head of the church is fulfilling the work of faith with power in his own heart, and experimentally apprehend that both He that sanctifieth and they that are sanctified are ONE! Farewell, dearly beloved in Christ.   Yours, &c.

No. XXIX.—TO REV. MR. K——.

"The Guide"—E—— street Church—One hundred witnesses—Revival—A local preacher—Long-continued efforts to obtain holiness—The sacrifice—The rest—Remark of Dr. ——. Sixty persons set apart for God—The camp prayer meeting—A passer-by arrested—A searching preacher—Revival in Baltimore—The work of God in A—— street in 1831—Morning meetings—Men and angels—Holiness the strength of the church—Satan's favorite instrument—A reproachful compliment—"And shall teach men so."

OUR dear Brother K—— asks if I have read Miss Littlefield's Letters? I have not, but should like to see them. If they are in tract form, could you not inclose some copies in the package containing our numbers of the "Guide?"

There has been a glorious revival of the work

of holiness in the E—— street Church. The minister stationed there called in this morning, and said, that at a love-feast held last night about one hundred testified clearly of the power of Christ to save from all sin. What a wonderful work, and all within a few months! I should have stated, that, besides this, several hundred have been converted within the same period. Perhaps there was never a stronger confirmation of the truth, "One shall chase a thousand, and two shall put ten thousand to flight," than is furnished by the history of this revival.

I am quite acquainted with its commencement and progress, and if you think it calculated to exhibit the faithfulness of God, and also to furnish useful instruction relative to the order to be observed in promoting revivals, you are at liberty to make use of it as may best promote the cause to which you are devoted.

A brother belonging to this charge received the blessing of holiness at camp meeting last summer. He had been struggling for two or three years to obtain it; and if wrestling all night a number of times; if fasting till the body was so nearly brought down, as to leave but little probability that the health will again rally; or if humility so deep, that though a local preacher, he has presented himself for the prayers of the people with the seekers of salvation; if by any way other than by simple *faith*

Believe God.   Everlasting Covenant.   Calm after a Storm.

the blessing were to be obtained; then this brother long since had gained it. But on passing a crowded tent one morning, he heard an humble disciple speak of the duty of *believing* God, after being assured that the sacrifice was upon the altar. She urged the present performance of this duty, by adverting to Abraham's sacrifice; maintaining that the offering *was* sanctified the moment it was laid upon the altar, and that to doubt it was to doubt the word of God. He now felt that it was his *duty* to believe, irrespective of frames and feelings, and also perceived that it was most important that he should enter into the bonds of an everlasting covenant with God, to be eternally given up to his service. The mode which had been presented he believed to be most Scriptural, and resolving at once to test it, he retired from the multitude, and in the sequestered wood again calmly surveyed the ground, and then most solemnly bound all upon the altar, and rested upon the word of God as an assurance of divine acceptance. He at once felt that he was founded upon the Rock of ages. Such a *rest*, after a tumult of years, can only be appreciated by those who, in like manner, have been driven about and tossed. His whole soul was at once filled with inexpressible longings that the church should see the duty of entire consecration and the simplicity of faith.

Dear Dr. —— had said to him in my hearing,

Surplus Grace to convert the World.   The Sixty.

"If the church would only get good measure, pressed down, shaken together, and running over, what would run over would be enough to convert the world." He seemed to be filled with faith and with the Holy Ghost at the time he said it, but I must confess that the expression struck me as extravagant. But the next I heard of it was at a meeting on the ground, where this brother was talking among the people with whom he stood connected in church fellowship. With power and demonstration of the Spirit, he assured them of the truth of Dr. P.'s assertion. He desired to know how many would bind themselves together before God, and before each other, to consecrate themselves wholly to God, and not to rest till they should receive the witness that the offering was accepted. It was not long before about sixty had thus solemnly set themselves apart for God.

At the camp prayer meeting, held a short time after their return, a number of those who were seeking the witness of holiness were so ardent in their desires for the blessing, that they rushed forward to the altar when the invitation was given for those who desired the prayers of the congregation, and it was then that the power of God began to be manifested in an extraordinary manner. Sinners from all parts of the house were seen making their way toward the altar of prayer, and what

A Passer-by.   Pardon and Holiness.   Baltimore.

may seem incredible, the power of the Highest seemed not only to rest upon all within the house, but upon those around it also. A person was passing by on business, when the awakening influences of the Spirit came down upon him, and turning into the church, he went forward to the altar crying for mercy. From this time the two branches of the work went on simultaneously. Numbers were wholly sanctified weekly, and scores were born into the kingdom of Christ. Some idea of what God hath wrought you may gather from the announcement at the beginning of this communication. This brother, with success somewhat similar, has labored at a number of places since. If I should give the characteristic mainly distinguishing his remarkable ministrations, I think it would be his uncompromising attitude, relative to an entire giving up of the world, and his earnest enforcement of the truth: "The time is come that judgment must begin at the house of God."

I have received a letter from the Rev. Mr. M——, of Baltimore, informing us of an extraordinary work going on at the M—— street Church. This work also began with the church. Meetings had for some time been held on the morning of each day, for the special benefit of those who were seeking the blessing of entire sanctification.

Brother M—— says, that he has "heard about thirty consistent witnesses testify at one of these

40 out of 120.   1000 converted.   Angels cannot preach.

meetings of the power of Christ to save from all sin. Meetings have been held in both the body and basement of the church at one time. Out of one hundred and twenty penitents forward for prayers, forty have during one evening been converted. The work is truly wonderful."

It was thus also that the extraordinary revival in the A—— street Church, of 1831, commenced, during which, I think, over a thousand souls were converted.

Morning meetings for the special benefit of the members were held from ten to twelve. It was through the instrumentality of these morning meetings that many became strong to labor for God, and prepared not only to point awakened sinners to Christ, but to nurse them after they had been brought into the way, and to lead them by the power of the Spirit into green pastures and beside still waters.

We bid you God speed, dear brother. Yours is truly a high and holy calling; a work which an angel might covet. But let us remember that men may do what angels may not do. Witness the case of Cornelius: the angel was not commissioned to proclaim Christ to Cornelius, but only to direct to a human instrument, which God had raised up, to tell him what he ought to do. Thus in the blessed work of telling men how they ought to come to Christ as their Saviour to the uttermost,

Great Designs greatly withstood.   Baptized Opposers.

God hath raised you up. We magnify the name of our Lord in your behalf. May he fulfill all the good pleasure of his goodness in you, and the work of faith with power. You are engaged in a great work, and your subtil enemy is doubtless very busy in his inventions to perplex, or to bring you down from your work. We have reason to believe that he generally proportions his opposition to the magnitude of the work to be performed. Personal holiness is a mighty engine for pulling down the strongholds of Satan, and he doubtless in a variety of ways withstands you. While laboring to promote it, sometimes he employs as his instruments those who stand committed before the world as the servants of Christ. When the enemy can get such as these to come out against the doctrine of entire sanctification, or to hold the truth in unrighteousness relative to this subject, he answers his purpose more effectually than by instrumentalities known to be at his disposal. Satan doubtless directs his most poignant arrows to your heart through some such. "Father, forgive them; they know not what they do." "They did it ignorantly" is, however, an apology I fear which can hardly avail, in the case of many of these baptized opposers of holiness in the church; or if volunteered for them, truth would claim to add, "Of this they are *willingly* ignorant."

Yet, in view of the rewards of eternity, how

truly deplorable the state of those who oppose truth, whether ignorantly, or otherwise! There are many, both among the ministry and the laity, who, apparently, with but little idea of the magnitude of the sin, speak lightly of the subject of holiness, and of those who profess the enjoyment of the blessing. "O he is one of the sanctified ones," say they; as if God had not in verity "*set apart*" the godly for himself. Such, on being questioned, may say that they are not opposed to holiness; but "the Lord knoweth them that are his." Their example goes toward weakening the force of truth. They do not profess to be living in the enjoyment of a state of holiness themselves, and in this they break not one of the least of God's commandments, but the first and great command, "Thou shalt love the Lord thy God with all thy heart, soul, mind, and strength"—enjoining holiness of heart in its fullest sense. O how many professors there are of this class, who thus break the command themselves, and, by the force of their example, "teach men so!" If there were a possibility of such characters getting to heaven, surely they would be called *least* in the kingdom of heaven, however dignified their ministerial calling or professions of piety may have been here on earth.

But, dear brother K., in view of the work in which you are engaged, how inspiring are the words of your divine Master, "But whosoever shall do and teach them, (these commandments,) the same shall be called great in the kingdom of heaven." Adieu, dear friend in Jesus.

No. XXX.—TO MRS. B——.

Mark xi, 24—1 John v, 14, 15—An illustration—Answers to prayer—"The faithful and true"—"In God will I praise his word"—The bank bill—The infidel minister—Faith and sense—The word personified—An end of the difficulty.

I RECEIVED your note of yesterday, in which you refer me to the interesting passage, Mark xi, 24. I respond with pleasure; but as my time is limited, I cannot hope to present you any very full exposition of my thoughts. The passage you refer to is in perfect keeping with 1 John v, 14, 15: "And this is the confidence that we have in Him, that, if we ask anything according to his will, he heareth us. And if we know that he hear us, whatsoever we ask, we know that we have the petitions that we desired of him."

For illustration, let it be supposed that sister B—— is a dear friend from whom I expect great favors. The granting of these favors is conditional. She has made known her *will*, involving a variety of points, and then referring me to this, says, "Ask what you will, and if *according* to the principles laid down, I will grant it."

Faith in Mrs. B——. How I have obtained answers.

If I have perfect confidence in sister B——, after ascertaining whether what I desire can be granted in accordance with her will, I go with confidence, and present my petitions, believing that I *receive* them, because I have *your word*, assuring me that I shall have them. If a friend, meeting me on my return from your presence, asks, "Have those petitions been granted?" I unhesitatingly answer, "*Yes*." "But I do not see the result," says the friend. "That does not make the case doubtful," I reply; "for sister B.'s word is as good as her bond, and I have her *word*, so you may rely upon it, just as firmly as though you saw me in actual possession of the thing desired."

The many gracious answers to prayer which I have received, on precisely the same principle, given in the illustration just presented, eternity will reveal to the praise of God. But I would not defer it till I have passed the bounds of time, to exhibit His *faithfulness*. His name is "FAITHFUL and TRUE."

I love to testify, by my words and actions, before God, angels, and men; yes, and before infernals too, that I do *rely on the faithfulness of God*. I am willing, if this be the will of God concerning me, to be brought into circumstances which may call forth an exhibition of my trust in God before a congregated universe. This, I believe, has been the spirit by which I have been actuated for several years past; I have had some thorough tests by outward circumstances, and inward exercises, and to the praise of God I say, I have not cast away my confidence, nor made shipwreck of faith.

We cannot honor God more than by trusting him, neither can we dishonor him more than by doubting his word. David loved to praise the word of God. With him my heart often exclaims, "In God will I *praise his word!*" Psalm lvi, 10. Upon no other subject does my heart labor for utterance as upon this, and never do I find language so utterly inadequate to express the views and emotions of my full heart, as when trying to present the Holy Scriptures as the WORD OF GOD. Should one express on this point all that language would convey, and this before congregated thousands, many of the company might indignantly respond, "Who does not believe the Bible to be the word of God?" And yet, dear sister B——, who *does* believe it?

It is a circumstance which does not seem to have arrested the attention of Christians generally, that a promise fully credited does in itself convey the thing promised. Thus a person owes you one hundred dollars. You call for payment, and he hands you a bill for that amount on "The —— Bank." "Did Mr. A—— pay you the amount he owed you?" asks a friend. "Yes," you say, "and I have the money in my pocket." "Let us see it," continues the inquirer: whereupon you draw out the bill and read, "The President, Directors, and Co., of the —— Bank, promise to pay, &c., one hundred dollars."

"Do you call that one hundred dollars?" rejoins your friend: "why, sir, it is only a *promise* of that amount." "True," say you; "but the paper of that institution is just the same with me as the gold." Here is *faith*—faith that recognizes the thing promised *in the promise.*

How pleasing to the proprietors of a moneyed institution must such demonstrations be, of confidence reposed in their veracity! Does not the above illustration agree with, "Whereby are given unto us exceeding great and precious promises, that *by these* ye might be partakers of the divine nature?" Thus it is that "faith is the *substance* of things hoped for."

Go where infidelity and skepticism are most deeply deplored, even to the ambassador for God, whose absorbing employ is to defend the Bible as the word of the Lord, and, with David, "in God to praise his word." Remind him of the requirement, "Be ye clean that bear the vessels of the Lord," and then ask, "Are you living in obedience to this command?" "No." "Why not?" "I cannot say why, unless it be my unbelief." *Unbelief!* In what does he mean that he lacks confidence? Not in himself; for he will tell you at once that he does not expect any good thing from himself. Not

What! believe without other evidence. What God *writes* he *speaks*.

in the ability of God to make him holy, for this he acknowledges.

Give him the oft-repeated direction, "Cast yourself wholly on Christ for salvation from all sin, and then claim the promise, 'I will receive you,' and thus 'cleanse yourself from all filthiness of the flesh and spirit, perfecting holiness in the fear of God,'" what would he say in reply? "What! must I rely upon the word of God without any other evidence?" As much as to say, "I do not conceive this to be a sufficient foundation for my faith to rest upon, and unless some external or internal communication apart from, or added to this, be given, I cannot believe that I receive the thing desired."

Does not this imply unbelief in the Scriptures, as the *voice* of *God?* Were that voice audibly uttered, would it be doubted? What makes the difference? Infidelity! Skepticism! Doubting whether the *written* word be in reality the same as the voice of God. If that voice were heard it would be believed: it is not heard, therefore it is doubted. Can these doubting ones say with perfect truth, that they *believe* the BIBLE to be the WORD OF GOD? It is, therefore, I express my painful convictions, that the Scriptures are not generally received as the word of God. Faith is not sufficient without sense. "Except ye see signs and wonders ye will not believe," is a reproof as truly deserved now, as in the days of Christ. The Bible is the WORD OF GOD. The awful sublimity of this truth is strikingly exhibited in Rev. xix, 13 : "His name is called The WORD OF GOD." Here the word is *personified* as Christ himself. Also John i, 1 : "In the beginning was the WORD, and the WORD was with God, and the WORD WAS GOD." "He that rejecteth me and receiveth not my Word, hath ONE that judgeth him, the WORD that I have spoken, the same shall judge him at the last day." In many other passages is the WORD OF GOD thus personified, as identical with God himself. In relying upon it, efficacious influences ought to be expected as confidently, as were healing influences from *touching Christ* when he was on earth; for in relying upon the word, we in verity rely upon Christ, and touch him as truly as though his bodily presence were with us, and we were permitted to lean upon him. But who believes the Bible to be the word of God? Does sister B——? Does brother B——? Lord help us to believe it; not as a "*dead* letter," but to apprehend it as SPIRIT and LIFE. Our difficulties about faith will all be at an end, when we *believe the* BIBLE to be the WORD OF GOD.

The grace of our Lord Jesus Christ be with your spirit.

   Yours, in the truth of the gospel.

"Believe that ye receive." Conditions.

No XXXI.—TO MRS. B——.

Presumption taken for faith—Doctrines abused—The assertion, "Believe that you have it, and you have it," not Scriptural—Importunate prayer unanswered—An unauthorized petitioner—The Pharisee—The seeker of sanctification—The lame and blind offered in sacrifice. The backslider's prayer—Divine direction sought in vain—Meddling with secret things—Why some parents cannot believe—Unholy hands lifted up.

My Dear Sister in Jesus,—Again I address you in further answer to your inquiry in relation to the text, "What things soever ye desire when ye pray, believe that ye receive them, and ye shall have them." In my former communication on this theme, the Lord blessed me with gracious refreshings from his word, while endeavoring to set forth his faithfulness. But the subject is so preeminently important, and so extensive in bearing, that I cannot feel satisfied without presenting some additional remarks, in order to a fuller illustration of my views.

There are conditions which must be carefully met; otherwise it is impossible really to believe that we receive. On this account, many who are continually asking and receive not, are disposed to regard this most precious passage as difficult to be understood. I have even heard those who have quoted it, as illustrative of the way in which the answer to their petitions had been apprehended, found fault with as not being orthodox.

"Shall we give it up?"   False Version.   No Answer.

I am aware that there are those who have wrested this, as they do other scriptures, to their own destruction. But shall we give up a portion from our Father's hand so replete with instruction in simplifying the way of faith? Shall we give it up, I ask, because it has been abused? As well might we give up the doctrine of free grace, or salvation by faith; for Universalists have abused the former, and Antinomians the latter.

I have occasionally heard, with grief, the remark, from persons whom I have regarded as entirely sincere, "Only believe you have it, and you have got it." This has been said when there was apparently an entire unfitness in the individual addressed for the reception of such an exhortation. And then, the phraseology is not Scriptural, and is liable to a construction wholly unauthorized by the passage of which it claims to be a version.

But there are those who shrink from this text, imagining that their experience does not furnish corroborative testimony in favor of its truthfulness. They fix on some given point, relative to which frequent prayer has been made, and attempts to exercise faith long persisted in; but in fruitlessness of result they have turned despairingly away, conscious that the things desired had not been granted.

Such may, on examination, find that they started from a wrong point. The thing desired

Started wrong.   The Pharisee.   Prayer for Purification.

may have been in accordance with the will of God, but the *petitioner* may not have possessed the qualifications which, according to the principles of God's law, entitle him to a favorable hearing. As has been stated, a variety of points is here involved, a few of which only at present can be mentioned.

In the first place, if he has come for pardon, his spirit may be unhumbled. It is only to the humble and contrite that pardon has been promised. "He shall save the humble person;" "He saveth such as be of a contrite spirit;" "Lord, thou hast heard the desire of the humble;" "Because thou didst humble thyself," &c. The unhumbled Pharisee went away, perhaps delighting himself with the idea that his boastful service had been received as true homage. But did his believing it to be so make it really so? Had his service been accepted, then the faithful and true Witness had gone aside from his WORD; for by this he was assured that it was only "To this man will I look, even to him that is poor, and of a contrite spirit, and trembleth at my word."

Another asks for the purification of his nature. "Can I doubt," says he, "whether it be in accordance with the will of God, that I should be 'sanctified throughout, body, soul, and spirit?' No; 'this is the will of God, even my sanctification.' Surely I may now ask, and believe that I receive." He asks, but does not receive. Why? Not because the petition is not in accordance with the will of God, but because there is an unwillingness in him to comply with the conditions upon which the blessing has been promised. He may be indulging in some practice which he has reason to believe inconsistent with the purification of his nature.

Sanctification implies a coming out from the world in such a sense as not to be governed by its opinions; a *crucifixion;* a cutting off a right hand; a plucking out a right eye. The petitioner, though consciously unwilling to submit to the painful process, still, with strong cries and tears, urges his plea, and in his expostulations says, "Lord, hast thou not said, 'What things soever ye desire when ye pray, believe that ye receive them, and ye shall have them?'" As well might they who came in the days of the prophet Malachi, with their polluted offerings, and covered the altar with tears, in their implorings for acceptance, have believed that God, contrary to the express declaration of his *word*, received the blind, lame, and sick, as acceptable sacrifice. Would their endeavors to believe that God did accept, have made it so? And yet who more desirous than they for the acceptance of their offerings?

The backslider in heart may come, asking for some less important good than his spiritual neces-

"If ye abide in me." Prayer for Wisdom.

sities demand. He asks, but does not receive, because he is unmindful of the condition, "*If ye abide in me, and my words abide in you, ye shall ask what ye will, and it shall be done unto you.*" He does not *abide* in Christ, and therefore has no right to expect the answer on these premises. He "asks and receives not, because he asks amiss, that he may consume it upon his lusts."

A sincerely disposed disciple of the Lord Jesus, feeling his need of divine guidance, asks wisdom; he then proceeds to the prosecution of the matter in hand, with much the same fearfulness and uncertainty that would have marked his course had he not asked divine direction. Though he asked in obedience to the will of his heavenly Father, yet his mind was not settled in the persuasion that wisdom from above would be given, to guide the affair to a heaven-directed conclusion. He may, perhaps, indulge a faint hope that all may be divinely ordered; but is the condition, implied in the tender of divine direction, met? He has not asked "in *faith, nothing wavering.*" "He that wavereth is like a wave of the sea driven of the wind and tossed; let not that man think that he shall receive anything of the Lord."

Another asks, and receives not, because he asks for that which it is not needful he should have. Perhaps he asks for knowledge of things of which God hath said, "*It is not for you to know.*"

Secret Things.   Children prayed for and indulged.

"Secret things belong unto the Lord our God; but those things which are revealed belong to us and to our children." Notwithstanding these dissuasives, he continues to ask. He may believe that he receives; but does this belief make it so? You have heard of those of late who have acted on this assumption, and the disastrous result seems to intimate that Satan answered the petition.

Another says: "I have prayed long and earnestly, that my children may be induced to choose the path to eternal life. Negligence, in training them up in the way they should go, may have marked the course of the parent. At the very time the petition is offered, those children may be indulging in practices of wordly conformity, from which the parent well knows they will have to depart, in order to get into the way to heaven. The reason why such cannot believe they receive when they pray, is but too evident.

But I might enlarge quite beyond the bounds of another sheet. The subject is prolific; beyond my power to present in detail. Suffice it to say, that the reason why very many petitioners ask, and receive not, may be inferred from 1 Tim. ii, 8: they do not "lift up holy hands, without wrath and doubting." In the eye of Omniscience, purity of motive is wanting; such ask, and may *not* believe that they receive what things soever they desire when they pray.

One Father.   Prayer for a Revival.

If opportunity should offer, it will give me pleasure to pursue this subject by way of telling you of some answers to prayer, received on precisely the principle laid down in the text, relative to which you have asked my views.

Yours, in love.

NO. XXXII.—TO THE MEMBERS OF THE —— CHURCH.

The church is a family—Intercessions—Revival prevented—The sin of one man—A reproach to Christ—Social gatherings *versus* class meetings—A wonderful deception—The convicted—Cruel friends—" Who ruined that soul?"—God's decree nullified—A revival in God's order—Death busy and the church idle—" Curse ye Meroz."

DEARLY BELOVED,—I have no explanation to offer for my solicitude on your behalf, other than that I believe God has himself given me a care for you. "We have one Father, even God." Children of one household are one in interest. That interest is the honor of the parent, and the good of the united family.

In view of your low state for some time past, my heart has been moved to cry earnestly to the Lord for a revival of his work among you. In my importunate supplications I have consciously realized the help of the Spirit, and have felt a firm conviction that what I desired was in verity according to the will of God. Indeed, I could not be more abundantly assured of a readiness on the *part of God* to work. But on becoming better acquainted with your state, by my recent visit, I am constrained to say, in faithfulness to you, and to the promise-keeping Lord whom I serve, that my prayers in your behalf have been hindered. I am convinced that God will not work in power among you, unless conditions are met on your part. I see agencies at work among you calculated to make your faith powerless, and to neutralize your prayers for a revival.

I well know that what I would say may not be applicable to all. When Israel was driven before his enemies, it was by the sin of *one man*, yet was not the great body implicated in the eye of God? The Lord of hosts had promised to go out with their armies, and to subdue their enemies before them, and now his promise had seemingly failed, for Israel had been smitten. O how greatly was his holy name dishonored among his enemies by this discomfiture! If you, beloved brethren and sisters, are not empowered to proclaim victory on the Lord's side, do you not see how the name of the Captain of your salvation may be reproached? He hath said, "How should one chase a thousand and two put ten thousand to flight, except their Rock had sold them, and the Lord had shut them up;" and if this promise is not fulfilled, do you not see how your *inactivity* may be the cause of triumph on the part of Satan?

While many among you are so absorbingly interested in a diversity of ways, as to prevent a regular attendance on your class and prayer meetings, and other stated means of grace, Satan is most busy. If you deem secular business, or meetings involving mainly secular interests, or the congratulations of friends, of more importance than an engagement to meet God at his house, can we wonder that he withholds the manifestations of his favor from you? Brethren, there is no neutral ground. It looks to me as if in every church seed were being sown, which will produce a harvest. Either the high and holy One, or the enemy of God and man, will quickly put in the sickle and reap.

By some it seems to be regarded as a matter of course, that the church should have its seasons of comparative inactivity. That this deception of Satan should have obtained to the extent it has, is wonderful. As before intimated, Satan in these times of declension is most *busily* engaged. *Now* he sows his seed plentifully, and may we not conclude, that on some of these occasions when the church has been aroused to put forth its most gigantic efforts, she has scarcely more than undone the wrong perpetrated during her previous inactivity?

Almost persuaded. "Why then don't my Friends warn me?"

That the lack of manifest zeal furnishes material for Satan to work with, I know from my own observation. Let me relate a case. On one occasion, while I was endeavoring to urge upon a sinner his awful condition, in view of his momentary exposure to the wrath of God, the Holy Spirit applied the truth to his conscience, and fearfulness and trembling took hold upon him. I had been pleading earnestly for his awakening, and now my heart leaped in joyous anticipation of his speedy transition from the kingdom of darkness. But the pious may conceive, though language cannot express, the anguish of my heart, when he said, "I have a brother who is a minister, and I have sisters also who are professors of religion; they have never talked with me in this way, and I am sure if I thought that they were in the perilous state in which you say I am, I could not *rest* day nor night without warning them." It was thus that Satan succeeded by the inactivity of these professors to quiet the conscience of this young man, who was possessed of talents for usefulness, which might have told on the salvation of scores of souls, but who, from the course which his convivial propensities inclined him to take, has probably finished his earthly career ere this. And upon whose skirts may his blood be found, when the Judge maketh inquisition?

I have seldom received more marked tokens of

divine approval, with a deeper consciousness of the Spirit *itself* making intercession, than when pleading for a revival of the work of the Lord among you; but after a better knowledge of your state, my heart with yearning emotions said, My prayer *cannot now* be answered. The people here are not now willing to have a revival by being *workers together with God;* and I well knew that in no other way could the petition be granted. Though the decree might have gone forth from the throne of God, you, brethren and sisters, may take upon yourselves the awful responsibility of making that decree null and void, by refusing to enter into the designs of God by being workers together with him. If you would have a revival, you must *set yourselves apart to work and live for it.* God works through human instrumentality, and if you would that he should work by you, you must put yourselves wholly in his hands—soul, body, and spirit—and then will your service be holy and acceptable. Then when you are individually instrumental in winning souls to Christ, how dear to your heart will be those who are newly brought into the fold; how deeply will you feel the importance, as nursing fathers and mothers, of leading the babes in Christ into the more excellent way; instructing them, by your example, to labor for the perishing around them! Were your prayers answered for a revival on other premises, it might result in little more than an ingathering of the names of such as would clog the chariot wheels of the Saviour.

But we must not forget that while the church lingers, *death is doing his work!* One after another is leaving you. Are you ready to meet at the bar of God those of your congregation who may have died out of Christ? Are you prepared individually to say, that your skirts are clear of their blood?

"*Unity is strength.*" If you would have a revival, the church must come up to the help of the Lord against the mighty. It is not left optional with herself whether she will obey the call of God or not. It is possible to stand on worse than neutral ground. My heart shrinks from appearing to be denunciatory, yet I must say, that unless favored with the blessing of God, we have his curse, and a bitter curse has been pronounced on those who come not up to the help of the Lord. "Curse ye Meroz," said the angel of the Lord, "curse ye bitterly the inhabitants thereof, because they came not up to the help of the Lord, to the help of the Lord against the mighty."

Your servant for Christ's sake.

No. XXXIII.—TO THE MEMBERS OF THE —— CHURCH.

Neglect of the stated means—A remark of Mr. Wesley—An engagement to meet a friend—Who broke it?—One in three at class—What Thomas lost—All strong, and all at work—"Begin at my sanctuary"—Six left of three hundred—An estimate—Nursing fathers and mothers.

WERE I to mention what I have thought your characteristic deficiencies, I would place among the most prominent your neglect of the stated means of grace. If you regard the church organization, under which you have voluntarily placed yourselves, as a divine institution, you should of course regard its apppointments as heaven-directed. Mr. Wesley says, "In all ordinary matters the voice of the church may be regarded as the voice of God." If so, then stated meetings, such as preaching, prayer, and class meetings, ought to be regarded as special seasons, at which the Lord Jesus has appointed to meet you. If such an appointment be slighted, does it not prove that you lightly estimate the presence of your Lord and Saviour?

Suppose a dear and influential friend to make arrangements for meeting you regularly, for the purpose of honoring and blessing you with his society: ever truthful, he comes at the hour specified, but does not find you there; often you are wholly absent; at other times you come quite

Too late. The Spirit came, but the church was not there.

after the hour specified. Would this conduct be calculated to assure your friend of your high regard for his friendship? If your repeated slights should move him to come to the decision no more to meet you, were the result other than might have been reasonably expected? and if an agreement to meet you should be thus broken, who would be the breaker of the engagement?

For a membership of three hundred not to number more than one hundred out on lecture or prayer-meeting evening exhibits a sad deficiency; yet, were you at your stated meetings to present even this proportion of your membership, it were more encouraging. Now can the Saviour believe that you as a people are greatly desiring the communications of his grace? Were the decree to pass his throne that on one of these stated occasions the Holy Spirit, in his reviving influences, should be poured out in unusual measure, how many of you would be as Thomas, who was absent when his Lord revealed himself to the other disciples!

O, if you really desire a general work of God in your midst, often be in waiting, as were the early disciples, and, with one accord in one place, look for the full baptism of the Holy Ghost. If thus strengthened with the might of the Spirit, you may confidently expect to be called out individually to work in the vineyard.

God's Ordination.   God's Order.   A Startling Question.

Less solicitude will then be felt about finely polished human instrumentalities, but a far more abiding reliance on the power of the Holy Ghost. This full baptism may be regarded as the act of ordination on the part of God, by which he empowers his disciples with the might of his Spirit, in order that they may bring forth much fruit, and that their fruit may *remain.*

The history of the church presents but little fruit of revivals where the order of God has not been observed. "And begin at my sanctuary," is the voice of God. The disciples were first baptized with the Holy Ghost and with fire, and then three thousand were converted in a day.

I may never forget some instances which have come under my special observation, calculated to confirm my mind in these views. A startling question presents, and my pen has lingered whether to give it the tangibility of words. It is this: Does not Satan gain by some church ingatherings? Let me instance. On one occasion, when in a stage-coach, about entering a place which two or three years previous had been favored with a gracious revival, the subject of religion was introduced to a gentleman sitting near me. "O, religion is a very good thing if people would only keep it when they get it," said he, in a very significant manner. I inquired his meaning, when he informed me that almost every one in that place had

Disastrous Results of a Revival without Holiness.

professed conversion but two or three years previously; and now scarce an individual of them could be found but had fallen away, and was worse than before. This relation pained me exceedingly, for I had expected to find the place as the garden of the Lord; and I well remembered the temptings of Satan, at the time the revival took place. I had been intimately acquainted with the minister under whose ministrations the revival occurred, and had once and again had earnest conversations with him relative to the order of God being observed; that *holiness* in the ministry and membership was important as a *foundation* for a revival. When this extraordinary ingathering was announced to me as having been brought about under his ministrations, the enemy tauntingly suggested that the position I had taken was not to be relied upon, and that the minister in question (who had the reputation of being a revivalist) would be abundantly satisfied that this order, though he at the time acknowledged it to be scripturally correct, was by no means important. But I still hoped that the state of religion in the place might not be quite so disastrous as represented, and soon afterward called on the minister for further information. I was told that out of the two or three hundred names taken in at that time, he did not think there were now as many as half a dozen on the church record, and he was by no means certain that one

Diminished by Increase. One shall chase a thousand.

remained steadfast. Probably there are but few such striking instances as this; but, alas, how often are scores of worldly minded professors enrolled on the church record during seasons of ingathering, who remain as weights, to retard Zion in her onward movements! One truly *Christlike* professor would do more for a church than a hundred of such professors; for it is of such that "one shall chase a thousand." It has been said, one sanctified may be counted upon as equivalent to a score converted. O may heaven speedily register scores of sanctified ones among the —— Church! then will you, as nursing fathers and mothers, receive to your embraces many who, by the power of the Spirit, have been born unto Zion. "Wherefore we pray always for you, that our God would count you worthy of this calling, and fulfill all the good pleasure of his goodness, and the work of faith with power; that the name of our Lord Jesus Christ may be glorified in you, and ye in him, according to the grace of our God, and of our Lord Jesus Christ. Amen."

Yours, in the faith and hope of the gospel.

A Book.   Reading for the Common People.

No. XXXIV.—TO ——.

Memoir of Mrs. ——. The common people—Good news—A commanding post—Ability equal to duty—Our calling as a church—"The high doctrines of our creed"—Mysteries—A popular young minister—Mr. Wesley's last advice—How others regard us—A dilemma—Professor —— Disappointment—A Presbyterian's opinion of a Methodist congregation—"What do ye more than others."

Dear Brother,—We thank you for your early attention to our communication of July 4th. * * * * * * As to the publication in question I trust the only desire of her friends in regard to it, is to furnish yet another example of the power of grace to transform in heart and in life. If yet another may be taken from the walks of ordinary Christian life, and added to the list of Jesus's witnesses of full salvation, I stand ready to do all in my power to serve the religious community.

Closer observations may perhaps convince me of a mistake, but at present I see not why a Memoir of Mrs. —— may not company with a Carvosso or a Rogers, though possibly of inferior intrinsic interest to those very special examples of the power of grace. Should it not be an object of ambition with us to furnish example and admonition for the *common people?* We may be instructed on this point by an observation of St. Mark touching the Saviour's ministrations: "The common people heard him gladly."

Holiness in High Places.   Ability equal to Duty.

We frequently receive communications from our mutual friends, Bishop and Mrs. ——. In one of her late communications, Mrs. —— says, "Dr. —— is now in the enjoyment of the witness of holiness." This has been a subject of continuous thanksgivings to God in your behalf. We rejoice in view of the bliss upon which you have entered: "For we who *believe* do enter into rest." We know that your heart has so *long* been desiring the rest of perfect faith, and we have been so long in prayerful solicitude for this object, that our hearts are indeed rejoiced. But though we greatly desired this because of our love to you, and our earnest wish for your personal happiness and safety, yet we may say that our desires were much more enlarged in view of your position in the church, and the responsibility, which, by virtue of this position, is laid upon you. We are prone to feel that this commanding post has not been assigned you by the mere will of man, but by the will of God; and though our solicitude might move us to tremble for you while we hear you say, "Who is sufficient for these things?" yet we well know that the Head of the church has not called you to a position which he will not empower you to sustain in all its various demands. To say otherwise would imply a belief that his ways are not *perfect*. Such an expression or thought were indeed impious.

That the church may be presented to Christ

Our Banner.   "High Doctrine."   "Mysteries."

"without spot or wrinkle, or any such thing," should surely be an object of primary interest with us as a people. Our responsibilities before God relative to the doctrine of Christian holiness are tremendous. The specific object for which the Wesleys were thrust out was "to *raise a holy people.*" A dispensation of the gospel has been committed to us, and we stand forth marshaled before the world, under the banner, "HOLINESS TO THE LORD."

I would not be captious, but will you excuse me while I venture a few thoughts which were suggested by your last very interesting letter? Speaking of two very distinguished ministers, you say, "I could wish that *such* would preach the *high doctrines of our creed:* I sometimes regret the efforts made by inferior skill and low experience to proclaim these holy mysteries." I confess, dear doctor, the expression, "high doctrines of our creed," and "*mysteries,*" elicited my jealousy. Does not the expression, "high doctrine," intimate something above ordinary attainment, as though the doctrine of holiness were something beyond the reach of the mass of professors? Your words, I fear, give but about a truthful exposition of the views generally entertained on this subject. But in view of the position in which we stand to this doctrine, is it well that we should look upon it as among the "mysteries" of our holy religion? Is it not because it is regarded in this light by very

The Ministry and the Laity. "How did you like the Discourse?"

many of our ministers, that it is not a matter of more general experience among the laity? Yet though your position may be truthful in the estimation of the church at large, and especially with the majority of the ministry, I am obliged to question its utility. This may look like temerity, but the harmful tendencies of the course are so apparent to my own mind, that I dare not be silent.

And yet I do not wonder that you should shrink from the ministrations of men of low experience and inferior skill. I have myself been placed in circumstances to sympathize with you herein. Some time since I heard a very popular young minister, who to my surprise took this as the theme of his discourse. But it was very evident that he could not say with Wesley, Fletcher, or Fisk, "We speak that we do know, and testify that we have seen." He afterward questioned me as to my views of the discourse. I dared not do otherwise than point at deficiencies. He pleaded, by way of apology, that he had so many engagements, that he really had not time to look into these deeper things of God—these high and holy "mysteries." Does this comport well with Mr. Wesley's last advice in relation to this our distinguishing doctrine? It reads thus: "Therefore, all our preachers should make a point of preaching perfection to believers *constantly, strongly,* and *explicitly;* and *all* our preachers should *mind this one thing,* and continually agonize for it." If this sacred charge had been kept, we had doubtless had scores of witnesses where we now have one. Then had we better fulfilled the designs of God in raising us up as a people. Indeed, it is by this doctrine of holiness that we have been mainly distinguished from other denominations. Besides, our close identification with this doctrine is the aspect in which, as I have often had occasion to observe, other denominations mainly regard us. I have known numbers of those who had been sincerely opposed to the doctrine of Christian perfection, who, on resolving to become Bible Christians, have found that holiness is a Bible doctrine. On perceiving this, their minds have at once been turned to us. Now, dear brother, what shall we do? If this grace be held up as an attainment, so high that but few even among the ministry enjoy it, where shall we direct these inquirers? I do not ask this question as though it were a merely supposable dilemma.

Such cases are more frequent than those who stand high in our church councils imagine. Would that it were not so: for were our responsibility in regard to this doctrine fully perceived by those in authority, then the note of alarm might be heard throughout our borders. To assure you that my solicitude is not needless, let me instance two or three cases in point.

Prof. ——. Our Creed and our Hearts. What would you have said!

Professor ——, of whose deep interest in the doctrine of Christian holiness you are fully aware, came to this city earnestly desiring to know the way of the Lord more perfectly. The first point of attraction was the M. E. ——; imagining that the enjoyment of the witness of holiness was the general experience of our ministers, he expected here to elicit much light and a ready response to his feelings. But he soon found, that though holiness was our distinguishing doctrine as a people, neither our ministry nor membership were generally distinguished by living in the enjoyment of it, as he had fondly anticipated, and with deep regret he mentioned his disappointment to us. What could we say?—for surely this was calculated to paralyze his own efforts in the pursuit of it.

At another time, a gentleman belonging to the Presbyterian Church had become so desirous of the blessing of full salvation, that the members of his own denomination had already begun to look at him as somewhat Methodistical. One evening he stepped into the church where I was worshiping. It was during a season of revival, and much ardor was manifested. As he stood overlooking the large congregation, he said earnestly, "I suppose all here enjoy the blessing of holiness." I cannot tell you how my heart was pained. And think how formidable the attempt at a reply. What would you have said, dear Dr. ——? Running my eye over the assembled multitude, I could not see one in fifty who professed to be living in the enjoyment of that state. But is the state of our congregations, generally, more encouraging even than this?

What does it avail that we hold this as a high doctrine of our creed? The fact of doing so but increases our obligations an hundred fold. It is the servant who knows his Lord's will, and does it not, that is to be beaten with many stripes. Unless we have witnesses to substantiate our theory, what do we more than others?

"Ah, what avails superior light!"

That there are so few comparatively among the membership who profess to enjoy the blessing may be attributed to the fact, that there is so little explicit and experimental testimony among the ministry on this point. Our dear brother is placed in a position to "begin at the sanctuary." You may remember that when you were so ill, that you entertained but little hope of ever again engaging in active service, we even then indulged the expectation that God might raise you up for the *special purpose* of arousing the ministry on this all-important topic. But where shall I stop? I fear I may weary you, and hasten to an item of business upon which we have been desired to address you.

* * * * * * *

Adieu, dear brother; pray for us that "God may

Property.   Given by God.   Unequally bestowed.

fulfill all the good pleasure of his goodness in us, and the work of faith with power."

Yours, &c.

No XXXV.—TO MR. J——.

Disposition of property—Inequalities of human condition—Responsibility graduated by possession—Prudent foresight recommended by Solomon—Of those who heap together riches—Comparative liberality—Censoriousness—" Are rich men required to give up all ?"—Community of goods—A debate.

DEAR BROTHER J—— asks to know my views in regard to the disposal of property. This is a subject so comprehensive in bearing, that it is not without earnestly imploring wisdom from above, that I venture to give my thoughts upon it.

" The silver is mine, and the gold is mine, saith the Lord of hosts." Nothing can be more evident than this fact, viz.: that God is the GIVER, whatever variety may appear in the distribution of his gifts. That God should dispense earthly good with a hand, seemingly, so unequal, is a subject at which skeptics have caviled. But when we remember that the great Master of the household is training subjects in this world for immortality and eternal life hereafter, and, to prove the fidelity of each, has placed at his disposal a given amount of his goods, that he may on his return receive his own with *usury*, the difficulty is solved.

Heaven's Nobility.   The Rich are to serve the Poor.

To some he has given, with but a small portion of this world's goods, much humble faith, and patient endurance. These, if they occupy faithfully till the Lord come, will, in the truest sense of the word, be of *heaven's nobility.* "Hath not God chosen the poor of this world, *rich* in faith, and *heirs* of the kingdom?" Those to whom he has intrusted much of earthly good, he has made the *servants* of his *chosen* ones; intending, if we "occupy till he come," faithfully, that we shall not be spiritually poor, but "rich in good works, being *ready* to distribute, *willing* to communicate."

Yet I daily feel that it is not a small thing that a man be found faithful. In reference to property, as well as other means of doing good, God will surely require his own, with *usury.* How will it be with those intrusted with a large portion of this world's goods, who are *hoarding* it up, while the interests of Christ's kingdom are making loud and incessant demands?

"But," it is said, "if none should lay up for seasons of emergency, how disastrously might sudden bereavements, such as are continually occurring, by death, or unlooked-for reverses, operate?" A prudent foresight may not be scripturally condemned; it is rather approved: see Prov. vi, 8. The example of the ant, who provideth her meat in the summer, and gathereth her food in the harvest, is presented, by way of re-

Prudent Foresight.   Hoarding.   God's Rule.

proof, to those who are prone to improvidence. But this furnishes no plea for those to whom it may be said, "Your riches are corrupted, and your garments are moth-eaten; your gold and silver is cankered; and the rust of them shall be a witness against you, and shall eat your flesh as it were fire: ye have heaped treasure together for the last days." I often fear that this passage may be applicable to some rich men of the present day, who name the name of Christ.

As I am more or less engaged, in several benevolent schemes, I must say that, as a whole, I have found persons in ordinary circumstances much more disposed to give, according to their ability, than the rich. The moral impropriety of this is apparent, and a reference to the Scriptures shows it to be palpably wrong. Paul says, "Let every one lay by him in store *as God hath prospered him:*" and no duty, on any point, can be more clearly demonstrated than this, viz.: that it is a *duty* to give *according* to the *ability* which God has given. For a man, then, who is worth $20,000, to give no more than one worth $1,000, other things being equal, is absolutely *sinful*. This may seem severe; but if it be absolutely sinful to disobey God, then he who does not give *according* to his *ability*, or, in other words, as God hath prospered him, is guilty of disobedience.

I hope I may not seem to favor that destroyer

Piety may coexist with Wealth.

of Christian unity, *censoriousness,* which is not unfrequently indulged by a class of persons who would unchristianize everything they cannot bring down to their own level.

From the early ages of the world there have been different classes in community. Abraham, who was eminently the friend of God, was *rich.* From his history, we may conclude that the position in the society in which he moved was commanding. David, the man after God's own heart, was a king, and of course was surrounded with the trappings of royalty. The devout meditations and the inspired hymns of the Psalmist, which furnish such precious food for the humble, holy soul, were many of them, doubtless, written in a king's palace. It would be well for those who are disposed to condemn such as have been raised, in the order of God, to a position somewhat above themselves, to remember this.

Joseph of Arimathea, the rich disciple, went and *craved* the body of Jesus, though the other disciples had forsaken him in his hour of greatest peril. Joseph was not ashamed to avow himself a disciple now, though adherence to his Lord exposed him to contumely and scorn. Duties would not have been laid down, regulating the conduct of the poor and rich—of masters and servants— were not such duties recognized by God.

I was not long since in a little company, where

"All Things common."   An Income spent for God.

the unity of the Spirit was marred by a little conversation, which ran about thus. The case of a deeply pious minister, who was reputed to be rich, was mentioned. A Christian brother remarked, by way of reference to this minister, that if the same kind of religion prevailed at the present day, as prevailed in the days of the apostles, the same effect would be produced; that is, we should have "*all things common.*" A friend, who greatly valued the Christian character of the minister in question, observed, that he was yearly, by his benevolent operations, consuming more than the interest of his money, and if the principal were expended, his ability to do good in this way must cease. This did not satisfy, and a censorious spirit, which ever seems to possess some infectious quality, was communicated to a friend present, who said, that she "never could understand how an individual could have the spirit of his Master, and yet see the heathen perishing, without giving up *all* he possessed." The minister's friend endeavored to maintain, by way of argument in his defense, that if the principal were expended, his present mode of doing good to thousands must cease, and that he could not, therefore, as a *faithful* steward, give up the entire of his property for present expenditures; but the brother who, perhaps, had never possessed means calculated to test his own fidelity on this point, remained unyielding in the opinion, that if the principles of holiness prevailed, a community of interests would be the result. These views being very confidently expressed, bore heavily on a deeply devoted person present, who was possessed of more means than either of the former, and who, doubtless, was far more *liberal* than those who, by their opinion, had condemned her. And thus the interview ended.

It is because I have known several cases where the unity of the spirit has been so sadly marred by similar views, that I have taken time to present this subject more fully. It is true, I cannot well apprehend a state of holiness, as otherwise than comprehending all with which we stand connected. The idea of being wholly the Lord's, and yet withholding our property from his control, implies an utter inconsistency. Yours truly.

No. XXXVI.—TO MR. J——.

A stumbling block.—"One hundred dollars instead of six"—The wealthy father and his two sons—Jacob's vow—Large income for the Lord's treasury—A broken vow—Obstacle to religious prosperity—Tests of fidelity—David's view of liberality—Systematic mode of giving—The tenth devoted—"Giveth and yet increaseth"—Missionaries.

DEAR BROTHER J——. It is because some seem to practice on the principle that they may be wholly the Lord's, and yet not exhibit the fruits of holiness in relation to giving, that the good way has

Worth $100,000.   Gives $100.   Two Sons spoiled.

often been evil spoken of. The eye of my mind is now resting on one who is said to be worth about $100,000. The amount he expends in benevolent operations does not probably exceed $100 per ann.; whereas, if he should but give the tenth, as was required under the Jewish dispensation, he would put at least $600 into the Lord's treasury yearly. But why should a *follower of Christ*, "who, though he was rich, yet for our sakes became poor, that we through his poverty might be rich"—why should such a one wish to hold so large an amount of his Lord's goods in his hands, while souls, for whom his Saviour died, are perishing in ignorance and want? I can assure you, brother J——, I would not be willing that my Lord should come and find me with so much of his goods hoarded up.

I was acquainted with two individuals, professors, of very dissimilar character, who have both gone to their account. The first died probably worth about 80 or $100,000, leaving his property to two unconverted sons, one of whom soon disposed of his portion by careless expenditures, making it of little account either to himself or others. His brother concluded that it were better not to risk his share in the chances of business, and consequently hoards it up, and is leading a life of *idleness*. Thus, what might have been expended by the father in laying up treasure in heaven, by spreading the light of the glorious gospel, is being spent by these sons, (who were spoiled by youthful indulgences,) in that which has been telling only to their hurt. In view of the reckonings of eternity, when such fathers shall be called to render an account of their stewardship, does it look desirable to die *rich?*

The case of the other friend differs widely. He commenced his business career with a solemn resolve to acknowledge God in all his ways. With the patriarch Jacob, he took upon himself a solemn vow, "*Of all that thou shalt give me, I will surely give the tenth unto thee.*" He also resolved, that he would never be what the world might term a *rich* man. Though at first he was often in straits, yet he had much to assure him that his vow was not unrecognized by God. He once related to me the following:—

"Calling one morning, as he went to his office, on a poor member of Christ's family, he found her unexpectedly destitute. He had but one dollar in his pocket, and he hesitated whether he could with propriety give it, but believing that she needed it more than himself, he gave it. During that day he made sixty dollars, and so sure was he that God had rendered him sixtyfold, that the enemy urged upon him afterward the singular temptation, that it would seem like bribing God to restore unto him sixtyfold, should he still persist in calling on the poor before engaging in the business of the day. During some portions of his life he was so greatly prospered of God, that, in fulfillment of his vow, he was enabled to put into the Lord's treasury several thousands yearly. He on one occasion related to me the case of a young friend, a member of his Bible class, who, by his advice, was induced to take upon himself the same sacred vow. This friend, at the time of his engagement, had a mother and sister under his care, and was receiving a salary of about $300. He devoted the tenth, and was enabled to live comfortably. The next year his salary was raised to $500. He still adhered to his vow, and abounded, of course, in yet greater comforts at home. His employers continued to increase his salary, until it amounted to $1200 per annum. He had for some time been uneasy from the idea that he was giving *too much*—more than persons, in his circumstances, generally gave, &c. Mentioning this to his friend and adviser, he observed, that he thought he ought to lay up more, as his mother was getting old. At last he yielded to the tempter, and actually ceased to perform his vow. He soon made "shipwreck of faith and a good conscience." Mr. —— continued faithfully to render unto the Lord according to his ability, until called to give an account of his stewardship.

I am sure that the day of eternity will reveal much sin lying at the door of the church on account of her deficiencies in giving. If men could behold the causes of spiritual leanness as God sees them, they would doubtless discover in this sin of covetousness the chief obstacle to the religious prosperity of thousands. "He that soweth sparingly shall reap sparingly." "God loveth the cheerful giver." The Dispenser of all good could say, Be ye warmed and be ye clothed, to every destitute being throughout the world, or could feed them by the hand of angels, as Elijah was fed, if it were not to test the fidelity of those to whom he has intrusted a sufficiency to meet this object. In like manner might every benevolent operation of the day, for the diffusion of light and truth, be sustained by means and influences wholly supernatural, if it were not that our gracious Lord has designed that we be workers together with him. But surely the ability to give ought to make us humble. With David we might say, "Who am I, and what is my people, that we should be able to offer so willingly after this sort? *for all things come of thee, and of thine own have we given thee.*" David apprehends a principle of giving which is not enough thought of, in the words, Shall I sacrifice that which "*doth cost me nothing?*"

I knew a husband and wife who commenced life with good ordinary prospects. They had not fixed their calculations on being rich. When objects of benevolence presented, they generally gave

A Husband and Wife.   The Tenth.   A Full Treasury.

in about an equal measure with the circle in which they moved, which was often composed of persons of much larger means than themselves. They, perhaps, never really thought that they gave too much. Still, when in the act of giving, the luxury of doing good might at times have been a little lessened by the thought, "Can I do this, and yet be just toward all men?"

One day the wife said, "Husband, let us have some systematic mode of giving. Suppose we fix on the tenth." "I think we give more than that now," he replied. "But everything," said the wife, "with which our heavenly Father has to do, is systematical; such beautiful order and symmetry pervade all his works, that we may well believe

'Order is heaven's first law.'

and we can easily give more afterward if needful;" and a conclusion was made that the *tenth* should be sacredly devoted. The result was, that they immediately found that the Lord's treasury was more fully replenished. Not a reasonable demand, when, as faithful stewards, they had a right to believe they ought to give, but could be in a moment met: not from their *own* treasury—no, it was only for them to dart a prayer to heaven, and say, "My heavenly Father, does this object meet thine approval?" and all was at once settled. A fact in connection with this mode of giving should be stated. Though they gave *more* than formerly, yet their means increased, so that they soon became possessed of a competency sufficient to meet ordinary emergencies. But they still maintained their former views relative to laying up treasures on earth. I have heard them say, "We never intend to be *rich*." If so, should they continue to prosper, I think it may not be long before they will be able to devote a fifth, and so on, until the whole be offered up to God. And why should not tradesmen, merchants, or professional men, as assiduously endeavor to prosecute a business with an intention of devoting its proceeds wholly toward promoting the interests of the Redeemer? I wonder why the Christian world does not furnish more examples of this kind. I have heard that such may be found who are thus manifesting their devotedness to Christ. Yet, do even such exhibit as much devotedness as the missionary, who not only sacrifices *all* his *time*, but often also health, friends, and all the dear delights of ripe society?

In love, &c.

The Great Theme.   Something Wonderful.

No. XXXVII.—TO REV. ———.

"Why cannot I believe?"—Plain dealing—An elevated position in the church—How attained—Our reputation belongs to God—Expulsions from the ministry—"Why insist on terms?"—A resolve to stand or fall with truth—Ashamed of Christ's *words*—The sin of ignorance—Acknowledgment—Objection to Scripture phraseology—Paul's conduct—Reputation—Not resigned to Christ—"How can ye believe?"—Fellowship with Him who made himself of no reputation—Christ's benediction on the outcast.

Rev. Sir,—My mind has been prayerfully interested for you ever since our first interview. I rejoice that your mind has become so powerfully influenced relative to the privilege of the believer. What more important theme than that of salvation from sin in the present life! Unless we are redeemed from all iniquity, and, as witnesses for Christ, live in the enjoyment of that state, the purpose for which Christ was manifest in the flesh remains unaccomplished. And how wonderful, with the Bible as the acknowledged standard of our faith and practice, that the doctrine of holiness, or entire sanctification, should have become a matter of controversy!

Yet, with those who love the truth in sincerity, and who consult the lively oracles for themselves, instead of following the *traditions of men*, this glorious doctrine will not long remain questionable. I am, indeed, most happy to know that your scruples have at length been wholly removed. But yet you

"Why can't I believe?"   Eminence.   "Who gave it?"

say, that you do not *experimentally* know of this doctrine. You, for some time past, have greatly desired this enjoyment, but why you are not enabled to believe and receive the end of your faith, with you yet remains inexplicable. I am happy to hear you say that the hinderance, whatever it may be, is with *yourself,* for you judge Him faithful who hath promised, who also will do it, as soon as you comply with the conditions upon which it is promised. I have conversed with many, who, to my mind, seemed to be on similar ground with yourself, and perceive what I imagine may hinder your faith from laying hold on the promises. I believe you wish plain dealing, and that as you have no fault to find with your Saviour, you would gladly know where the fault may be.

I know you will give God all the glory, when I allude to the fact, that you occupy a commanding position in the Christian world. In the order of Providence, you have influence with prominent men in the ministry and the laity, who are opposed, some of them violently, to the doctrine of salvation from all sin in the present life. By your pen also, you are favorably known in the literature of the day, and thus stand before the Christian community of Europe and America as a theologian of sincere, earnest, and enlightened piety. Now, should I ask you how this commanding position was attained, in looking back upon every step which you have ascended, you would acknowledge the helpful Spirit of grace, and with humility and gratitude you would ascribe to God, glory in the highest. Then you know that your reputation already belongs to God. Have you rendered, or are you now rendering, it back to Him? Let me, as in the presence of the high and holy One, solemnly urge your prayerful examination of yourself on this point, for *here* I think you may find the difficulty. Is it your intention that the avowal of your belief in this doctrine shall be coextensive with your influence? You now in blameless reputation stand enranked with men who have thrust from their midst those who were, and are now, experimental witnesses of the attainment of holiness. The blamelessness of their lives, and their increased zeal and success in winning souls to Christ, were fully and freely admitted by the brethren who refused them church fellowship. "But your doctrine! That is what we do not like." "Holiness, sanctification, or Christian perfection—these are terms which we do not approve. Renounce them, and you are still one with us, and together we will fight against sin, the world, and Satan. Refuse, and we use the awful power delegated to us by the Head of the church, and we not only thrust you from our ranks, but we depose you from the Christian ministry, and henceforth you are to us as a heathen man and a publican."

"Why not call it Consecration?" Ashamed of Christ's words.

And why could not these dear brethren accede to your wishes, and call the state into which the Saviour had brought them, a state of "consecration," or "the assurance of faith," instead of sanctification or holiness? Because, the doctrine of entire sanctification and holiness is set forth as you acknowledge you have found it, clear as noon-day, in the Bible, and they had in reality given themselves up to be as their Master, even "of no reputation," and they had also fully purposed to stand or to be thrust out with the truth. JESUS, THE WAY AND THE TRUTH, was with them, and when you thrust them out because they were not ashamed of Christ and his WORDS before this adulterous generation, did not the Saviour say to the hearts of those of you who had thus proved that you were ashamed of his words, "Of him also shall the Son of man be ashamed before his Father and the holy angels?"

In the judgment of Christian charity it may doubtless be said of some of them, "Brethren, I wot that through ignorance ye did it:" but does this make repentance and confession less necessary? "*If* we *confess* our sins, he is faithful and just to forgive us our sins, and to cleanse us from all unrighteousness." If the condition be not complied with, that is *confession*, the first point in the process is not met, and of course forgiveness and cleansing cannot follow. *Eternal* consequences hang

The Creed and the Bible. "Why must I use those Words?"

upon your prompt compliance with this condition. Is the purification of the heart by faith a light matter, when God hath said, "*Without holiness no man shall see the Lord?*"

I am aware that it is a doctrine of your creed, as a people, that salvation from all sin may not be expected until the hour of the soul's dismission from the body; but you have frankly acknowledged, in social intercourse with friends who have embraced the same views of truth as yourself, that the Bible does not authorize this creed. The Sun of righteousness has risen upon your heart, and you *see* and *feel* that you must be saved from sin, and in the daily epistle of your life and conversation exhibit the power of Christ to save. Yet, should the Lord bring you into this state of salvation, you are not willing to come out and confess it in *Scriptural words*. "Why, when these words are so objectionable," you ask, "should I be required to use them? May I not live in a state of entire devotion to God, and profess the assurance of faith, and entire consecration to the service of Christ, without using the objectionable words, holiness or sanctification, and thus save my reputation, that I may be more extensively useful?" No! for then would the offense of the cross have ceased. And the very idea seems to imply, that you were to be in some way the gainer by being ashamed of the words of Christ. "But does not Paul speak of being all things to all men, that he might gain some?" As well might Paul have maintained his rank among the persecutors of his Lord, after he had ceased his hostilities, from a persuasion that if he should lose his reputation with them, he might remove himself from a position in which he might be useful to them.

Whereas, the very fact of his having been in reputation among the Jews, "having sat at the feet of Gamaliel and been taught according to the perfect manner of the law of the fathers, being zealous toward God, and persecuting this way unto death;" was a very commanding reason why he should come out, when convinced of his error, as a zealous promoter of truth, and endeavor that his influence and zeal in defense of the truth should be coextensive with what they had been in defense of error. I would not intimate that you have persecuted this way; what your former course may have been is not known to me, but this I know, that you *now* feel not only a union in doctrinal sentiment, but a sweet cleaving of Spirit to those who profess to enjoy this grace. But so careful are you of your *reputation*, that even in this you are seemingly afraid of being brought out. Why all this, if your reputation were not dearer to your heart than TRUTH? O, be no more ashamed of Christ and *his words*. Has he given you honor? Lay this thy gift also upon the altar; and if you value your hope of eternal life, O

"One Thing thou lackest." "How can ye believe?"

think not more of the gift than of the altar upon which your gift is sacrificed, and by which it is sanctified. How soon may the gift which is not used in promoting the divine glory be withdrawn from you! You may in sincerity have thought that you were living in a state of entire consecration; but unless you have laid your reputation, as well as everything else, upon the altar, you are not thus living before God. To be candid, from the first interview I had with you, I have believed this to be the difficulty in the way of your exercising that faith which brings into the enjoyment of present salvation from sin. If a Jew had brought to the altar a sacrifice which he knew to be in any degree imperfect, would he have any authority from the word of the Lord for believing it holy, acceptable? Imagine that he had lingered long at the altar in most earnest desire for the reception of his gift, would the God of the altar have been moved, because of his importunity, to accept and seal the blemished offering? As well might we imagine that the God and Father of our Lord Jesus Christ could deny himself, and that with him were variableness and turning. "*How can ye believe which receive honor one of another, and seek not the honor that cometh from God only?*"

The mention of this passage reminds me of a dear friend, who for years stood about in the same experience and belief as yourself. I may also say, that he was a minister in good repute in your communion. One day, after he had been speaking of the many years he had been a believer in the doctrine of holiness, and of his earnest desires for the blessing, &c., I said, "How can you account for this, brother, that you should with so much sincerity and earnestness have been seeking the blessing for years without obtaining it?" He quickly replied, "that just so soon as he was willing to give up that honor which cometh from the world, and to seek that honor which cometh from God *only*, he found it perfectly easy to believe." Will my dear friend try this short and easy way? O give up your reputation! Consent to a fellowship with Him who "made himself of no reputation:" "who, for the joy that was set before him, endured the cross, despising the shame, and is set down at the right hand of the throne of God." For consider Him that endured such contradiction of sinners against himself, and resolve, if need be, to follow his example of patient endurance. Be willing, in obedience to the command of the high and holy One, to "sanctify the Lord God in your heart, and let him be your fear and your dread." Come out, and be separate in verity and in profession, touch not the unclean thing, and then the promise at once meets you, "I will receive you." But be assured, on the authority of God's word, that you will not be able to believe with the heart, until you are willing to make confession with the mouth. The purpose of God in making us the *receivers* of his grace, is that we may be its *dispensers* also. " Give, and it shall be given you."

If all of your denomination who are in heart believers in the attainment of holiness as a doctrine of the Bible, should stand out fearlessly in the defense of truth, what a revolution might be produced! Perhaps it is only for *you* to come out with an avowal of your views, in order to bring others to the point who are standing in about the same position as yourself. If you have more influence than some others, for this talent, which might be so favorably used on this subject, you are responsible.

The churches are gradually coming to the light. It is my earnest prayer that the Lord may raise up instruments in the denomination to which you belong, to hold up this precious light. How do you know but it may be the design of God to assign you a prominent place among those instruments, so that you may say rejoicingly,—

"And I enjoy the glorious shame,
The scandal of the cross."

The Lord save you from declining this honor, if it be his will concerning you. But should it be given you in behalf of Christ, not only to believe on his name, but also to *suffer* for his sake, why not glory in this your inheritance? Your Saviour hath said, "Blessed are ye when men shall hate you, and when they shall *separate you from their company*, and shall reproach you, and cast out your name as evil, for the Son of man's sake. Rejoice and be exceeding glad, and leap for joy, for great is your reward in heaven, for in like manner did their fathers unto the prophets."

Yours, &c.

No. XXXVIII.—TO REV. MR. H——.

Heaven's nobility incog—Views presented by the Spirit on the subject of confession—A sanctified soul hails from heaven—The force of the clause, "in earth as in heaven"—An angel on earth; his singleness of purpose; his heroic zeal—"My boast in the Lord."

We have daily been expecting the return of brother W——, to forward the inclosed $10, which, though he is now absent from us, have been gained in part through his instrumentality; in answer to your request, for your friend, who though poor in this world, is, it seems, rich in faith. Heaven's nobility often goes incog here on earth. It is an honor to be coveted to be counted meet

> "After our lowly Lord to go,
> And serve the heirs of heaven below."

And now, what cheer, dear brother? Is your blessed Saviour still in close companionship with you? Let me say, to the praise of his grace, that I have never proved his sustaining power more gloriously than of late. The significant passage, "For ye are dead, and your life is hid with Christ in God," has been apprehended in my recent experience so deeply, that language fails to express what I would say.

Some views which I received on the memorable hour, when I was permitted, through the blood of the everlasting covenant, to enter within the veil, have recurred to my mind with much force within a few days. They were the communications of the Spirit, and, as such, I am sure will ever be useful to me. I do not remember ever to have mentioned them to you, and it has been urged upon my mind, that it may be well to present them to my beloved brother.

Just prior to the reception of these views, it had been suggested that I might be called to testify of this grace before hundreds and thousands. In view of this, it was proposed, "Can you do it?" I was startled at the thought! Not from an unwillingness to profess the blessing before an assembled universe, if such were the will of God concerning me; but the remembrance came up before me, of the many times I had resolved to confess Christ before men, and had failed by yielding to the plausible reasonings of the deceiver. "How possible to mistake duty!" with a variety of similar suggestions, would be urged, until the opportunity had passed, and when too late, my foe stood ready to taunt me

Suggestion. A Member of the Body. I will rather die than yield.

with the victory he had gained. And now it was suggested, that this was the way I should lose the blessing, and you will not wonder that I was startled at the thought.

I saw it was necessary that some principles should be established in my mind, relative to what might constitute duty on this point. The matter was resolved thus. On any occasion, when I had reason to believe that a declaration of what God had done for my soul might be helpful to my own spiritual interests, even though another might not be specially benefited, this should fix the duty relative to my own soul, and might have a bearing upon my neighbor also, inasmuch as I was but a part of the great body, and, for the ultimate good of the whole, it was needful that I should be in a healthful state.

You may at once perceive by analogy, how duty to my neighbor, in relation to confession, was made plain also. After perceiving what should constitute duty, I was enabled to resolve, that if it literally cost me my life to go forward, I would make that sacrifice rather than yield to the shrinkings of the flesh.

It was at this point that the Lord gave me to see more fully the nature of the blessed state upon which I had entered. I had said, "Into thy hands I commit my spirit, for thou hast redeemed me, O Lord God of truth." It was suggested, Had your

A Soul committed to God.   We belong in Heaven.

spirit actually returned to the God who gave it, at the time you made this solemn surrender, and were it said, after having mingled for a little time in adoration with the burning spirits before the throne, You are now required to return for a little time to earth, to confess Christ before men, as a Saviour, able to save unto the uttermost, would you hesitate in declaring the object of your mission before hundreds and thousands?

I at once perceived that I would have no more to do with the world, so far as being influenced by its opinions, than would Gabriel, or any inhabitant of heaven who might be commissioned for the performance of a work on earth; and my burning spirit only needed an angel's wing to bear it through the habitable earth, to proclaim "full salvation through faith in the blood of the Lamb." I now apprehended in my experience the meaning of the prayer, "Thy will be done in earth as it is done in heaven." The beautiful words of our poet,—

"Let us, to perfect love restored,
Thine image here retrieve,
And, in the knowledge of our Lord,
The life of angels live,"—

had power and point in them. In experimental verity I now realized the truth of the Saviour's words: "Ye are not of the world, but I have chosen you out of the world, therefore the world hateth you." How unreasonable did it appear to expect sympathy from the world, Christ's avowed enemy!

An Angel on Earth. Fidelity. Zeal.

Let us conjecture, dear brother H——, what might be the sentiments that would inspire one of those angel spirits who have been centuries past doing the will of God in heaven. Were it said to such a one, You are commissioned by the will of your holy Sovereign to perform a mission to earth. It may require threescore and ten years of time, according to earthly computation, and while there, you must lay aside your angel wing, and your flaming spirit must be enshrined in just such a form as mortals wear, and to the various vicissitudes to which men are subject you must submit. He comes! But conceive the sentiments which inspire him to action. Is he influenced to be as much like the world as he may be, or does his ardor, in the performance of his work, reprove the world, and show a regardlessness of its smiles or frowns? And in relation to the reception of his message, has he not such an assurance that it is not his *own*, but the message of his Lord, as to make it his only concern to deliver it *faithfully*, that he may, in the most expeditious manner, accomplish his great work? Think you not that the aspirations of his heaven-born soul might incline him to efforts far more ardent than the children of this world, or even some professed Christians, might think necessary?

And now, let me make my boast in the Lord, and say, Somewhat similar are the sentiments which have influenced my heart ever since I was enabled, by the power of the Holy Spirit, to set myself apart wholly for God. O what a deadness to the world do I continually realize! I have received the sentence of death in myself, that I should not trust in myself, but in Him that raiseth the dead, and I experimentally apprehend that he hath raised me to entire newness of life. I feel that I have but one work, and that is to do the will of my heavenly Father. Heaven is my *home*. Christ is my *Saviour*. Exalted be his name for ever! Yours, &c.

No. XXXIX.—TO REV. MR. M——.

Questions proposed—" What is the witness of the Spirit ?"—Wesley's definition—" He that believeth hath the witness"—A promissory note—Ten years' experience—Whether we believe or not is matter of consciousness—" What are the evidences of entire sanctification ?"—" The Spirit itself beareth witness"—" By what marks may we know that we are entirely sanctified ?"—Sympathy with Christ—The mind of Christ—Continuous walking in Christ.

Our beloved brother M.'s letter should not have remained so long unanswered had time permitted an earlier reply. You make several important inquiries which it would give me much pleasure to answer were my abilities equal to my wishes. Not that I regard the subjects of inquiry obscure, for to my mind they appear plain, but because, as one says, "it is hard to find words, in the language of men, to explain the deep things of God."

Witness of the Spirit.   Wesley's Views.

"*What is the witness of the Spirit?*" stands first in importance among your questions. In answer to this inquiry, Mr. Wesley says something like this, "It is an inward impression on the soul, whereby the Spirit of God immediately and directly witnesses to our spirit, that the grace which we have desired is imparted." With me, this witness has, I think, invariably been given the moment I have *unwaveringly* believed God. We have received of that Spirit whereby we *know* the things freely given to us of God. The Spirit *itself* beareth witness with our spirit. In all my experience God has honored an implicit reliance on his *word*, and immediately on believing, my heart is ready to exclaim, "He that *believeth*, hath the witness in himself."

I cannot well conceive how it may be otherwise, than that the believing one should receive, and in conscious possession enjoy, the precise object which his faith has grasped. *According* to our faith it is *done* unto us. "Said I not unto thee, If thou wouldst believe, thou shouldst see the salvation of God?" Faith is the *substance* of things hoped for, the evidence of things not seen. If I may have so much confidence in the promissory note of a fellow-man, as to make it at once available for whatever articles I may need in food, raiment, &c., with how much stronger confidence may I say of the promissory notes of my heavenly Father, "Faith

Christ the Word of God. "He that believeth hath the Witness."

is the *substance* of things hoped for, the *evidence* of things not seen!" Christ says, "The words I speak unto you they are *spirit* and they are *life*." And where are the wonderful words thus endued with *spirit* and *life* to be found? Surely it were wisdom to know, for who would have the temerity to pronounce a faith resting on these *lively* oracles, a dead faith?

"Say not in thine heart, Who shall ascend into heaven? that is, to bring *Christ* down from above; or, Who shall descend into the deep? that is, to bring up *Christ* again from the dead. But what saith it? The WORD is nigh thee, even in thy mouth and *in* thy heart;" here the WORD is used as being identical with Christ—the eternal WORD speaking in person. Thus it is, that I apprehend, in resting upon the WORD, I rest upon Christ as truly as though the WORD were again made flesh and dwelt among us. These important truths, I trust, I have realized in my experience for more than ten years past, and it looks to me strangely incongruous for one to say, "I *believe*, and yet have *not* the witness in myself." This form of expression, or something similar to it, is not unusual with many sincere persons, who probably do not perceive the enormity of their fault. In our communications with each other, each is conscious whether he has confidence, and reposes unwaveringly, on the words of the other. How unreason-

What is the Evidence of Entire Sanctification?

able then is the idea, that we now receive the communications of the Holy Spirit through the written word, and not have the *witness*, or, in other words, the internal *consciousness* that we do believe!

"What is the evidence of entire sanctification?" is another inquiry. How might an offerer at the Jewish altar arrive at an evidence that his offering was sanctified? In the first place, God had explicitly made known just the sacrifice required, and the manner in which it should be presented. If the offerer had complied with these requirements, he, of course, knew that he had done so, or in other words, had the testimony of his own spirit to assure him of this fact. In immediate connection with this, the witness of the Holy Spirit is given as a consequence of relying upon the faithfulness of God. The moment his offering was laid upon the altar, he had the *evidence* of God's word that his offering was sanctified. "But is there not an evidence apart from the WORD?" The Holy Spirit always speaks to my heart by the word, and when I believe it, let me again say, that I at once experimentally apprehend, as Christ hath said, "that his words are spirit and life." David says, "Thou hast magnified thy WORD above all thy name." If the word were only looked upon in the light which emanates from it, the exclamation would never again be heard, "What! believe with no other evidence than the word!" If the word is given as

Marks of Entire Sanctification.

identical with Christ himself, the same as though his living voice were sounding in our ear, then we who believe it may with strong confidence exclaim, "He that believeth hath the witness in himself!" "The Spirit itself beareth witness with our spirit," &c.

And yet another inquiry: "By what marks may we *know* that we are sanctified?" I am endeavoring to meet your questions in the order in which they stand in your letter, but the foregoing infers that we now have the testimony of our own spirit, and also the Spirit bearing witness with ours that we are wholly sanctified. We were brought into this state by reposing all upon Christ. If we abide in Christ, we shall walk even as he walked. Our sympathies will be blended with his. The prayer,

> "My spirit to Calvary bear,
> To *suffer* and *triumph* with thee,"

will be answered in our experience. We shall as truly submit to be with Jesus as the man of sorrows, in labors abundant for the salvation of the perishing, as on the mount, beholding his excellent glory. But where might I cease in enumerating the marks by which we may know that we are wholly sanctified? "Let this mind be in you which was in Christ Jesus," is perhaps as marked a characteristic as can be given. If we have the mind which was in Christ, it will induce a life which will correspond, in a degree, with what his was when on

A Growing Assurance. Stability. From Faith to Faith.

earth. Such a life may, in return, bring upon us trials which will *mark* our onward progress, much in the same way as was His when on earth; for, "In the world ye shall have tribulation."

The beginning of my confidence has generally been as the light which shineth more and more unto the perfect day. The way in which my heart has become divinely assured, has not been by *sudden* disclosures of truth, or extraordinary internal or external manifestations, but generally, by a solemn conviction that God *cannot* be unfaithful. He cannot deny himself; but, as the immutable Jehovah, is ever bound by the law of his nature to fulfill his promises to the trusting one. The rest of my soul has been, not in extraordinary emotion, but "in quietness and assurance." "Knowledge and stability shall be the strength of thy times." So saith the Spirit by the prophet Isaiah, and these words happily exhibit what my experience has been. "We who believe do enter into rest;" yet it is not enough that I, by a definite *act* of faith entered. That act was but one of the many successive acts by which I am accomplishing my passage to the skies: "For therein is the righteousness of God revealed from faith to faith, as it is written, The just shall live by faith." The work of the Father, the Word, and the Spirit, seems, to my apprehension, to have been equally blended, both in bringing me into this state and in my sustainment

All Revelations from God are by the Spirit.

since I have entered. Of the Spirit it is said, "He shall not speak of himself," and his silent operations on the heart may not always at once be discerned as distinct from the testimony of our own spirit. Yet we should ever bear in mind, that whatever revelations of the Father or the Son are made to the believing heart, they are all the work of the Holy Spirit.

It is thus, my dear brother, I am enabled to rejoice in the conscious operations of the Holy Spirit on my heart. In receiving the Bible as the voice of the Spirit, I take the glorious revelations therein set forth as revelations made by the Spirit, to exhibit God the Father and the Son to my believing soul. The ineffable glories of the Father and the Son could never in any degree have been apprehended, had not the Spirit taken of the things of God and revealed them; and it is thus, my beloved brother, that we through the eternal Spirit are brought into communion and fellowship with the Father and the Son. May the grace of our Lord Jesus Christ, and the love of God, and the communion of the Holy Spirit, be with you! Amen.

Your sister in Jesus.

No. XL.—TO MISS S——.

The divine image borne and reflected—The doctrine of entire sanctification at conversion considered—It is anti-Wesleyan—Unscriptural—Christians urged to go on to perfection—Desires for holiness the result not of backslidings, but of an active and growing faith—Humiliating confession of an errorist.

. . . . Brother and sister —— are now with us. They desire me to present their warmest Christian regards. We feel it to be a great privilege to enjoy the society of these precious disciples of the Lord Jesus. They bear the divine impress so truly, that it tells with great sweetness and power on the entire circle in which they move. How often, in beholding these burning and shining lights, have I ejaculated,—

> "Jesus, let *all* thy lovers shine,
> Illustrious as the sun,
> And bright with borrow'd rays divine
> Their glorious circuit run!"

You speak of your friend, a minister who is promulgating the opinion, that a soul justified, is also, and at the same time, fully sanctified. That the soul is partially sanctified when brought into a state of adoption, is, I believe, scripturally correct. But, on the contrary, the notion that at the moment of adoption the entire sanctification of body, soul, and spirit, is accomplished, is, I believe, dangerous heresy. Dangerous, inasmuch as it induces the

Paul's Exhortations to Unsanctified Believers.

Lord's redeemed ones to stop short of the prize of their high calling.

You and I profess to be Wesleyan in our views, and you know Mr. Wesley took much pains to arrest this unscriptural doctrine, which began to develop itself in his day. I say unscriptural, because it cannot be legitimately drawn from the Bible. Its partisans affirm that it may, but with no more truth than other dogmas of the day are said to be thus deduced.

Paul was writing to his Christian *brethren*, when, presenting to their view the promises of conformity to the divine image, he says, "Having these promises, dearly beloved, let us cleanse ourselves from all filthiness of the flesh and spirit, perfecting holiness in the fear of the Lord." Would the apostle have urged them to the attainment of a state of entire holiness, were they already in the enjoyment of it? Surely they had not yet cleansed themselves from all filthiness of the flesh and spirit, when he thus exhorted them.

On another occasion Paul addresses his brethren thus: "I could not speak unto you as unto spiritual, but as unto carnal, even as unto babes in Christ." Here then were babes in Christ, for inspiration acknowledges their adoption, but yet they could not be addressed as wholly spiritual. In view of their many unsanctified doings, they had merited the reproofs of the apostle. The significant question,

Adopted, but not wholly sanctified.

"Are ye not carnal?" seems to leave room for the conjecture, that some even in that day might have had an impression that they were wholly spiritual, as a concomitant of their adoption. Paul seemingly presents their wrong doing as a proof that they were not wholly sanctified, and, in the manner above stated, urges them on to the attainment of that state.

The same apostle, in writing to the Thessalonians, in affectionate acknowledgment of their spiritual condition—children of his heavenly Father—says, "We beseech you, brethren, and exhort you by the Lord Jesus, that as ye have received of us how ye ought to walk and to please God, so ye would abound more and more. For ye know what *commandments* we gave you by the Lord Jesus." Now, mark the command to which first and special reference is here made: "*This is the will of God, even your sanctification.*" If already wholly sanctified, why this solemn declaration?

In closing up his epistle, he again reminds them of his absorbing desire for their entire sanctification by the prayer—"The very God of peace sanctify you *wholly;* and I pray God that your whole spirit, and soul, and body, be preserved blameless, unto the coming of our Lord Jesus Christ. Faithful is he that hath called you, who also *will* do it."

Had Paul been disposed to urge upon his brethren

Wrong Teachings.   Disastrous Alternatives.

the views advocated by the minister you have mentioned, he might have said, My brethren, beloved in the Lord, when you were first brought nigh by the blood of Jesus, and freely justified by his grace, then ye were no more in any degree carnal, but were wholly sanctified, throughout spirit, soul, and body. If by your subsequent daily, yet nearer, approaches to the Sun of righteousness, any remains of the carnal mind be discovered, it is because you have either fallen from grace, or what is more probable, have been mistaken in thinking yourselves converted at all; for if you were ever truly converted, you were at the same time wholly sanctified.

I have spoken of this unscriptural, anti-Wesleyan doctrine, as dangerous heresy; and would not either of the foregoing alternatives be calculated to tell disastrously on the soul convinced of the necessity of entire sanctification? To yield to the impression that he had fallen from grace, and that the enemy which had been entirely expelled had been permitted to re-enter, were only calculated to move him to seek for a reinstatement in his former condi-

proximity to the Sun of righteousness, and the heavenly radiations have only been permitted to penetrate his soul in order that the discovered deficiencies may be fully removed by the all-cleansing power of his Saviour. Thus, such as God hath not grieved would be grieved, and instead of being encouraged to an onward course, from the conviction that he had been gaining a more thorough knowledge of his necessities, by drawing nearer to God, he is driven back to first principles, laying again the foundation of repentance from dead works, and of faith toward God.

On the other hand, if the light revealing the remains of the carnal mind be resisted by submitting to the wrong teaching of men, rather than the oracles of God, the consequences would be yet more disastrous than the former alternative. A little leaven leaveneth the whole lump. Could Satan devise a scheme better suited to his purpose of getting the soul partially or wholly under his control, than to induce us to wrap ourselves in the persuasion that sin is all destroyed, while the remains of corruption are still working within? No wonder that he so often transforms himself into an angel of light, by getting ministers, and now and then other good persons, to help him by their sophistry in defending this doctrine. I have myself witnessed singular incongruities in theory and practice with some who, with an exhibition of unhallowed zeal, have defended these views, while, at the same time, and by their own confession, their experience and theory were contradicting each other. It was said to one of these on one occasion, "Brother, are you living in a state of justifi-

Are you wholly sanctified?   The Two States.

cation?" "Yes," was the reply. "And have you the evidence that you are wholly sanctified?" "No."

This is a subject on which I feel much interest, for with much pain I have witnessed its baneful effects. I had intended to say more, but will write you soon again.

As ever, in love.

No. XLI.—TO MISS S——.

Mr. Wesley's views—The author's habit of mind—Evidence of justification previous to entire sanctification—Movement of the denominations toward the unity of the faith—Tuesday meeting—A charming sight—Quotations from Wesley—Experience of David—The apostles—A cloud of witnesses—Caleb and Joshua—The danger of refusing to go on to perfection.

. . . . Your own experience furnishes such conclusive testimony relative to the two states, justification and sanctification, that I do not wonder at the solicitude you express in reference to ministers who so recklessly controvert this point. I very much venerate the opinions of Mr. Wesley, the founder of Methodism, under God. But I am so constituted, that it seems to be a habit which the law of my nature demands, to analyze sentiments let them come from whom they may, before I can really receive them as my own. Thus I seemed to be turned away from all mere human opinions, previous to entering into a state of justification. In like manner, yet with more distinctness, prior to apprehending the state of sanctification, was I turned away from human helps, "to the law and to the testimony." I have already informed you of the clear witness of justification which preceded my entering into the enjoyment of holiness, and the distinctness of my perceptions relative to my absolute need of that state. And then, on being led by the Spirit through the blood of the everlasting covenant into the holiest, you know something of the manner in which the Holy Spirit took of the things of God and revealed them unto me. I could just as well doubt my existence this moment, as to doubt my own justification some time previous to being brought into a state of sanctification. This I know was brought about by the teachings of the Spirit *through* the *word*, for every progressive step, as you may remember, was distinctly directed by the waymarks laid down in the *word* of God.

It is now no small satisfaction for me to know, that the views received, by thus carefully testing every onward movement by the law and the testimony, are so fully in accordance with Mr. Wesley's views of Bible truth. The more I search the Scriptures, the more I am confirmed in the belief that Wesley was a man eminently taught of God, and "mighty in the Scriptures." The deeply devoted

The Wesleyan Theology.   Unity of the Faith.

of all denominations seem to be verging toward that point, "the unity of the faith," where the watchmen see eye to eye. Should it not be cause of gratitude with those who adhere to Mr. Wesley's expositions of Bible truth, that as the watchmen in Zion approach the point of union in view, they seem more and more to appreciate the Wesleyan theology?

I know these sentiments might seem egotistic, should they fall under the eye of some. But I think I may be permitted to speak with a degree of assurance. Perhaps few have had better opportunity to judge on this subject than myself. Though your stay in our city was short, yet, by your visits at our house, and your attendance on the Tuesday afternoon meetings, it is easy for you to imagine the ground on which the watchmen may see eye to eye—the point at which we may arrive, where we may find ourselves "in the unity of the faith." It is a usual thing for ministers of different denominations to meet with us on the common ground of holiness. Here we may say,—

> "Even now we speak and think the same,
>   And cordially agree;
> United all in Jesus' name,
>   In perfect harmony."

I have observed at one meeting, side by side, Presbyterian, Baptist, Congregationalist, Moravian, and Methodist brethren, united in sentiment, heaven beaming in their countenances, sitting under the banner of love, breathing the atmosphere of heaven.

But I have digressed. I began with the intention of responding to what has been said of those ministers among us who maintain that they are one in doctrine with Mr. Wesley on this point, that when justified we are at the same time fully sanctified. Mr. Wesley cannot be made to favor these views without greatly distorting his words.

I have just been at pains to get his precise words on this subject:—" From what has been said we may easily learn the mischievousness of that opinion, that we are *wholly* sanctified when we are justified; that our hearts are then cleansed from all sin. It is true, we are then delivered, as was observed before, from the dominion of outward sin, and at the same time the power of inward sin is so broken, that we need no longer follow, or be led by it; but it is by no means true, that inward sin is then totally destroyed, that the root of pride, self-will, anger, and love of the world, is then taken out of the heart, or that the carnal mind, and the heart, bent to backslidings, are entirely extirpated. And to think the contrary, is not, as some suppose, a harmless mistake. No; it does *immense harm*; it entirely blocks up the way to any further change: for it is manifest, ' They that are whole do not need a physician, but they that are sick.' If, therefore, we think we are quite made whole

Mr. Wesley's Refutation of an Unscriptural Doctrine.

already, there is no room to seek any further healing. On this supposition it is absurd to expect a further deliverance from sin, whether gradual or instantaneous."

Mr. Wesley, in another place, goes on to bring other arguments against this "new and unscriptural doctrine," as he terms it, which I may not now take room to transcribe, at the close of which, he says, "I cannot, therefore, by any means receive the assertion that there is no sin in a believer from the moment he is justified. First, because it is contrary to the whole tenor of Scripture. Secondly, because it is contrary to the experience of the children of God. Thirdly, because it is absolutely new, never heard of in the world till yesterday. And lastly, because it is naturally attended with the most fatal consequences; not only grieving those whom God hath not grieved, but perhaps dragging them into everlasting perdition." I have quoted largely, but you may not have his Works at hand, and as I believe I have not read the portion here given myself for years, I have been glad of the opportunity of again refreshing my own mind. Had I known that my views of Scripture on this point so nearly accorded in word with his, I might before have given his in place of my own.

These views accord with the religious experience of men of all ages. After David had said, "He hath brought me up out of a horrible pit, out of

Experience. David. The Apostles. A Cloud of Witnesses.

the miry clay," he further said, "And *establishea my goings.*" Doubtless this *establishing grace* was given in answer to the prayer, "Wash me *thoroughly* from mine iniquity, and cleanse me from my sin:" "Create in me a clean heart, O God." Previous to the day of Pentecost the disciples could dispute among themselves which should be the greatest; and Thomas could not believe unless he saw signs and wonders. Various other wrong doings exhibited the remains of carnality among them. After the full baptism of the Holy Ghost was given, strifes, cowardice, and unbelief, were put away, and in entire devotion to the service of Christ, they gave themselves up to the work of establishing his kingdom on earth. Unequivocal demonstration was given that the old leaven was purged out.

What a great cloud of witnesses has since arisen! By the word of their testimony, and the blood of the Lamb, they have overcome. Thousands of living witnesses could now be adduced of the attainableness of this state. But O how important it is that those who have entered this rest should be explicit in their testimony! It was not only through the "blood of the Lamb," but by the "*word of their testimony,*" that they of whom the Revelator spake overcame.

I am reminded of Caleb and Joshua, who, after having spied out the good land, gave in "the word of their testimony" thus: "We are well able

More Witnesses wanted. The Fallen. Old Professors.

to go up and possess the good land." Had only a few more of the spies added their voice to the weight of Caleb and Joshua's testimony, is it probable that the Israelites would have yielded to their doubts, whether God would bring them into the land which he had promised, saying, "Go up and possess it?"

Ah, little do those who are not adding their voice to the testimony, "We are well able," &c., think how the cause may be suffering through their deficiency. The carcasses of those who fell in the wilderness furnish a faint resemblance of the many thousands who have been brought out of spiritual Egypt, and are now commanded to go up and possess

"The land of rest from inbred sin,
The land of perfect holiness;"

but who, because of unbelief, refuse to go up. Alas for the thousands who fall or have fallen in the wilderness! I sometimes fear that the blood of many of these may be found on the skirts of old professors, who, though they may have spied out the good land, do nevertheless by their own experience virtually say, "We are not able to go up and possess it."

Mr. Wesley, in his sermon, "*Let us go on unto perfection,*" says, "That the doing of this is a point of the utmost importance:" the apostle intimates in the next words, "This will we do, if God permit." For it is impossible for those who were once enlightened, and have tasted of the good word of God, and the powers of the world to come, and have fallen away, to renew them again to repentance." As if he had said, If we do not "go on to perfection," we are in the *utmost danger of falling away.* "And if we do fall away, it is impossible (that is, exceedingly hard) to renew us again to repentance."

I have indeed written a long letter, but you are so critically and also responsibly circumstanced with respect to the topics presented, that I will not apologize.

Your devoted friend.

No. XLII.—TO MR. C——.

The willing and obedient—Profession and practice—The cross—" I will guide thee by mine eye"—Lessons of experience—The importance of immediate action in the use of present grace—A temptation not to speak *definitely* yielded to—Sad effects—Reproved, but not rejected—God doth not afflict willingly—Holiness may be forfeited by neglect—A strange testimony—Reply—Acknowledgment—Lingering in duty—Its consequences—Views of personal obligation.

You say that you know you must be willing and obedient, if you would eat the good of the land. I have thought, my dear brother C., that the Lord had taken much pains to teach you this lesson; but has not your experience taught you, that it is

Consecration. A Cross shunned. "What do ye more than Others?"

one thing to receive a lesson, and quite another thing to retain it? My heart assures me, my precious brother, that you are sincere before God; and as you have earnestly asked my advice, I am sure you wish me to be candid.

Permit me, then, to say, that grace, I think, has done much for you. I see no reason to conclude, that you have been mistaken as to your state, in conceiving it to be one of consecration to God; but yet I have observed, what, by some, might be deemed discrepancies between your conduct and profession, which may retard your own progress and also hinder your success in testifying of Christ as your full Saviour. Let me instance. Not long since you were asked to take part in the exercises of a meeting where your services were really required. It was evident that there was not another present to take your place, but you yielded to the shrinking of the flesh, and declined before several who do not profess to be wholly sanctified, saying, "I do not feel free to it." Here was one professing to be wholly sanctified, unwilling to perform a duty rendered obvious by the providence of God; and how could those not professing the blessing reconcile the conduct and the profession? If the thoughts of most present had been uttered, doubtless the response of many hearts had been, "What do ye more than others?" I must confess that, though fully aware of the sincerity of brother C., yet I could not but feel that a profession carried out thus was hardly to be desired.

Imagine that the Saviour, when about to bear the cross up the hill of Calvary for you, had yielded to the shrinkings of nature, and said, "I do not feel free to it." You have given yourself up to follow the Lamb whithersoever he goeth; but I need not say to you, that you cannot do this, unless you take up your cross *daily* and follow after him. The warfare is against the world, the *flesh*, and Satan. Doubtless every successive day of our pilgrimage will present "something still to do or bear," from which the flesh may shrink; but shall we yield? If so, we are the servants of him whom we obey. But I am persuaded better things of brother C., though I thus speak.

I am thankful that your heavenly Father reproved you on the occasion referred to. In his great love he sometimes permits us to be convinced, by *painful* experience, of our errors. We who are parents take pains to instruct our children, in order that they may gradually come to a knowledge of the various duties of life, and after having once clearly assured them of a duty, we expect them to act accordingly. We do not *condemn* a child for not knowing, but if he disobeys subsequently to his being convinced of duty, then *condemnation* follows. Now, dear brother, in more instances than the one referred to, have I feared that you

Guided by a Look.   A Silken Cord.   Bliss.

would come under condemnation. Your Lord and Master says, "I will instruct thee, and teach thee in the way which thou shalt go; I will guide thee with mine eye." How quiet and gentle his sway! It is true, he holds the reins which are to guide us through all the vicissitudes of life, and its various duties; yet they are held by the hand of infinite wisdom and love; and the silken cord, which holds us in the way, is a bond of love. I heard one, who is now eminent for the holiness and usefulness of her life, say, on her first entrance upon the way, "I resolved to obey every intimation of the Holy Spirit, even the faintest of them." Richly does her experience prove the faithfulness of God, "The willing and the obedient shall eat the good of the land."

If I were to be guided by the eye of another, what constant watchfulness were necessary; but if my inmost heart were wholly possessed with the idea, that, to turn my attention off from that eye of light, were to leave me, perhaps in one moment, to take a step which might end in darkness, misery, and death; whereas, on the other hand, obedience to its dictates were only submitting to what was, in the highest degree, necessary for my well-being—O that were bliss indeed! What a privilege to be guided by an eye whose every motion is dictated by love—infinite LOVE! Please turn to the thirty-second Psalm, and read from the

Bit and Bridle.   Lessons learned.   "Why don't you do it?"

eighth verse to the close. How evident it is, that our heavenly Father would have us obey the *gentle* monitions of his Spirit! "Be not as the horse, or as the mule, which have no understanding; whose mouth must be held in with bit and bridle." How our hearts yearn in love over a child who exhibits a ceaseless desire to know and obey our wishes! Such a child may my dear brother C. ever be.

I am endeavoring to be willing and obedient; yet, it is by painful experience that I have occasionally learned some useful lessons. I will attempt to give you a glance at the way a few of these were learned; and I think the relation may help to expose the devices of Satan. A few days after I first received the witness of holiness, I was at a meeting where there was a number of persons deeply agonized in spirit for the salvation of God. Some were groaning for justifying grace, and others for full redemption. O, thought I, if there were only some one here to talk about the simple way of salvation by faith! "Why do you not do it?" was suggested. O, thought I, it would require a *special* commission to undertake a duty so formidable; for among the suppliants for full salvation were one or more ministers, and other persons of influence. I was at a camp meeting, and I hastened to a retired place, that I might, without interruption, inquire of God. But I had scarcely knelt before I received the gentle chidings

Reproved.   Opportunity lost.   "Don't be definite."

of the Spirit thus: "Did you not, in supplicating guidance for the day, ask that you might be filled with the knowledge of the will of God, with all wisdom and spiritual understanding?" &c. When you asked, did you not believe that you received the thing you desired? Why then did you not let your conduct correspond with your faith, by acting *promptly?* Before I called, God had answered, and I hastened back to the meeting; but it was only to learn that my omission had frustrated the design of God; for I had scarcely reached the place before the meeting was closed, preparatory to public exercises from the stand. I felt so deeply mortified that Satan should thus have robbed me of this opportunity for usefulness, that I believe I have not needed a repetition of the lesson.

A short time after this I was at a love-feast. My heart was rejoicing in the blessedness of full salvation; and the privilege of sounding it abroad to the ends of the earth would, indeed, have been blissful. It was presented, You have mentioned it before in this church; and, perhaps, the most here have heard your experience on this point; and here are others who profess to enjoy this blessing, yet they do not speak so *definitely* nor so *often* on that subject, and it will appear more humble to be more reserved. I concluded I would not speak *definitely* of enjoying the blessing, but would leave it to be inferred. I rose to testify, but felt no liberty. I was startled, said but little, and sat down. I thought, Can it be that it was not my duty to speak? No, that duty was clear. If the Lord required the testimony, why did he not help me, was the next question? I inquired the cause. My Saviour was most graciously near and precious, and truly did I feel that he did not condemn me; but, in love he assured me, that I had chosen my *own* way to speak, therefore I had no right to expect the special help of the Holy Spirit. I was pained indeed. I saw that I had not honored God as I might have done; yet the transgression had not been willful; but it surely was one which needed the atonement of Christ; and had it not been every moment available, impurity, sufficient to banish my soul from his presence, had been contracted: yet I still felt that I loved God with all my heart; that I still kept *all upon the altar*, and, consequently, could still say, The blood of Jesus *cleanseth*. To the praise of God I believe I may say, that Satan has never again had the advantage of me on this point.

I would urge the importance of looking well to the things which we have gained. A lesson once learned should ever be retained. We as parents would feel ourselves grieved and dishonored by a child who is ever learning, and never coming to the knowledge which we desire to impart. Our heavenly Father is intent on teaching us the lessons

The Divine Tenderness.   Danger of being drawn back.

of his grace, and if we will not learn otherwise than by *painful* experience, his love may move him to treat us accordingly. Yet in all our afflictions he is afflicted; and shall we move the heart of infinite love to painful correctives, in order to make and keep us right? It is because the bowels of compassion are yearning toward us, that he says, "Be not as the horse or as the mule." O may our dear brother C. be guided most peacefully, and gently, in every heavenward step, by the eye of LOVE!

In other cases than the one in question, have I observed your proneness to shrink from the cross. In this you say your heavenly Father reproved you; and, doubtless, he has before reproved you. It is my impression, that the next time you do thus, he will remove the light of his countenance, and you will be numbered among the many who once enjoyed the blessing of holiness, and have lost it. Think of the position in which Israel would have stood, if after they had once, by the power of God, entered upon their promised inheritance, they had been driven back again into the wilderness by their enemies. What cause of triumph would this have been to their foes, and how dishonoring to themselves and to their God! O what a struggle with the powers of darkness had my dear brother before entering this his rightful inheritance, and shall his enemies yet again prevail, and drive him back? Jesus, Captain of our salvation, forbid it! Sooner cut short thy work in righteousness, and take him to thyself in heaven.

I have yet a little room on my sheet, and there are other lessons which with me have been somewhat painfully learned; and, as they involve points about which we have conversed, I will mention them briefly. I told you that the Lord had assured me, that it was not for me to wait for *impelling* influences, but rather to act from the dictates of a sanctified judgment, (and if we render up mind, memory, and will, every moment, to Christ, are we not to believe he *sanctifies* all these powers?) We may often be required to act with *promptness* where the circumstances will not admit of delay. The promptings of the Spirit may often suggest, as was said to David, "Do what is in thy heart, for the Lord is with thee;" or with Joshua, when he was lying on his face, and it was said, "Up, for Israel hath sinned."

I was present at a meeting for testimony on holiness, where, after it had for some time progressed most profitably, an influential individual arose and said, among other inexplicable things, "When I experienced religion I was as happy as I could live; but afterward, when my mind became interested on the subject of sanctification, I lost all my enjoyment, and have never regained it since." I had expected much from the meeting, but, for a

Silent Watchman.   Taking Sides with God.   The Result.

moment, all seemed lost. Several ministers were present, and I earnestly hoped some might defend the precious doctrine of holiness from the aspersion which had been implied; but they were silent. I had been solicited to be present, to help forward the exercises of the meeting, and the enemy tauntingly suggested, If you reply by way of reproving this brother, it will look as if you were indeed willing to be a teacher among teachers. But shall any one be left to conceive, from such high authority, (for the one who had spoken was a minister,) that as soon as they really resolve on obedience to the command, "Be ye holy," they are to lose all their enjoyment in religion? I could not abide the thought, and said, If others will not do their duty, by taking sides with God, they must settle it before God for themselves; it is the Lord's most precious truth which suffers, and he can use this feeble instrument in its defense.

I spoke; and the Lord not only took care of his truth, but he took care of my influence in the minds of those present, as I plainly saw afterward. The next day, the individual who had spoken so questionably came to me, and with tears acknowledged that he had permitted his mind to get into great darkness on that point. He seemed very sincere in his resolves that he would seek till he obtained the blessing.

It was only during the ensuing week that I was

Boisterous.   Stand up for the Truth.   The Delay.

again present, under similar circumstances, at a meeting held quite remote from the one just referred to. A minister had said at the opening of the meeting, "Sister —— is with us, and will instruct us in the way of holiness." The enemy made this a source of some temptation to me, but the way of the Lord seemed to be preparing for a baptism of the Spirit, when an illiterate man, seemingly of boisterous habits, began to tell of an experience made up of signs and wonders. After telling of great ecstasies, he concluded by saying, with much emphasis, "Brethren and sisters, if you are happy you are holy." I longed, for the sake of the cause, that some one would set him right; but said the enemy, "If you should attempt to do it, they would certainly think that you thought yourself capable of instructing them." The Spirit said, "Stand up in defense of truth: did not God take care of your influence, last week, under similar circumstances, and will he not do it now?" I lingered, saying in my heart, The views which this person has presented are so palpably wrong, that any discerning individual may discover their falsity; and thus I reasoned, neither really decided not to speak in defense of truth, nor fully resolved that I would do so, until the gracious influence, which had before prevailed, seemed to be withdrawn from the meeting, and I saw that I had grieved the Spirit of holiness. Never since that time have

Reputation.   Let us keep what we get.   Established.

I dared to be otherwise than fearless in the defense of truth. I do not judge *others;* to their own Master they stand or fall, but *my* duty is plain. I have given up my *reputation* to God; and I cannot consistently make a profession of being wholly given up to the service of Christ, or of having received his Spirit, without standing out faithfully in defense of the blessed doctrines of the gospel, and manifesting that spirit, by a corresponding sympathy, when his cause suffers.

The Lord help us to "look to ourselves, that we lose not those things which we have wrought, but that we receive a full reward," and may we ever be found perfect and complete in all the will of God.   Yours, in the fellowship of the Spirit.

No. XLIII.—TO MRS. D——.

Establishing grace—God's worthies—Few excel—Instability—Unlike God—Let your yea be yea, and your nay nay—The seal of the Spirit—Our Father's testament—Spiritual ambition—Ann Cutler.

O it is indeed a good thing, my sister, that the heart be *established* in grace. If God himself hath pronounced it a good thing, surely it must be pre-eminently good. How confirming it is to the pious heart to look upon one who, year after year, pursues the even tenor of his way with undaunted step! God has his worthies, even in the present day, and the eye of my mind is just now resting

"Of whom the World is not worthy." Few excel.

with inexpressible delight on some of those of whom the world is not worthy. I have beheld them while the fires of tribulation have burned hotly around them, and yet,

> "Like Moses' bush,
> They flourish unconsumed in fire."

And again have I beheld them; and the world, the flesh, and Satan, in close array, would fain have triumphed over them, but thus far have they overcome by the word of their testimony and the blood of the Lamb, and, still strong in faith, they endure as *seeing* Him who is invisible. It is not wise to say, "The former days were better than these."

But yet in view of the extensive provisions of grace, taken in connection with the inspiring fact, that "God is no respecter of persons," how small the number of those who excel!

> The King's highway: how narrow is the road,
> How few there be that find it: yet the abode
> Of God—the Christian's home—lies at its end,
> And none can reach the goal but they who bend
> With purpose all unyielding—steady, true,
> And step undaunted, though all hell pursue.

Instability is an evil of far greater magnitude than is generally apprehended. It is composed of elements which are wholly unlike what God loves. As well might an attempt be made to unite Christ and Belial, as to unite an unstable soul enduringly to "Jesus Christ, the same yesterday, to-day, and for ever."

Instability.	Immutability of God.

For the honor of the cause of God, I have greatly desired that the evil of instability might be looked upon with the abhorrence which it merits. To the degree a thing is unlike God, it must be hateful in his sight. With the immutable Jehovah there is neither variableness nor *shadow* of turning. Yet, alas! how unlike God are many who profess to have received his nature! Their career is but a continual exhibition of *variableness* and *turning*. On one occasion you may find them flaming with ardor in the cause of Christ, and seemingly dead to the vanities of earth, and again, perhaps, in a few short months, they are found spiritless and worldly. And many there are of a higher grade of experience, who sadly mistake the mark here. How often, in view of the firm foundation laid for their faith, have they said before God, "I will believe!" "I do believe!" But when called to endure the trial of their faith, they are *variable*, and *turn* away from the believer's only resting place, forgetful that their yea should be *yea*, and their nay *nay*, with God. Ever do such find that "whatsoever is more than this cometh of *evil*." "*Unstable* as water, thou shalt not excel," was said of one in ancient time, and alas for the cause of holiness, that the experience of so many should illustrate the melancholy prediction!

I wonder why the *sealing of the Spirit* is not oftener an object of special faith and entreaty?

The Spirit's Seal.   Our Inheritance.

The Scriptures present it as the privilege of the believer: "After that ye believed, ye were sealed with the Holy Spirit of promise," Eph. i, 3. And again, as though those addressed had already received the seal, it is said, "Grieve not the Spirit, whereby ye are sealed unto the day of redemption." Paul surely had received it, or he had not said, "I am persuaded that neither death, nor life, nor angels, nor principalities, nor powers, nor things present, nor things to come, nor height, nor depth, nor any other creature, shall be able to separate us from the love of God, which is in Christ Jesus our Lord." I adore the God of my salvation, by whose grace I was moved to plead for the sealing of the Holy Spirit. The Bible presented it as my privilege, and this was enough to inspire my faith in pleading for it. Never did I more consciously realize that the Spirit itself maketh intercession, than when groaning before God for this establishing grace. It was the Holy Spirit that placed it distinctly before my mind, as a privilege included in the believer's inheritance.

The believer's *inheritance!* How glorious! How wonderful the privileges purchased by the sufferings and death of the Son of God! all of which are now made over to every child of God, through faith in Christ Jesus. When an earthly parent leaves his last will and testament, setting forth in specific terms the inheritance bequeathed, how

The Heir opening the Will.   Ann Cutler.

minutely does each inheritor examine the document in order to ascertain the extent and validity of his claims! If fearful that his own judgment may be defective, he eagerly inquires of those who are skilled in law, until assured that all the privileges granted by virtue of his father's will are fully apprehended. Why are not the children of our heavenly Father more ambitious to secure their rights? Truly, the children of this world are wiser in their generation than the children of light. It was said of Ann Cutler, a worthy of Wesley's time, that it was her daily practice to search the Scriptures with earnest prayer, in order to ascertain just what it was her privilege to expect, and after being assured of the will of God concerning her, she made it a point never to rest until the promised blessing was hers. What an inspiring example! May the Lord help us to do likewise.

Yours, &c.

No. XLIV.—TO MRS. E——.

Disappointment—Our recent interview—Sad change—Fault-finding *versus* prayer—Ministers need encouragement—" Our minister is not popular "—Harmful effects—Speaking evil of ministers—A false light—Confession—A stumbling block—" Touch not mine anointed "—A family regulation with respect to the reputation of ministers.

My beloved sister and myself were both somewhat disappointed on the occasion of our recent interview. But I hope, my dear E—— has learned to regard all her disappointments as emphatically God's *appointments*. If so, obedience to the command, " In *everything* give thanks," has become one of your most pleasant duties.

But I fear that this may not be your state before God. You were *unhappy* last evening, and not only your words but your very looks expressed unhappiness. The interview previous to that of last evening, which I remember to have had with you, was spent in conversation on the all-important subject of " HOLINESS TO THE LORD." That theme stood absorbingly before you, and seemed to be engraven on all your intentions. Instead of being much concerned about *self*, and ways and means for the bringing about the consummation of your own wishes, you were mostly concerned in the establishment of the pure and peaceable kingdom of Christ in the hearts of those with whom you communed.

Fault-finding *versus* Prayer.

Do I mistake, when I say, I fear that it is not altogether with you as in years past? I believe that my beloved sister wishes to stand perfect and complete in all the will of God, and if so, she will bear with me while I breathe aloud thoughts and fears which have oppressed my heart concerning her. Has not the deceiver, as an angel of light, beguiled you by his sophistries? By turning the eye of your mind so intently upon what you deem to be the failings of your minister, has he not succeeded in turning your attention away from "the beam that is in thine own eye?" Had the time which has been spent by yourself, and a number of your friends, in perhaps *prayerless* talking and thinking about your minister, been spent in seasons of fasting and prayer for the holiness of his life, and the success of his ministrations, he might by this time not only have been eminent as an example in faith, in purity, and in doctrine, but yourself and your friends, standing prominent as you do in the church, might have been greatly instrumental in promoting its purification and prosperity.

The day of eternity only can reveal what loss yourself, and friends, and also your minister, and the cause generally, has sustained by this disaffection which you have manifested toward your minister and his administration. Instead of holding up his hands, which surely, by the ordinary duties of his responsible station must need support, you

Bear ye one another's Burdens. What have you accomplished?

and your friends have added greatly to this accumulated weight. How, O how can this course appear in the sight of the meek, lowly, loving Saviour, who hath said, "Bear ye one another's burdens, and so fulfill the law of Christ?"

"But," say you, "we think him deficient in piety, and though he seems to preach well, yet he has other faults; he is not generally popular, and to us his ministrations are not profitable." Now, my dear sister, had yourself and friends first went to Jesus, as did his disciples of old, and told him all, had you done this without even mentioning your dissatisfaction to one another, I have little doubt but you would have had one of the most prosperous conference years you ever enjoyed.

Do you think that your expressions of dissatisfaction have in any way improved the piety of your minister? Have they tended toward making him more generally popular? Or have they made his ministrations more profitable to yourselves? If none of these important results have been attained, then there is every reason why you should take shame and confusion of face to yourselves.

But let me tell you, that there are humble, holy souls, in church fellowship with you, who have found the word of life, as dispensed by your minister, precious food. While you have been scattering here and there and gathering nothing, and are now almost starving, for your very looks say, "O

The Wrong Path.   A False Light.   Make Confession.

my leanness, my leanness!" these have been feeding richly on the dainties of heaven. O what have you lost, and what has the precious cause of Christ lost, by your turning out of the highway into this by-path, and alas for those who have followed you through these delusions of Satan!

I say "these delusions of Satan," for, truly, as an angel of *light*, has the deceiver decoyed you into this path. If, in your imagination, light beams upon it, beware; it is the glare of the fires of perdition, and it will lead you, if you persist, and those who follow you, eventually to the point whence it emanates.

I see no way to get back upon the right track, but to acknowledge your error, and return. "If we confess our sins, He is faithful and just to forgive us our sins, and to cleanse us from all unrighteousness." "Make confession!" "Why, this would be coming down from the position in which I have stood, and my influence would thereby be injured, and my attitude be less favorable for usefulness than formerly." No, my sister, you have put a stumbling block in the way of the people, and in their sight you will have to return and take it up, that they may see that you have pursued a course which it would be dangerous for them to follow. And then the Lord may reinstate you among the leading spirits of his sacramental hosts, otherwise it were not safe to follow you.

> Christ and his Ministers. "Touch not mine anointed."

I do not mean by my remarks to intimate that your minister is faultless. I should, on the contrary, think that his demeanor may, in some respects, be reprehensible. But, as ministers are of like passions with ourselves, should we not, in sympathy with the spirit of the Saviour, be touched with the feeling of their infirmities? The chosen ambassadors of Christ, those who have been called, as was Aaron, must be peculiarly dear to the heart of the Saviour. Their influence stands inseparably identified with the promotion of his kingdom, and whoever touches the influence of these chosen ones, touches the heart of Christ. But must we not speak, in order that evils may be corrected? No, not unless you have taken the case to Christ *first*, and told him all the matter in all its bearings. And then, if after much prayer, and close communion with the Head of the church, he requires, for the well-being of the church, that the matter be brought out, let it be done with much prayerful caution and with a *single* eye to the glory of God, and not for the redress of a mere *personal* grievance.

Personal grievances should, in most cases, be taken *only* to God and to the individual concerned. Husband and I make it a point not to mention little matters we hear of this kind, even in our family, and often we do not mention them to each other. "Touch not mine anointed, and do my prophets

Evils cured by Prayer.   Solicitude.

no harm," stands prominent among our family regulations. In common with others, I sometimes see things in ministers, which, for the honor of Christ's precious cause, I could wish were otherwise, but the more my heart is troubled, the more constantly and earnestly do I keep the matter before God. Among the greatest victories I have ever gained, have been the curing of these evils in this *noiseless* manner. I have left no room on my sheet for apologies, in view of this plain dealing.

Yours, in Christian love.

No XLV.—TO MR. K——.

Solicitude—A twenty years' seeker—The longer and the shorter way—Remarkable experience in the steam cars—A meeting established for the promotion of holiness—How holiness sustains in the hour of trial, exemplified—The difference between willingness and obedience—A quotation from Mr. Wesley.

Your omission to write, lest my reply should make an unnecessary draft upon my time, has cost me more time in perplexing inquiries after the reasons of your strange silence, than would have been consumed in a long response.

I have felt most affectionately and prayerfully solicitous for your spiritual welfare. I hoped that ere this your goings had been established in the way of holiness. I am sure, dear brother, if the prophet had told you to do some great thing, you would have done it. But now, when it is only to cease your endeavors to save yourself, and by an act of faith cast yourself wholly on Christ, believing that he *fulfills* his promises to you, you shrink, and linger, just at the base of the fountain, unwilling to make the venture.

My dear brother, why do you not *now*
"Plunge into the purple flood,
And rise in all the life of God?"

By waiting thus you grieve your Saviour, for you ought long since to have been a witness of the full power of saving grace. This you may prove at any moment when you will, with your whole heart, trust in Christ as your present Saviour.

A beloved brother, who, for many years, had been earnestly longing for the witness of holiness, said to me, "I think I have not as deep and painful conviction on this subject as I ought to have, preparatory to the immediate reception of it. Mr. Wesley says, that often deeper and more painful conviction precedes it, than is experienced previous to justification." In return I observed "If all the deep feeling and earnestness of desire which you have felt during the past twenty years were gathered up within the compass of a few weeks, or a few days, would not the amount be great indeed?" He readily acknowledged it would. "Imagine," said I, "that you were to die within two minutes, what would you do?" With much solemnity he said, "I would cast myself upon the merits of my *Saviour!*" "Do you think he would save you from all your sins?" "I believe he would." "What! without any *more conviction?*" With emotion he acknowledged the conclusion to which he had brought himself, and yielded the point. He has since made the venture, and cast himself believingly on Christ, resolved to rest upon the authority of the word of God, as the evidence of his entire acceptance. As an able minister of the New Testament, he is now, in turn, proclaiming to others the excellency of that Word, upon which, as an immovable foundation, his faith is based.

I regret that you are not redeeming the time relative to this subject. If you were clear in the experience of this grace, how much more successful might you be in your endeavors to help others into its enjoyment! You say you now perceive, that you had reason to conclude you were in the enjoyment of the blessing at the time referred to in your last. Then why did you not at once, on perceiving this, again resume the confidence which you had cast away. If you have not yet resumed it, why may you not do so this moment? It is wonderful how the adversary gets the advantage of some, by keeping them lingering on the borders of the promised land, while others, at a single bound, leap over, and then exultingly gather its fruits, and tell of its blessedness to others.

Remarkable Experience in the Cars.

Let me tell of one who was not twenty years in getting into the way. He had, for some time previous, known the joys of pardoned sin. But he had not been much in communion with those, whose absorbing employ was to "praise the beauty of holiness," and on being thrown into the company of such, his heart became greatly enamored with its beauties, and earnestly did he long to enter upon its enjoyment. Just in this simple manner he obtained the desire of his heart. We were about to respond to an invitation to visit his residence, in order to spend a little season in communing on the subject; and while on the way in the steam cars, I said, "Brother J., are you sinning *now?*" "No, I believe I am not." "*How* are you saved from sin?" "I do not know, unless Christ *saves* me." "Do you think he would save you another moment, if you should continue to rely upon him?" "I believe he would." "Will you do it?" "By the help of the Lord, *I will.*" And that help was granted. He continued, with every moment, to gather fresh strength. I soon said, "I will not ask you what you will do to-morrow, nor what you will do five minutes hence; but, if you should now have the opportunity, would you be willing to say, Jesus *now* saves me from all sin: 'For with the heart man believeth unto righteousness, and with the mouth confession is made unto salvation?'" "By the help of the Lord, I will." He was an in-

Meeting for Holiness established.   A Fiery Trial.

fluential man, and both Presbyterian and Methodist ministers were in habits of intimacy at his house. That afternoon, I have reason to believe, that numbers were made acquainted with his interest on the subject. He shortly afterward established a meeting at his house for the promotion of holiness, ministers of different denominations have there met, with members of their charge, and ever since it has been kept up for the diffusion of light, and the edification of the lovers of holiness. Yesterday he visited us. He seems to be most truly going on from strength to strength, evidencing the power of Christ as a full Saviour before the world, amid the toils and perils of an extensive business.

Several weeks after he thus began to rest upon Jesus to *save* him under every diversity of circumstances, he was aroused one night to behold his extensive printing establishment in flames. He had had a similar calamity some time previous, which made this seem doubly disastrous. But the Saviour even here assured him, that there might be reasons why it were not better for him to lay up treasure on earth, and with sweet placidity of mind he was enabled, while yet beholding the devouring element, to sink down more closely into the bosom of love, with the inspiring assurance, "All things work together for good to them that love God."

Dear brother, why will you not *now* rest upon

Christ to *save* you? If you do not expect to save yourself in any degree, but depend wholly on the merits of Christ for salvation, why should you not this moment begin to trust him, to cleanse you from all your uncleanness. He now says to you, "I will, be thou clean;" but you do not *manifest* your willingness to be made clean, until you cast yourself as *you are* upon Christ, believing that he now *fulfills* his promises to you. You can no more be saved the present moment for the future than you can breathe for the future. You grieve the Holy Spirit while you stay away, and instead of getting a greater fitness, are every moment rendering yourself more unworthy; inasmuch as the Spirit has, for months past, been urging you to the open fountain, and Christ has been saying, "Come, for all things are *now* ready." Months since, you ought to have added your testimony to those who are already cleansed, and kept clean, and with them have said, "We are his witnesses of these things; and so also is the Holy Ghost whom God hath given to them that *obey* him."

I would not seem causelessly to upbraid a dear brother for whom I feel so affectionately desirous, but I am sure, if you linger after this hour, that the Saviour will upbraid you for *your* unbelief. It is not only the *willing*, but the *obedient*, that shall eat the good of the land, that is, they who *show* their willingness by their obedience. Your child may assure you of his willingness to obey your commands, but how lightly would these repeated assurances tell on your heart, unless he demonstrate it by doing what you require. Your mere willingness to believe will not itself bring you into

> "The land of rest from inbred sin,
> The land of perfect holiness,"

If Israel had for a long time stood upon the borders of their promised inheritance, continually saying, in obedience to the command, "Go over and possess the good land," "We are *willing*, and stand here all ready to go over;"—would this expression of willingness have brought them any nearer the point? Rather, would not their lingering have grieved their gracious God, who had led them through the wilderness, and brought them to this point, just in order that they might *now* enter in? O may our dear brother never be doomed to wander back into the wilderness of unbelief!

Mr. Wesley says, "Certainly you may look for it *now*, if you believe it is by faith. And by this token you may know whether you seek it by faith or by works. If by works you want something to be done *first*, before you are sanctified. You think I must first *be*, or *do* thus or thus. Then you are seeking it by works unto this day. If you seek it by faith, you must expect it *as you are;* and if as *you are*, then expect it NOW. It is of importance

Expect it by Faith.   Expect it as you are.   Expect it now.

to observe that there is an inseparable connection between these three things. Expect it *by faith*. Expect it *as you are*. Expect it *now*. To allow one is to allow them all. Do you believe that we are sanctified by faith? Be true then to your principle, and look for the blessing just as you are, neither better nor worse, as a poor sinner that has still nothing to pay, nothing to plead, but '*Christ died.*' And if you look for it as you are, then expect it now. Stay for nothing, why should you? Christ is ready and he is all you want." In another place, he adds, "To this confidence, that God is both able and willing to do it now, there needs to be added one thing more, a divine evidence and conviction that he *doeth* it. In that hour it is done, God says to the inmost soul, '*According to thy faith* be it done unto thee!' Then the soul is pure from every spot of sin; it is clear from all unrighteousness. The believer then experiences the deep meaning of these solemn words, 'If we walk in the light, as he is in the light, we have fellowship one with another, and the blood of Jesus Christ, his son, cleanseth us from all unrighteousness.'"

I hope my long letter may not prevent you from writing quickly in return, if it at all consist with your other duties. If your usage of Henry Clay, as a correspondent, is given as a sample of what I may expect from you, I shall regret it. I love

Reference to the Experience of Mrs. U—— and Mrs. L——.

to receive long letters, but I think I shall never again presume to send so long a talk as this in return. I so much desire to hear that you have entered into the rest of faith, that I am prone to forget myself while urging you on this point. The last experience in the "Riches of Grace," is from the pen of Mrs. Professor U——, of B——k, Maine. There is also another in that work to which I would refer you, on page 115, experience 19; you will find it also in the Guide, vol. 3, page 8. This is the experience of my beloved sister, Mrs. L——, the reading of which, I think, may be confirming to your faith. My dear husband, and all the members of my family still remember you most affectionately. My Christian salutations to Mrs. K——. Yours, &c.

NO. XLVI.—TO MISS D——.

A little child learning to walk—The Divine Sympathy proportioned to our feebleness—"I will hold thy right hand"—Shrinkings from duty—"I have ordained you"—The weak made strong—"Worldly Christians?"—A light in the world.

Your note came to hand, and has been cause of thanksgiving to the God of all grace, who hath made such great grace abound toward you. As you have received the Lord Jesus to the full salvation of your soul, I have been longing to hear how you have been enabled to *walk* in him.

A Little Child learning to Walk.

You speak of yourself as a little child coming to its parent, just learning to walk. Sweet and inspiring thoughts present themselves to my mind, in viewing this as your state. I regard my sister as having entered upon the road, which, by the fiat of the Lord of the way, "*shall be called, The way of holiness.*" He who hath cast it up for the express purpose that the redeemed of the Lord may walk therein, is with her every moment, guarding every step, and assuring her in every strait, " I the Lord thy God will hold thy right hand, saying unto thee, Fear not, I will help thee." The little child just learning to walk, commands more of the careful attentions of the parent, than one who, by previous training, has attained a firm gait. The love and ceaseless attentions of your Saviour are bestowed upon you, just in the proportion that your feebleness demands.

You are not favored with the companionship of many friends, who are walking in the highway, and you feel your loneliness. But O, what are earthly companions and loves, compared with the companionship and love of such a Friend as your Jesus purposes to be. Keep close to his side, and you will ever hear him saying to you, "Lo, I am with you alway, even unto the end of the world."

"But why do I grasp him with a trembling hand?" you ask. Let me in reply again refer you to the precious words: "I the Lord will hold thy

Divine Sympathy.   Expect a Daily Cross.

right hand." While your trembling hand is held in the firm, unyielding grasp of the Almighty, need you fear? Commune with your Saviour upon this question, and he will assure you that *his* strength is *your* strength. He knows the weakness of your flesh, but does he love you less because you cleave to him tremblingly. No! rather does he look upon you with yet greater tenderness, while he compassionately says, "The spirit indeed is willing, but the flesh is weak." When prone to sing,

"I hold thee with a trembling hand,"

may you ever be constrained to add,

"He holds me with his mighty hand,"

"Aye, he encompasseth my entire being within the hollow of his hand."

"Why do I feel it a cross to declare what he has done for me," you inquire. Expect a *daily* cross. "If any man will come after me, let him deny himself, and take up his cross *daily*, and follow me." In reference to some duties, even sanctified humanity may shrink; but if the human will is subject to the divine will, and submissively says, "Not my will but thine be done," I do not see why this does not imply a perfect state of the affections. I hope my dear sister will ever, through grace, " Cast aside that enthusiastic doctrine, that we are not to do good, unless our hearts are free to it." With David, may you ever be disposed to call upon all that fear the Lord, and tell what great things he hath done for your soul.

And now, my dear sister, do not be startled, when I tell you that you have been *ordained* for a great work. Not by the imposition of mortal hands, or a call from man. No, Christ, the great Head of the church, hath chosen you, "and ordained you, that ye should go and bring forth fruit." O my sister, yours is indeed a high and holy calling. Alas for you, if you are not found faithful to the trust committed!

But you have much to encourage you. Why should you not bear much fruit? "It is God that worketh in you." You are ONE with Him, who of God is made unto us Wisdom, Righteousness, Sanctification, and Redemption. O how mighty may you be as an instrument in the hand of God! "He holds you by the right hand, and with you, though but a worm, he may thrash a mountain."

How powerless, and even unseemly, were the instruments through which the walls of Jericho fell. Had the combined force of the mighty of the earth been called into requisition, for the accomplishment of this enterprise, then the excellency of the power might have been ascribed to men, *not* to God. And now our God will not give his glory to another. When he intends that the strong citadel which sin has raised in the hearts of men should be assailed, if he chooses instruments as impotent, or as unlooked-for, as were those rams' horns, we will not question his wisdom. Let us not say, What doest thou? but, without reasoning, resign ourselves into his hands.

In regard to the individuals to whom you have referred, I could but exclaim, O how strong and high is the barrier which renders the hearts of some, who profess love to the Saviour, impervious to the light, respecting the doctrine of salvation from all sin. May we not fear, that in many instances, it is because "the god of this world hath blinded the minds of them which believe not?"

Worldly-minded Christians! Does not the expression imply an agreement between Christ and Belial? an agreement which the Scriptures most strongly deny. Yet, alas! in what a variety of ways is the friendship of this world courted, by some who profess union with Christ. Should it be said to such, "Ye adulterers and adulteresses, know ye not that the friendship of this world is enmity with God; whosoever, therefore, will be a friend of the world, is the enemy of God," they would be amazed; yet this passage exhibits the true state of worldly professors toward God.

May you, my beloved friend, keep your garments unspotted. Amid a crooked and perverse generation, may you shine as a light in the world. If this prayer is answered in your experience, your

Expect Persecution.   Specified Wants.

daily walk and conversation will be a reproof to such professors as would join in affinity with the world. Expect persecution from such. "If ye will live godly in Christ Jesus, ye shall suffer persecution;" therefore make up your mind to this, and may God give you great courage, and ever, through sustaining grace, may you be

> " Bold to take up, firm to sustain,
> The consecrated cross."

Your sister in Christ.

No. XLVII.—TO REV. MR. H——.

Specified wants; presented, supplied, doubted—The inference—The great exchange; a man given and a God received—"Was God unfaithful?"—Mr. H——'s statement of his experience—A precise answer to a specific request—Confession delayed; urged—Witnesses of perfect love needed in the ministry.

BROTHER H—— kindly permits me to ask questions, or present truth, in any form, and I gratefully avail myself of the privilege.

A picture presents itself to my mind. Brother H—— has a son, whom he much loves. The boy has been in perilous circumstances, and comes to his father hungry, thirsty, and *all* want. His heart has been abundantly assured, from a knowledge of your nature and the resources at your command to gratify the promptings of your benevolent wishes, that he has but to come and present his case, to have all his need supplied. He

"It may be something else."   A Questionable Position.

has heard his father say, "Ask what you will, my son, and it shall be given you." Thus, at your bidding, he begins to specify his wants, and says, "Father, I am thirsty, give me water." The request is answered; he drinks, and at once feels precisely the effect anticipated.

I ask—"Did your father give you water?" Should he, with perhaps a saddened countenance, reply, "I do not know; I only know that it was *water* I wanted." "But did not your father assure you, that he would give *just* what you asked; and does not the effect answer your anticipations?" "Yes, my system is indeed greatly invigorated, but yet I cannot determine—it *may* be something else."

"But your father knew that you needed water, and it was because he saw your need, and had a plentiful supply, that he told you, you should have it, if you asked for it; and how can you reconcile the conduct of your father with truth? Does the general bearing of his conduct toward you warrant this *want* of confidence? Do you not know that you cast a shade upon the character of your father, by indulging in this mode of reasoning? The paternal love—ability—or fidelity, of your father, seems to be involved." Which of the three would you have me question?

Your son looks toward me reproachfully, and thinks me unkind, and yet I know not how, from his statement of his case, to arrive at other conclusions; and however much he may be pained, he alone is responsible for the untrue, or unkind thoughts I may entertain of his father.

Brother H——'s spirit was all athirst for the fountain of life and purity. His heavenly Father had given him to see the image of his Saviour *infinitely* desirable. The conditions upon which it was to be received, were set before you, and your spirit complied. The Holy Spirit urged you to *take* the image of your Saviour, assuring you that HE had taken yours. You made the exchange—"gave him your sin, and took his purity—gave him your shame, and took his honor—gave him your helplessness, and took his strength—gave him your death, and took his everlasting life." Yes, you made the exchange.

It was not in your own strength, that you were enabled to exchange your own vile image for the blessed likeness of your Saviour. But you *did*, through grace, do it, and here was fidelity on *your* part. Was God *unfaithful* in the performance of *his* part of the engagement? How can it be otherwise, if the position which you occupy be correct? If the want of fidelity on the part of God is not implied in the attitude in which you stand, I do not apprehend your experience, and must wait to be further informed.

Now, dear brother, do you not think this posi-

Mr. H——'s own Statement of his Experience.

tion inconsistent? "Does it not intimate a *fault* on the part of your Saviour?" And yet your whole heart is saying, "I have no fault to find with my Saviour," his name is "*Faithful* and *True*." You have acknowledged, that at the moment you made the "*exchange*"—the surrender of self, He was at once *true* to the performance of his part of the engagement. To use your own words, "His omnipotent hand was laid upon me—I felt it not only outwardly but inwardly—it pressed upon my whole being, and diffused all through and through it a sin-consuming, holy energy. As it passed downward, my heart, as well as my head, was *conscious of the presence* of this soul-cleansing energy, under which I fell to the floor, and, in joyful surprise, at the moment cried out with a loud voice. Still the hand of power wrought *within* and *without*, and wherever it moved, it seemed to leave the impress of the Saviour's image."

Now, brother, was God *true* and faithful? Your own confession has thrown the want of fidelity on *yourself*, and here I know you would have it rest. But will you, by *word*, *thought*, or *look*, in future be instrumental in cherishing, in any one heart, the impression that your heavenly Father, after having induced you to *specify* your wants, *might* possibly have given *something else* in place of that he had caused you to ask for? I think the lessons in *doctrine, reproof, correction*, and

The Three Loaves. Confession should have been made.

instruction in *righteousness*, contained in the first paragraph of the 11th chapter of Luke, meets your case precisely.

A specific request is here made, the friend wanted *three* loaves. Because of his importunity, his friend rises, and gives as *many* as he needs. And then the Saviour says, " Ask and it shall be given you, &c. If a son shall ask bread of any of you that is a father, will he give him a *stone?* or, if he ask a fish, will he give him a serpent? or, if he shall ask an egg, will he give him a scorpion?"

You know, dear brother, that your heavenly Father gave *just* the blessing you asked for, and your error has been in not confessing with your lips his *faithfulness* in fulfilling his promises. Your heart has believed, but your *lips* have not fully, freely, and habitually made *confession*. And thus *your* part of the work has been left in part unfulfilled. Do you not think, brother, that the time past should suffice? Would not God have been much more honored through your instrumentality, had you not *refrained your lips*, but fully and freely declared with David, to the great congregation, the faithfulness of your God? O! no longer *hide*, in any degree, his righteousness within your heart; redeem the time, and be assured, that the more you hold up the light that God has kindled, the more gloriously will your own soul become illuminated.

How the Creature may be Humbled.   An Encouraging Thought.

A very holy man once said, he felt it his duty to confess to the *outside* of what he enjoyed—assured that it not only honored God, but *humbled the creature*. And, dear brother, I know you will find it so in your own experience. I think you must begin to feel that you have been kept back from more open confession, by a well-circumstanced device of the enemy of God, of holiness, of your soul; and, if you continue longer thus, will not the enemy secure a partial triumph? Are you as strongly empowered to serve the cause of holiness, and honor your Saviour, who has imparted his image to you, as if you were enabled to declare at all times, unhesitatingly, that he *sanctifies* and *saves you fully?*

An encouraging thought presents itself. You know it is said that the wrath of our enemies shall praise him. Now, brother, should you not take pains to give publicity to your failure, in not confessing more specifically the great work that God has wrought for you? Your testimony might reach, and bring out many more among the dear brethren in the ministry, similarly conditioned with yourself—and surely this would not be a small service to the church.

You know how much the cause requires witnesses among the *ministry;* witnesses "that speak of that they *know*, and testify of that they have *seen*," and for want of such testimony, the work is less prosperous among the people than it would otherwise be. You know the Word directs us for example in faith and practice to the *ministry*, "whose faith *follow*"—"For the priest's lips should keep knowledge, and the people should seek the law at his mouth."

If such is the responsible attitude in which God's ambassadors stand, surely Jesus says, more appealingly to them than to us, "Ye are my witnesses;" and the account of their stewardship, when called to present every man perfect in Christ Jesus, may be found to be vastly less satisfactory, from the very fact that the testimony of their own experience had not been more fully brought out before the people.

Faithfully yours.

No. XLVIII.—TO MR. C——.

Impelled to activity by the Word—An enthusiastic doctrine—A nice point—Quietism—Abraham pleading for Sodom—Moses pleading for Israel—Christ in the person of his saints.

IN answer to your inquiry I will say, I do not think I have less faith in praying for the unconverted than formerly. "If so," you ask, "how has it been nourished and retained?" I answer, not generally by what may in one sense be termed *impelling* influences, but from the obvious requirements of the WORD, "Be ye steadfast, immovable,

Talents must be used.   God wills the Sinner's Salvation.

always abounding in the work of the Lord;"—"Instant in season, out of season;"—with kindred passages implying the utmost vigilance, and requiring the most skillful management in the employment of talents intrusted for usefulness. Otherwise, how can we, as faithful stewards, return his own with *usury*?

Mr. Wesley, in accordance with these Scripture enjoinments, says in his rules for the Methodist Societies, " Casting aside that enthusiastic doctrine, that we are not to do good unless our hearts are free to it." The greater the good to be accomplished, the more powerful and subtil will be the dissuasives which Satan will interpose. It is the will of God that sinners should be saved, and that the most energetic and unremitting efforts should be made in warning, entreating, and even compelling them to close in with the offers of mercy. So when we pray for the unconverted, whether we feel like it or not, we may have this confidence, that we ask that which is according to the will of God, and divine influences will descend upon them in answer to the prayer of faith, whether they will hear or whether they will forbear—it is thus that we are workers together with God—a sweet savor of Christ in them that are saved, and in them that perish. The manner, then, in which I have been enabled through grace to retain and nourish this " sympathy with Christ," is by continuing to labor

Labor.   Shrinkings.   God's Purpose changed by Prayer.

with him in saving the souls for whom his most precious blood was spilt; and this I endeavor to do on the same principle upon which I would perform other duties, and oftentimes amid the shrinkings of nature and powerful temptations to unbelief. Perhaps you say, Is it not the Spirit that makes intercession, and can I, without this moving of the Divinity within me, present acceptable prayer? This is a nice point, and only by comparing Scripture with Scripture can we resolve the matter. Had Abraham been disposed to lean toward Quietism, he had been less importunate in pleading for the Sodomites, and possibly righteous Lot might not have been delivered, yet God did not reprove him for unsubmissiveness. God had declared his purpose to Moses, and rebellious Israel was doomed to destruction; had Moses carried out the principles of the sect referred to, and calmly awaited the event in fancied submission, may we not presume that the sentence of divine justice would have been fulfilled? But was it not the Spirit of the divine Intercessor working mightily within Moses, that thus moved him to importune for the forgiveness of the rebels? Just so Justice may doom the sinner, but the WORD assures us, "Whatsoever ye shall ask in my name, that will I do, that the Father may be glorified in the Son." And notwithstanding the many exceeding great and precious promises given unto us, yet God hath

Sum of Religion.   Conformity to the Will of God.

declared, "For these things will I be inquired of by the house of Israel."

"The life of God in the soul of man," is said to be the sum of religion. "For ye are dead, and your life is hid with Christ in God." If Christ is our life, will not our lives be an exhibition of what his was when here below? His whole life was one continuous effort for the salvation of man, and to the degree we partake of his nature, we will exhibit before the world what he was when on earth. It is thus I am ever prone to measure my own attainments in grace. It is blessed indeed to sink into the will of God; but in order to know that we are in his will, we need a revelation of it, so that we may measure ourselves by its standard. This revelation we have fully exhibited in the life of Christ, and now it is for us to sink down "into the purple flood, then shall we rise moulded in his image, and present a glorious pattern, before men, of *conformity to the will of God.*"

Yours truly.

No. XLIX.—TO MRS. ——.

Led by a right way—Domestic cares—A Mother's Trials—Tests of grace should be welcome—Predictions—Trials—Triumphs—Mrs. Susannah Wesley—Daughters of Sarah—The Wesley Family—Influence of American republicanism on American wives—Quotation from Mrs. W.'s biography—Apology.

YES, beloved, he hath, indeed, led us by a *right* way. Only think of a Father infinite in goodness, wisdom, and love, leading forth his children, and in every strait which the fearful, disquieting career of life may present, saying,

" Cast off the weight, let fear depart,
And every care be gone,"

"For I, the Lord thy God, will hold thy right hand, saying unto thee, Fear not, I will help thee. Led by the hand of the infinitely wise, omnipotent Jehovah! How truly, then, may we encourage and confirm our hearts in the knowledge that we are in verity being led forth in the *"right* way." We have committed ourselves to his guidance, and none ever trusted in him and was confounded.

Your beloved babe confines you mostly from those outward active services to which you have been accustomed,—services which you were permitted to see promotive of the kingdom of Christ, and in the performance of which, your own soul was also quickened in the heavenly way. Well, you do not need me to assure you that this is "the *right* way " for you at the present time ; your letter furnishes most conclusive testimony of your confidence in this particular.

One of your own sweet privileges is hereby granted, and you are thus permitted to *test,* and also to *exhibit* the power of grace to sustain, in circumstances where thousands of pious mothers are placed, and where, alas! too many are prone to let go their hold on the provisions of grace.. How many who have adorned the doctrine of God their Saviour, when free from the vexatious cares of a little family, have, when their quiet has been thus broken in upon in the order of Providence, become weak as others.

You are aware of the opinion which has obtained with a large class of house-keepers, as to the difficulty, and some might say, impossibility of maintaining unbroken peace, and unquenched zeal, amid the unceasing trial of patience, and untold vicissitudes, to which a mother is exposed in rearing a family.

More especially have I observed those possessed of a higher grade of mind, inclining to pursuits calculated to tell extensively on the world, exposed to severe mental conflicts on this point. And here I must indulge in sorrowing reflections—I have seen the mighty fall!

Now, beloved, can I doubt but that our God is bringing you forth by "the right way," when to the gaze of the world, and also to the knowledge of your own heart, you stand forth confessedly of the class alluded to. And will not my dear sister acknowledge herself signally blest, in being brought through the ordeal, maintaining unbroken peace, unabated zeal, and yet deeper devotedness to the service of her Redeemer.

"Yes," I hear you ask, "Is it not matter of rejoicing and thanksgiving, that we have the *privilege* of testing the power of that grace which is so abundantly bestowed in time of need. With you, my dear sister, my whole heart responds, "Glory be to God for these tests." Not unfrequently it is said, "If Mrs. —— only had this and the other trial to endure, she might not so confidently affirm the sufficiency of grace under *all* circumstances." Similar expressions have been made relative to the unworthy one addressing you; and then when called to pass through trials of like nature, and grace has triumphed, observant lovers of Jesus have informed me of the sentiments expressed, which were before unknown to me, and then have I been constrained to say most exultingly indeed, "He hath led me forth by the right way."

How my admiration of the grace of God has been raised in contemplating the character of Mrs. Susannah Wesley. Surely here was an intellect of the highest order, which well fitted her to shine

Mrs. Wesley. Family Jurisdiction. Republican Principles.

with no common lustre either in the religious or literary world. She was endowed naturally with the most marked independence, originality, and correctness of thought, which capacitated her to act (under God) for herself beyond ordinary ability. Yet, even an inspired Paul would not, I think, have hesitated in ranking her among the most favorite daughters of her who called her husband, lord.

Scarce would I dare breathe a thought that would reflect other than the highest honor on the memory of the father of the illustrious Wesley, yet I think there are few who have read the interesting history of the Wesley family, but will join me in saying that the husband's lordly prerogative was maintained quite to the bounds that Scriptural propriety might warrant, and perhaps a little beyond what the gallantry and republicanism of the present day would justify. Can we survey the character of Mrs. Wesley from a more elevated position than this? Had she contended the point of family jurisdiction, from a consciousness of her intellectual superiority, how disastrous had the consequences been to her own peace and the well-being of her family. Modern usage might possibly have sanctioned this. I have known the peace of an entire household shipwrecked here; and from what I have frequently observed, have feared that our republican principles may have affected our

American wives somewhat unfavorably, inducing a forgetfulness of some express Scriptural injunctions on this point.

Mrs. Wesley's biographer says thus of her: "Notwithstanding she allotted two hours of the day for meditation and private prayer, no woman was ever more diligent in business, or attentive to family affairs than she. Remarkable for *method* and good arrangement, both in her studies and business, she saved much time and kept her mind free from perplexity. She had *nineteen* children! (think of the amount of physical suffering and care,) ten of whom at least grew up to be educated. This duty fell upon her; and it were scarcely possible that they should have had a better instructor."

Yet all this, with the advantages which wealth insures, might not by some be pronounced extraordinary excellence. But let it be remembered that this wonderful woman was often called to grapple with poverty and its attendant circumstances, and surely it will be said, though "many daughters have done virtuously, thou excellest them all."

And now, my dear sister will wonder at such a long chapter on such an unlooked-for subject; and without intending the infliction, I may have taxed her, by gratifying my own feelings in tracing a character so amiable. You will surely

Ill health.   A Letter received as a Gift.

imagine my health improved to admit of writing such a long letter. But though somewhat improved, yet it is still but seldom I dare take my pen, and when guilty of what my too careful husband might call the *ungracious* act, I dare not continue its use but a little while at a time; yet I think I can as easily conclude this to be "the right way for me at the present time, as I can conceive it to be "the right way" for you to write your excellent letter, "a line or two at a time, with your dear babe in your arms." That the Lord moved you to write as you did I cannot doubt, for I had been longing and praying for a letter from you, and when I received it I knelt and thanked the Father of mercies that his Spirit had induced you to write.

May He who has undertaken to lead us forth by a right way to the city of habitation, preserve us unto his heavenly kingdom, and after having been led forth through this changeful world by the right hand of omnipotent love, may we hail each other in the abode of ever-during rest; and may we also be permitted to greet each member of our beloved households in the city of our God.

Yours ever, in changeless love.

"I hate Vain Thoughts."   Satanic Resistance.

No. L.—TO MRS. H——.

Wandering thoughts—Satanic resistance—A strong testimony in the midst of temptation—Satan defied—God tempted by questionings—A life of faith—The cost counted—Unwavering reliance—Fruits of faith—A precious gem—Shortness of time—Sudden death contemplated.

You speak of *wanderings in prayer*. I am a sister in tribulation with you in this matter. But all I can do is to cast myself on Jesus, as a *Saviour*, to save me from *cherishing* them. He knows my integrity, and I dare to believe he pities me, when I repeatedly say before him, "I hate vain thoughts." And does not the *fact* that we so truly abhor them, assure us that they are only a class of those endless temptations from without, which so long as we are in an enemy's land, we may expect? I have thought that it is only because the enemy conceives he can *perplex* me more at present, with this mode of warfare, that he so long persists.

You also observed, that "when laboring with others, endeavoring to encourage, &c., you are so tried within." Can you expect otherwise than that Satan should withstand you, when you are endeavoring to do the work of your Master? The warfare is not so much against *you*, as against the kingdom of Christ. He is at enmity with *God*, and to the degree you exert an influence in bringing souls under the reign of Christ, Satan will try to

A Strong Testimony in the midst of Temptation.

perplex, and in every possible way withstand you.

But, dear sister, did you not make use of too strong language in speaking of *"endless doubtings."* You surely do not, in thus laboring with others, or in giving in your testimony, *doubt* whether you will be sustained? You labor for, and with others, because the Holy Spirit moves you to it. What other influence could move you to labor for the establishment of the kingdom of your Redeemer in the hearts of others? Satan, divided against himself, cannot stand.

You desire to be delivered from these, so that you may bear a "stronger testimony." I think I sometimes give in a *stronger testimony* when tempted to doubt, than when all is quiet. If Satan could induce me to yield so far as to weaken my testimony, it would, on my part, be a partial closing in with his designs, and doubtless if he should succeed once, it would only embolden for an attack on every such occasion. So I make it a point, when most powerfully tempted, to speak most *confidently*. You may wonder, but I have proved the benefit of this course. At the Tuesday meeting two or three weeks since, I practised on this principle precisely. The *accuser* for several days had been withstanding me at every point. He would fain have accused me in every word, thought, or action. Added to this, sensible assurances of the love of my Saviour were in a great measure withheld; and thus, with an indescribable sense of unworthiness, but with a consciousness of resting on *Christ*, I gave in a *"stronger testimony"* than usual. The feeling that possessed my soul was, that of defying Satan in the name of *Christ;* the enemy every moment saying that my state of grace did not warrant the testimony I had given. After I had finished, I felt such a conscious victory over the powers of darkness that my soul was filled with triumph. I afterward enjoyed blessed satisfaction in telling them, that the strong testimony I had given in was not founded on any state of *feeling* I at the time enjoyed, but because I *knew* I was by faith resting on the strong basis of the immutable word to sustain me in all I had said, and even in using much stronger language if it were possible.

You know Israel *tempted* God, in saying, *"Is the Lord with us or not?"* Let us not tempt him by doubts, either in *thought* or *expression*. We cannot honor God more than by trusting him. Let us *" trust* in him and not be *afraid."* If we were continually possessed of *sensible* manifestations, should we have occasion to exercise our *trust* in God? *Trust* and *faith* seem to imply much the same thing, and neither favors the idea of long-continued *sensible* manifestations. You may remember that a part of your letter was in allusion to this subject.

The Cost counted of living a Life of Faith. Temptations.

When I set out to *live* a life of faith on the Son of God, I counted the cost. I thought of the "father of the faithful," who "by faith journeyed, not knowing whither he went," and made up my mind that I would be contented to follow God blindfolded as long as I lived, if such were his requirement. I saw *holiness* to be a *state* of soul in which all the powers of body and mind were given up to God, and I perceived that the enjoyment of this state was in perfect consistency with extreme sorrow, as well as with exceeding great joy. Through grace I was enabled to say,

> "Give joy or grief, give ease or pain,
> Take life or friends away."

These were among my first expressions on entering upon this *state*. It has often since been suggested that I gave myself up so fully to live a life of *faith*, that God had taken me at my word. And will you believe, the enemy sometimes tries to tempt me to be *sorry* for it. But he has never *succeeded* in causing me to regret it for one moment. But you would hardly conceive how often he tries to make me think my faith a mere *intellectual knowledge*. I meet him by saying, it is founded on principles laid down by the eternal Mind, and consequently immovable in *faithfulness*. God has promised such results as the *fruits* of faith. I *trust* him, and on the authority of *his own word* declare in *strongest testimony*, his faithfulness in

Fruits of Faith.　　Worth of the Promises.　　Shortness of Time.

fulfilling his promises. The *fruits* of holiness follow—I dare not doubt it. A consuming zeal in the cause of God, which gathers within its grasp my whole being, is continually inspiring corresponding efforts. "My soul shall make her boast in the Lord, and the *humble* shall hear thereof and be glad." "*One* promise is worth more than a mountain of gold reaching to the heavens." How rich are *we*. Unto us are given exceeding great and precious promises. I found an inestimably precious gem a few days since, which, in view of what my temptations had been, was precisely in point. "*Wisdom* and *knowledge* shall be the *stability* of thy time, and strength of salvation :* the fear of the Lord is his treasure." Isa. xxxiii, 6. Satan seems to have mostly done with my *intellectual* faith since. I have, dear sister, through grace, a good hope of immortality and eternal life. Our hope of seeing each other is deferred. But as it is by our heavenly Father's appointment, our hearts are not sick. With us,

"This note above the rest *does* swell,
Our Jesus hath done all things well."

We are *sisters in the Lord*, and our hearts are united for *eternity*, and as we are only to take in a small fraction of *time* here, we will rejoicingly say,

"No matter what cheer
We meet with on earth ; for eternity's *here!*"

Time seems very short, and I have some thoughts

* *Salvations.* Margin

Thoughts in Relation to a Sudden Departure from Earth.

I would like to express. But I see your affectionate heart is too easily moved, and you well know how often people have impressions which are never realized. But I will say that a *sudden* departure from earth seems to me calculated to glorify God, just as much, if not more, than a protracted illness. And if either our beloved brother or sister were thus taken by surprise, and required to "open unto Him *immediately*," I should think of it as in the case of Emory. The church was then roused through the length and breadth of the land, to feel the solemn import of the words, "Be ye also ready, for in such an hour as ye think not the Son of man cometh."

I am trying to have my work "*all* done up," and to do what my hand findeth to do, with my might. So many are comparatively easy without having on the white robe, that I have thought, if my being taken at a moment's warning would arouse the many for whom I have been interested to feel abidingly the importance of being *ready*, I would be willing to be laid a sacrifice upon the service of the faith of the church in this matter also. Shall we not strive with *pen* and *voice*, and in every possible way, to work while the day lasts?

Yours, as ever.

No. LI.—TO REV. MR. ——.

The children of God are one in interest—Obligations vary according to relationships—Abraham's unheard-of path of duty—Remarkable requisition—Satan's subtilties—Just where light meets us—Willing is not doing—The appearance of evil—A questionable practice cripples faith—Crucifixion of the flesh required—David's sacrifice—God will help you—An old habit broken.

My dear brother in Christ will be pleased to hear that his letter was rightly directed. So far from requiring an apology for writing to one of the children of your heavenly Father, it surely should rather require one for not doing so, if you were impressed that it might be serviceable to you. My mind is so fully possessed with the assurance, that all the children of God are members of *one* body, that I am not prone to conceive of separate interests.

I was not at home when your letter reached the city of New-York, but it was brought to me at this place. I hasten to reply, though not favored with facilities for writing, nor opportunity for maturing my thoughts as I might otherwise do.

Your case, dear brother, does not appear to me inexplicable. I have met with a number of cases somewhat similar. Not, indeed, in regard to the precise object to be given up, but where the power to exercise faith on proper principles has been withheld, until the object required had been surrendered. We cannot, in all cases, make duties

Obligations vary.   Abraham's Faith manifested by his Obedience.

one for the other, because our obligations vary from a variety of causes, being as diversified as are the positions in which we are providentially placed.

Abraham was called to sacrifice Isaac. He did not know at the time, why such an unheard-of duty was enjoined. It was enough that God had made the demand. But it was the design of God, that Abraham should stand out before all succeeding generations, as the father of the faithful—the friend of God. "Ye are my friends, if ye do whatsoever I command you." Over four thousand years, Abraham has been reaping the fruit of his obedience. He knows now why the sacrifice was required, and we should be willing to wait till the day of eternity reveals the wherefore, for this or the other requirement, assured that the Judge of all the earth will do right. Infinite wisdom can require nothing but what will be for the promotion of the divine glory, and for our ultimate good.

It was thus that I was required to sacrifice an object, which, at the time, I was not aware stood in any degree between God and my soul. As far as the state of my affections was concerned, I could see no reason why I should make the surrender. I had never even heard of any one under like circumstances, being called to a similar trial. Satan, on this ground, urged that this must be temptation. How he loves to carry out his deceptions, by transforming himself into an angel of

Satan may tempt us that we are tempted.

light. If he can only succeed in causing us to pronounce upon the workings of the Spirit, as the workings of his own fiendish power, he is as well satisfied with the transformation, as though it were accomplished by any other process. But relative to the sacrifice to which I was called, the Holy Spirit suggested, Though Abraham did not know, when called to sacrifice his son Isaac, why such a requirement was made, yet he knows now; and are you willing to wait till you are an inhabitant of that world where knowledge is made perfect, in order to know why this sacrifice is required at your hands?

Praised be the Lord my strength, through whose power I had now come, not only to a *willingness* to be holy, but to the *decision, I will now be holy*, and lay *all* upon the altar, though the sacrifice be dear as life itself. The surrender was made. *Then*, and not *till* then, did clear light beam upon my mind. All was *not* upon the altar till I came to this point. When I came to this, I was met, as usual, by the words, "*If* any man *will* do his will, he shall know of the doctrine." "God is the Lord which hath showed us *light:* bind the sacrifice with cords, even unto the horns of the altar." Psalm cxviii, 27.

We have no authority from the word of the Lord, to expect clear light, *until* the sacrifice is bound to the altar. The clear beamings of the

Coming up to the Light. Touch the Altar. Questionable Practices.

Sun of righteousness ever shine the same upon the King's highway; but it is not till the traveler arrives at the last point, and actually comes to Christ, and gives up the last vestige of sin and self, that he enters, through the blood of the everlasting covenant, into the holiest. Here the bright rays from the throne of the Eternal beam at once upon his soul, and the simplicity of the way of faith is discovered. The WORD, as you will remember, does not say, "If any man is *willing* to do his will, he shall know of the doctrine;" but, "If any man will *do* his will," &c. What a vast difference it would have made in ancient times, if those who were commanded to present the required sacrifices had contented themselves with a *willingness* to lay their offerings upon the altar, without ever actually coming to the point of making the surrender! It was not until their sacrifices *touched* the altar, that they were made holy. As well might they have kept them at the distance of a mile, as to have kept them within arm's-reach.

It is said of the way of holiness, "The *unclean* shall not pass over it." If we are in the practice of that which is questionable, we must either become "fully persuaded," or come under condemnation. "He that doubteth, is damned." "Whether ye eat or drink, or whatsoever ye do, do all to the glory of God." The command, "Abstain from all *appearance* of evil," is equally binding with that which requires abstinence from evil itself. You speak of a habit in which you have indulged for many years which gives you uneasiness. Whatever may be thought of the necessity of using tobacco by some well-meaning people, we know the general voice of the deeply pious is against it. A profession of holiness, and a continuance in this practice, would subject many minds to questionings which would make your testimony less useful. "Could I enjoy a state of holiness, and yet indulge in this unseemly, and worse than useless, habit?" would be the inquiry with many a precious one for whom Christ died. Should your persistence in this habit make you less successful, as a minister, in presenting the claims of holiness, with but one individual, may you not conjecture that your Redeemer would look chidingly upon you in that day, when you will be called to present every man perfect in Christ Jesus?

I was about to say, I am glad you were not brought into a state of holiness while continuing in this practice. But I am reminded by referring to your letter, that you thought you were once in the enjoyment of this blessing, though this habit was not at the time relinquished. I hardly know what to say to this, only that "the time of this ignorance God winked at," &c. Your mind was not then as fully enlightened in relation to the harmfulness of this practice as it now is. And may **not** your *misgivings*, even at the time, ultimately have crippled your faith in such a way as to prevent a firm hold on the blessing? To me it looks probable, that till this time you might have held fast your confidence, had it not been for this difficulty.

* * * O, I am sure you will thank God that he has thus, in answer to your oft-repeated petitions for *light*, enabled you to perceive the object; and though the surrender may be crucifying to the flesh, yet with David you will say, "Neither will I offer burnt-offerings unto the Lord my God of that which doth cost me nothing."

Yours, in Christian love.

No. LII.—TO THE REV. MR. M——.

Can persons who are sincerely pious be deceived?—Satan transforms himself—A visit from a fiend clothed in an angel garb imagined; he quotes Scripture—How Christ received such a one—Satan loves a shining mark—A sure method of finding him out—The Bible the only chart—Satan may answer petitions presented on wrong premises—Gracious assurances may be counterfeited.

How is it possible that so many sincerely pious persons should be deceived, may be asked? Did they not take *the* book—the only *book* to guide poor erring men to heaven? Was not this their only chart? And did they not say, By this one and only sure guide we stand or fall? And also was not the Holy Spirit, which has been promised to guide into all truth, earnestly implored? How, after this careful, Bible-directed mode of procedure, can these mistakes be accounted for? And can we conceive otherwise, than that, after all the apparent failures, we must be mainly right?

In answer to the question relative to the possibility of sincerely pious persons being deceived, I would say, To me it seems very possible. I now tread on ground where I would proceed with the most humble dependence upon Christ as my wisdom, and will endeavor through his grace to present no idea but what may be fully qualified by a reference to the "law and to the testimony." The arch deceiver is represented in the Scriptures as capable of transforming himself into an angel of light. I have such confidence in your piety, dear sir, and also in the Christian integrity of very many who have adhered to your views, that I fully believe you would turn away from the deceiver, if he should present himself in his native robe. How far would you be from receiving an opinion from one that you know to be a fiend of the lower regions! But would it not serve the interests of the prince of darkness, whose coming is in all *deceivableness*, if he could get a sincere Christian, especially one of elevated piety and extensive usefulness, would he not, I ask, serve the interests of his kingdom by a corresponding extensiveness, if he could so *transform* himself as to appear truly as an angel of light, and thus get such a one en-

A Fiend clothed in an Angel Garb.   A Shining Mark.

gaged in carrying out his designs? Should the deceiver, thus clothed in light, rise up before us this moment, would not the first impression be, to regard him really as an angel from heaven? And then to cap the climax of deceivableness, if he should bring *detached* portions from the blessed word, as he did to our Saviour, and tell us, "*It is written,*" how hastily we might be prompted to yield! But what would be wisdom in such a dilemma as this? The Saviour has set an example, just in point. He brings up the detached portions, and by the light of truth, symmetrically arranged, Satan is vanquished. From the example just presented, and from the history of the world, from Adam down to the present time, we are furnished with assurances that Satan

"Loves a shining mark;"

and that he should fix his eye on one so distinguished for piety and talent as the lamented and distinguished individual referred to in our last, is just what might have been expected; but that he should have succeeded with his deceptions, so far as to turn his eye off from the one direct path, and to divert his devoted heart and labors from the *one* thing needful to those lesser matters of endless genealogies, &c., I confess not to be so easily accounted for.

"If such sincere persons may thus, with Bible in hand, be deceived, how can we come at any certain standard of truth?" may still be urged. This leads to a more explicit answer to the second question. David says, "Thy word is a lamp." It is the light that maketh manifest. We are admonished to believe not every spirit, but *try* the spirits whether they be of God. And by what standard are we to try them? "To the law and to the testimony; if they speak not according to this word, it is because there is no light in them." It is only thus that a fiend of darkness, when *transformed*, can be discerned from a true angel of light. It is by holding up this lamp, and with prayerful scrutiny drawing aside the assumed vestments, that we are enabled clearly to discover his deceptions.

In answer to the question, "Whether you did not take the Bible, as the one and only foundation of your faith," I answer, No. You *added* thereunto, by making a faith necessary to salvation which could not be understood without the addition of *human* calculations. This, you know, is most expressly prohibited by the word: see Rev. xxii, 18, "If any man shall add unto these things," &c. You surely will not now say, that your peculiar views relative to the *time* of the second advent can be adduced from the Bible *alone*. In that blessed book, the way to heaven is set forth so plainly, that wayfaring men, though fools, shall not err. But who would ever have thought of

An Illegitimate Faith.   Supernatural Influences not always divine

arriving at your views from the simple word of God, without the aid of *human* calculations? You may say, what has been added in making up the sum of the advent faith has been gathered from accredited history, of which all may inform themselves, if they will only be at the pains to do so. And if they should do so, and come at your faith, would it be a faith made up from the Bible? As it is, our best historians and commentators differ as to the *date* of events, both ecclesiastical and profane; and if any one, or half dozen of them, had been permitted to add their calculations to the sacred text, what a Bible should we by this time have had? But have you not, in a sense, done this? And I think you can hardly conceive of the perplexities in which many sincere minds have been involved, in fruitless endeavors to bring out your faith from the Bible.

"But was not the guidance of the Spirit of truth earnestly implored in these investigations, and have not spiritual influences, which cannot be accounted for otherwise than from a supernatural source, given corroborative evidence of the propriety and truthfulness of the impressions thus gained?" These influences can only be accounted for from the fact, that one step aside from the direct line marked out in the chart to heaven is exceedingly perilous. There is but one way in which we can *rightfully* claim answers to prayer, and this is directly on the ground of *Bible truth.* "This is the confidence we have in him, that if we ask anything *according to his will,* he heareth us." 1 John v, 14. Was it not straying from the direct line of the word, when you asked to know the precise time of the second advent? Were you not withheld admittance to the court of heaven by the word which says, "Secret things belong unto God; but those which are revealed, unto us and to our children." Should you still urge your way, you are still peremptorily warded off by the "sword of the Spirit." "It is not for you to *know* the times or the seasons which the Father hath put in his own power."

Looking at the matter thus, I see not how a petition, relative to knowing the *precise* time of the Saviour's advent, could be answered from the court of heaven; and being presented on *wrong ground,* might not the answer to the petition come from a *wrong source?* If the adversary of God and man can transform himself into an angel of light, quote Scripture to suit his purpose, &c., why may we not presume that he would be at pains to counterfeit gracious assurances? We read that the working of Satan is "*with all power, and signs, and lying wonders;*" and may not some extraordinary spiritual influences, which have been experienced relative to this subject, be accounted for thus?

Yours, sincerely.

God will reveal it.   A Class Leader questioned.

No. LIII.—TO MR. L——.

Witness of holiness lost—Unholy class leaders responsible for lowness of piety in the membership—The faithfulness of God proved when the blessing was lost—A light may be extinguished—Gifts derived from God must be diffused—Necessity of coming back—Promises may not be appropriated until the conditions are met—In what a state of holiness consists.

AND now, dear brother, I have been presenting you before God in the arms of faith and prayer. I very much regret that you have lost the witness of holiness. Do try, through the merits of your Saviour, to get so near the throne of light, that you may discover *just how* you lost the blessing. You know God hath said, "If in anything you be otherwise minded, he will reveal even this unto you." And will he not reveal that which so vastly concerns, not only your own eternal well-being, but also that of those intrusted to your care, those whom, by the great Shepherd's appointment, you are over in the Lord?

Can you, dear brother, urge the present attainment of holiness, with the same point, and power, upon the members of your class, as though *you* were in the enjoyment of the blessing? If not, may you not have their dwarfishness in religion, or even their backslidings, measurably to answer for. Do you, as their leader, expect them to go in advance of you in faith and practice? God called you out to occupy this prominent position. Did

A Leader should be an Example in Experience.

he intend to fix the eyes of others upon you thus, without empowering you to be an *example* in *experience* as well as an instructor in word and doctrine? The sentiment dishonors God, and I am sure brother L—— will not indulge the thought, but will recognize the responsibility that rests upon him, not to give currency to it, in the minds of others, by his own example of deficiency in experience. I do not wish to upbraid one I so much respect and love, but if Truth reproves, surely you will not deem *me* unkind.

Of late my contemplations have been more than usually on the character of the Eternal, in his *unchangeableness* and *truth*. I should love, dear brother, to lay open my whole heart to you on this subject. The immutable Jehovah has been teaching me gracious lessons, which, to the praise of his grace, are daily becoming more established into settled principles. I dare not do otherwise than let my "yea be yea, and my nay, nay." My mind is continually confirming in the assurance, that whatsoever is more than this, cometh of *evil*. Surely, brother, when we practice to the contrary, we exhibit that which is so unlike the character of God, that we greatly grieve and dishonor him.

You know the design of redemption is not fully answered unless the *image* of God be restored to the soul. How unlike conformity to the eternally

The Offering sanctified.   Cautious in professing.

Faithful and True are we, if we are continually vacillating in our faith and purposes! With God there is neither *variableness* nor *shadow of turning*. More than once has God given you the witness that you were wholly his. God was faithful. The very moment you laid all upon the altar, that moment the altar sanctified the gift. All, for some time previous to this, seemed laid upon the altar, with the exception of your *will*, which required signs and wonders; but your will was at last given up also. The sacrifice met the divine requirement, and was at once sanctified.

You continued to prove the faithfulness of God. So long as you *kept* all upon the altar, the promised results followed. Yes, you were *sanctified*. And when you *lost* the blessing, you also proved the faithfulness of the Lord Jehovah. You were warranted from his word in anticipating just the loss you sustained. It was the *necessary* result of the course you pursued. To use your own language, you became "*cautious in professing* the blessing." You ceased to pour out to others, and to the degree you did so, God ceased to pour into your own soul. You know it is said, "*Give*, and it shall be given you." Now when you ceased to comply with the condition, by withholding from those around you the testimony of the great salvation God had imparted—yes, *hid* the righteousness of God within your heart—and did not with David abundantly utter the memory of his great goodness—ceased to declare it, as you will remember you at first resolved on doing, to the great congregation, why wonder that to just the degree you indulged in this, your evidence should become darkened? And when at last, as you acknowledge, you ceased to speak of it at all—hid your light altogether under a bushel—why wonder that it should be extinguished? Was it not just what you might have expected? How could God have been unchangeable in his purpose, and have awarded you a different experience?

You say you "could not have told at the time, nor have you been able to discover since, the occasion of your declension." If I have judged correctly, you lost it by degrees, in precisely the ratio you became cautious in professing it. And this doubtless is the way in which hundreds lose the blessing. God does not impart his blessings to us for our own exclusive enjoyment. It is his design that we should be vessels sanctified to his use, through which he may communicate to the perishing around us the knowledge of his great salvation. It was his purpose that you should have been used as a channel, through which should flow out to the greatest possible number a knowledge of full salvation—a redemption from all iniquity. Only see how you have disappointed the expectations of his mercy. And what a loser you have been! How

| Come back. | God's Work. | Man must act. |

many stars might you have had in the crown of your rejoicing, had you persevered!

Now brother, you see the point from which you have wandered. The changeableness has been wholly on your own part. Will you not come directly *back?* This may be humbling to your spirit, but I am sure you will have to come to this decision. You need not expect any more light until you make use of that which you already have. Come, brother, let those who are following your faith, know that you apprehend Jesus Christ the *same* yesterday, to-day, and for ever. Lay all upon the altar just now, resolved that you will now believe upon the bare declaration that God has given in his word. Here is a solid foundation. Heaven and earth shall pass away before one jot or tittle shall fail. Resting thus upon God's eternal truth as the only foundation of your faith—irrespective of frames and feelings, your goings will become established. And thus in your degree, you will be continually deriving power to perfect holiness. Do you observe that it is present grace that flows out to you on condition of a *present act on your part?* God will not perform *your* part of the work, but *gives* you the power. He worketh in you to will, and now he requires that you should *do* his good pleasure. I need not say that he stands ready and infinitely desirous for the performance of the work *now*. You hear him saying,

"Come, for all things are *now* ready." Do not forget that it is a present salvation received *momentarily* from above. In view of the conditions being complied with on your part, He says, "I will receive you." Comply, and then you have a *right* to lay hold upon the promise; and upon the bare authority of the immutable Word it is your duty to say, "Thou *dost* receive me." The blood of Jesus *cleanseth* from all unrighteousness. O dear brother, leave your feelings out of the question, and now begin to *live*, not for an hour, or a day; but begin to *live a life* of faith on the Son of God, for the just shall *live by faith;* and I pray you no more proportion faith to feeling, for here has been your error. Joy, peace, love, &c., are the *fruits* of faith, and must necessarily *follow*, not *precede*. Surely my dear brother will not regard it as optional with himself whether he will live in the enjoyment of this salvation or not. If holiness is a state of soul in which all the powers of the body and mind are wholly given up to God, the *duty* of living in the possession of it is most obvious. And this consideration will—yes, *must* settle the matter with you. Now, to him that is able to keep you from falling, and to present you faultless before the presence of his glory with exceeding joy, to the only wise God our Saviour, be glory and majesty, dominion and power, both now and ever. Amen. Yours, in the fellowship of the gospel.

"I have no greater Joy."   A Mother's Solicitude.

No. LIV.—TO MRS. J——.

Responsibility of parents in regard to the salvation of their children—A memorable struggle—The Spirit's intercession—Prayer answered—Parents should resolve on the salvation of their children—Children under sentence of death—A child born of the Spirit—Young converts may be holy—An interesting disciple—Remarks of a minister.

MY BELOVED SISTER,—Yours of August 24th was received yesterday. "Blessed be the God and Father of our Lord Jesus Christ, which, according to his abundant mercy, hath begotten us again unto a lively hope by the resurrection of Jesus Christ from the dead." Next in importance to the happiness of knowing that we have been elected unto eternal life through sanctification of the Spirit and belief of the truth, is the knowledge that our children are walking in the truth. Truly may we unite with the beloved apostle and say, "I have no greater joy."

The responsibility of parents, in regard to the salvation of their children, seems to be so nearly allied to what our obligations are in relation to the salvation of our own souls, that the connecting link scarcely stands dissevered in my mind. The promises are to the righteous and their seed. I have had seasons of deep and earnest solicitude in wrestling with God for the salvation of my own soul, yet these, I think, but lightly compare with the unutterable travail I have at times endured, since I have been a mother, for the salvation of my chil-

"Death or Victory." Agony of Soul. Help of the Spirit.

dren. One of these occasions I may never forget through time or eternity.

I had said, "I will not let thee go," resolved rather to die in the contest than to yield the point. For months my soul had been burdened, and Satan had seemingly been permitted to withstand me more successfully on this than any other subject. And strange to tell, on every other point the throne of grace seemed more accessible than on this. I think I may say, that the resolve now was "death or victory." So intense was the agony of my spirit, that my physical nature could not have endured the struggle much longer, and it was not until several days had elapsed that my health regained its former tone. Shall I say that I felt that heaven could hardly be a state of bliss for me, if the offspring of my body were doomed to everlasting burnings? With Moses, I seemed almost constrained to say, "If thou wilt not, blot my name out of thy book." Why this remarkable trial of my faith and patience was endured, I perhaps may never know in time; for, for several hours the saddest part of my cup was that I seemed left to struggle alone. It was only a little before deliverance came, that I said, If I have the help of the Holy Spirit, let me have some apprehension of it, whereupon I received an indescribable view of how the Spirit *itself* had been making intercession during all the hours of that memorable day before the

Victory.   Resolve on your Child's Salvation.

throne, in behalf of my child. O what a consciousness was given, that the Holy Spirit had made my heart its abode, and that the Lord was making me the instrument in the salvation of the child! From that moment faith seemed almost changed to sight, and so assured was I, that it was the Spirit *itself* that maketh intercession, that my own identity seemed for the time in a manner lost, and I could only think of myself as an instrument, given up wholly through the power of the Spirit to God.

It seems to me, as if no truly pious parent need ever be disheartened in view of the ultimate salvation of his children, if the resolution, that they shall be saved, be determinately persisted in. This resolve must, of course, include the purpose that every earthly consideration shall be subservient to this object. I fully believe if I had been less importunate, or less persevering on the occasion referred to, that I should not have prevailed with Israel's God; for, as I have intimated, he did not seem to regard my prayer, but rather to say, "Let me alone." Had Jacob's courage failed one half hour before the blessing came, would he have been called Israel? But we had better go limping all our days, or die in struggles for the salvation of our children, rather than that they should dwell with everlasting burnings. How pious parents can enjoy life, and go on as happily as though all were well, while their children are under the *sentence of death*, is surprising. Were their children under the sentence of temporal death, from having broken the laws of their country, would we expect to see these parents enjoying life, and as much at ease as though all were well? Such parents would be thought destitute of natural affection. And how can God and angels look upon parents, who are comparatively at ease, while their children are under a sentence, which, without an hour's warning, may be executed, and their offspring doomed to a fate more fearful than the death of the body a million times told! Have such parents faith in God? Do they believe that the sinner is condemned already?

I do not wonder that you so greatly rejoice that your beloved J—— has been born of the Spirit. Our hearts respond with yours in the exclamation, "Glory to God in the highest." May he be "steadfast, immovable, *always* abounding in the work of the Lord." Either for the youthful disciple, or for the more mature Christian, this is an important admonition. In about the same measure we abound in labor for the salvation of those around us, God dispenses blessings to our souls. "He that watereth, shall be watered also himself." If dear J—— has fixed his aim on being a decided follower of the Saviour, I hope he is expecting a *daily* cross. It may perhaps be a cross from which

Young Converts may be holy.   An Interesting Disciple.

the flesh may shrink, to tell his young friends what great things the Lord has done for him; but in doing this, his own soul will be greatly strengthened, and he will at once begin to be a preacher of righteousness. May my dear friend commence at once to gather stars for the crown of his rejoicing!

I hope, dear J———, will bear in mind that young converts may be holy. I witnessed an encouraging exemplification of this on Tuesday. An intelligent lady, who experienced religion about four weeks since, was at our afternoon meeting. Her husband and herself were both skeptical, and, at the time of her conversion, grace made a wonderful transformation. By the permission of her husband, she at once commenced family prayer, and also other religious duties, such as asking a blessing at meals, laying aside her gay and costly apparel, &c. The pious minister who was instrumental in her conversion, loved holiness, and took pains to instruct this interesting disciple in the way. He gave her the "Way of Holiness," and other books also were sent to her; but one book she had which eclipsed all others: for this, she said, was full of holiness. This book was the BIBLE. She had been telling me how she felt, while endeavoring to sustain the family altar in the presence of her husband. I said, in return, "What you now want to enable you to bear up triumphantly amid these trials, is the blessing of holiness." This she was dis-

Forty Years in going an eleven days' Journey.

posed to acknowledge, but soon said, "Why is it that so many professors seem to know so little about this blessing? I told an aged minister my feelings in reference to it, and he said, I was yet too young in experience to expect the blessing."

I assured her that it was not with the example nor the opinions of men that she had to do, and recalled her acknowledgment that the Bible was full of requisitions to be holy, and for the moment the tempter seemed silenced, when she brought up the experience of an aged brother which had been given in during the meeting; which experience went to say, that he had been forty-seven years a full believer in the doctrine of holiness, and though he had sincerely and earnestly coveted the attainment, he had not yet received the desire of his heart. "Why," she continued, "should others be so long in arriving at this point, if I may gain it so soon?" "And why were the Israelites forty years in arriving at a point which might have been reached in eleven days? Was it not because of their unbelief? More than eleven days have passed since you were brought out of spiritual Egypt, and surely you will not limit the Holy One of Israel, and provoke him to send you back to wander in the wilderness. You have come up to the borders of the promised land. Will you not now step over into

'The land of rest from inbred sin,
The land of perfect holiness?'"

Sinful to doubt God's Willingness or Ability *now*.

With looks expressive of unutterable desire, she said, "I believe the Lord will bring me in." "*When* do you think he will bring you in?" "I do not know, but I think it will not be long." "He has assured you of his willingness to save you *this* moment, and it is sinful to doubt either his ability or his willingness to save you *now*. Do you believe that God would be faithful to his word, if you should now venture body, soul, and spirit, wholly and for ever upon Christ?" "I believe he would." "Will you begin to trust him, and by a continuous act rely momentarily on your Saviour for salvation from all sin? The poet says,—

> 'But is it possible that I
> Should live and sin no more?
> Lord, if on thee I dare rely,
> The faith shall bring the power.'

Now you would not dare dishonor your Saviour so much as not to believe that he would save you from sin this and every succeeding moment, if you would trust him." Her faith gathered strength, and she said, "I know he would save, and I will trust him." "Why should you not believe that he is *saving* you, if you are *now* relying upon him for full salvation? If you are being saved it is because Christ is *saving* you; and do you not feel that you are this moment saved, and can you not say,—

> 'Thou from sin dost save me *now*,
> And thou wilt save me evermore?'"

With emotion she said, "Bless the Lord, I am saved."

A Young Convert sanctified.   Remarks of a Minister.

A gracious baptism of the Spirit was given, and in the full assurance of faith she cried out, "O I am sanctified; glory be to God!" A little band of devoted ones had lingered with us after the close of the meeting, and we fell upon our knees and ascribed glory to the Father, Son, and Holy Spirit.

God is no respecter of persons; what he has done for one, he is willing to do for another. If J——'s mother received the witness of holiness, when she was but little over ten years old, so clearly, that she has never since doubted that she was then made the partaker of this precious grace, why may not J——, thus early in his Christian life, set out to receive the full impress of the Holy Spirit? A minister of deep and enlightened piety, in exhorting the friends at the Tuesday meeting, said, That from careful observation, he had become settled in the conviction, that by far the most successful time to urge the attainment of holiness, was when the mind was tender from its first reception of regenerating grace. Now, said he, is the time to give it the mold, before the young affections have learned to be truant, and the mind has become used to parley with the tempter, and to yield to his suggestions.

Present my regards to brother J—— and all the members composing your pleasant family circle.

Your ever devoted sister.

A Memorable Day.　　　Temptation.　　　Humiliation.

No. LV.—TO REV. MR. U——.

Of the act of faith—Humiliating perceptions—Shrinkings from a profession of holiness—The direct path—A ceaseless sacrifice—The key which opens the door—What is the act of faith?—Terms of the covenant—Faith, not works, the ground of acceptance—The blessedness of purity—Why do some receive the blessing sooner than others who are equally sincere?—How example may hinder—How the blessing may be obtained—Tears of desire shed, yet a willingness to be holy not attained.

CHRISTMAS day was rendered memorable by my receiving more definite and confirmed views of the precise act of faith, which brings present salvation from all sin.

These views were preceded by an uncommon humiliation of spirit. During the day a temptation to hastiness was continually pressing upon me, and as the tempter had an object to act upon, the suggestion was, that I had, more or less, yielded to its influence. On examination, I could not bring the conviction that I had offended, and consequently did not feel condemnation; yet I was most deeply humbled, under a sense of my unworthiness. While confessing my want of higher degrees of holiness, and lamenting this before the Lord, I was led to question how it was, that I had been enabled to hold fast the beginning of my confidence, and continually witness that the blood of Jesus cleanseth.

I felt that I had not deceived myself, and could

appeal to the Searcher of hearts that it was not merely a blessing in *name* that had been gloried in, but an actual realization of his saving and cleansing power. Yes, thought I, in verity I do know, that the blood of Jesus cleanseth—*cleanseth now!* With feelings which even the recollections of that hour reproduce, causing tears of grateful joy, I could say with Paul, "To me, who am less than the least of all saints, is this grace given." Yet, for reasons almost undefinable, but which perhaps cannot be more fully expressed than by saying, the appearance (in the eyes of some) of assuming, by professing this blessing, a higher state of experience than many others whose piety I so much venerate, and especially some of Christ's beloved ambassadors, whom in love I highly esteem for their work's sake, I felt a shrinking tenderness of spirit, relative to the testimony I had given before the world on this point. And yet I realized that the vows of God were upon me, and wo is me if I do not profess this blessing, and urge its attainableness on others. And must I continue to urge its reasonableness, even though it may assume the appearance of taking higher ground in the Christian walk? I felt that I could weep, and even now do weep at the thought. But the plain, direct path, cast up for the ransomed of the Lord to walk in, still presented its track, lit up by the rays of divine truth, as luminously as ever. The way was

Duty ours; events the Lord's.   Irrevocably given up.

not to be mistaken. I saw what would be the result of a willful turning, either to the right hand or to the left. It was a blessed thought that I had given my influence into the hands of the Lord, and could unhesitatingly leave it there, and know that *duty* was mine, and *events* the Lord's. I also most deeply felt that it was not because I was more worthy than others, that I had been enabled, for years past, to bear testimony to the possibility of living in the enjoyment of the *witness* that the blood of Jesus cleanseth from all unrighteousness.

But I would not assume the ground, that I have not trespassed in thought, word, or deed, since that time. No. But in this, through grace, I will glory,—I have not, since the memorable hour that witnessed the entire consecration of all my powers, taken myself from off the altar, but have ceaselessly endeavored to present a living sacrifice of body, soul, and spirit. Since that period, I have not felt as if any of these redeemed powers were for one moment at my disposal. When duty has been presented, however much nature may have shrunk from the requisition, I have been enabled to act upon the principle, that I have given myself irrevocably to God. Though life might be the forfeiture, I have estimated the favor of my God better than life. Neither have I, since that period, knowingly transgressed.

Yet, I do not take this as the precise ground of

A Key which opens the Door. What is the Act of Faith?

my confidence; but this state of soul, in conjunction with an act of faith, which as a key opens the door, and brings the soul into the actual possession of full and complete redemption, is that which I have been enabled to render continually available, and by this I have been permitted to enter into that state of light and liberty which is spoken of 1 John i, 7.

But what is this act of faith which brings the soul into the enjoyment of full salvation? By the help of the Lord I will state it, as also the way by which I continue its exercise. I saw that God had erected an altar, whereunto I was commanded to come with faith, nothing doubting. And still further, that he did not require that I should believe, without a thorough foundation for my faith. Perhaps I cannot better explain, than by adverting to what my expectations would be, if a will, which I knew to be in every possible way legally executed, were placed in my hands, and I authorized, from undoubted authority, in believing myself the rightful heir of an inheritance. Would I hesitate in availing myself of its provisions, and think it mysterious that I was to come into possession by merely believing the validity of the document? And yet the knowledge of the fact, without the act of taking possession, would leave it just as unavailable for my present necessities, as though there were no such inheritance for me.

God's Requisition. The Offering accepted and sealed.

Thus I saw that God had declared it his will, even my sanctification, and that he had also rendered that will very explicit by the command, "Come out from among them, and be ye separate, touch not the unclean thing," conjoined with the declaration, "I will receive you." In view of this declaration of my heavenly Father, had I any reason to doubt that it was his will, even my sanctification? What then remained for me, but, through the strength of grace, to "come out and be *separate?*" With this requisition I was enabled to comply. Would it not have been strangely inconsistent, after having come to this point, not to have believed that God would accept? And did it require any extraordinary effort of faith to believe that I was indeed one of his covenant people? It was thus, therefore, in the simplicity of my heart, I was ready to exclaim, Why, it is hardly of faith, but rather of knowledge; it is so easy. It is all here. I have given myself wholly to God. He has accepted the offering, and sealed me irrevocably his. And would it not be strange, and in effect doing great dishonor to the faithful Jehovah, by an intimation of inconsistency, if, when he had required the entire surrender, and enabled me to comply, I were not to believe he would be true to his own part of the engagement?

But to get at the more definite answer that presented itself in reply to the inquiry, how I, so

Sincerity and Devotion insufficient without Faith.

unworthy, was permitted to be clear in the enjoyment of this blessing, when there were so many whose piety I held in such high esteem who were not? The only explanation I could give was this: I have faith in God, and believe fully in the validity and feasibility of the plan devised by infinite wisdom, by which the polluted may be cleansed.

The plan, in perfect consistency with the nature of its Author, is unalterable. The devotion that might induce its possessor to pass through the flames, or to weep tears of blood, cannot produce an alteration or the least swerving from the principles laid down. By the right of purchase, God demands, and beseeches, that we present our bodies a *living* sacrifice. We present the offering, and are cleansed. We continue to present it, and continue to be cleansed. The Lamb slain from the foundation of the world, with garments newly dipped in blood, is continually present before the throne; and it is but to know that we lay all upon the altar, and believe in the infinitely meritorious efficacy of his blood, in order to realize, with all the blood-washed company, that we

> "Every moment *have*
> The merit of his death."

It is then, and only then, that we can fully mingle in song with the spirits of the just made perfect around the throne. Who does not feel the impotency of human language, when the full soul endeavors to bring out in words the transcendent blessedness of conscious purity: when the spirit exultingly joins with the redeemed in the song, "Unto him that loved us, and washed us from our sins in his own blood, and hath made us kings and priests unto God and his Father, to him be glory, and dominion, for ever and ever, Amen!" And yet there are those who are appropriating this language, from a blessed knowledge of its glorious import. But alas! there are those also, who, by the will of their heavenly Father, have an equal claim in the covenant of grace: those who have expressed joyous confidence in the declaration, "God is no respecter of persons;" yea, those even whose energy of spirit in the cause of their God would lead them to pass through fire and water,

"Into that wealthy place,"

who do not feel that they have yet been brought to possess

"This land of rest, from inbred sin,
The land of perfect holiness."

O! why is it thus? Would that my heart were as a mirror, to reflect, in living characters, the answer that its deep emotions dictate to the inquiry. May the Spirit of holiness communicate the answer to every sincere, inquiring Christian, while I attempt a reply.

There are, as has been said, certain unalterable requisitions laid down by the immutable Jehovah.

The Offering brought.   Feeling *before* Faith.

With God there is "no variableness, neither shadow of turning." His requirements cannot be varied or set aside, however sincere or devoted the inquirer. These individuals have, doubtless, again and again, brought their all *to* the altar, but, in so doing, they have not firmly believed that God would be true, and, at the moment they presented, accept the offering at their hands. They well know it to be the sacrifice that he requires: Rom. xii. 1, "I beseech you therefore, brethren, by the mercies of God, that ye present your *bodies* a living sacrifice, holy, acceptable unto God, which is your reasonable service." And that they could not even have brought the offering without his assistance: John xv, 5, "For without me ye can do nothing." But they hesitate to believe, because they do not *feel* that he has accepted, *before* they have dared to venture upon the veracity of his word. He has required the sacrifice, and has positively affirmed that he *will* accept: 2 Cor. vi, 17, "Wherefore, come out from among them, and be ye separate, saith the Lord, and touch not the unclean thing, and I WILL RECEIVE YOU." He has given the ability to bring it to the foot of the cross, and yet they *will* not *believe* that he *does* receive, merely because some state of *feeling*, which has been pictured to the mind, does not immediately follow.

The experience of many might be portrayed by

Abraham watches a Consecrated Offering.

what would have been the conduct of Abraham, if, after having brought the offering required by God, he had concluded, instead of remaining by the altar, driving away the fowls from polluting the sacrifice, he had reasoned thus: "The fire of heaven does not descend as I had anticipated; and though I well know that God has required that I should lay this sacrifice upon the altar, yet why does he not consume it? Why is my faith thus tried, and I constrained thus long to *wait*, preserving this hallowed offering from the touch of pollution? And who can determine how long I may be required to linger in this disheartening suspense? Already the sun begins to retire; a horror of darkness comes over me: surely there must have been some mistaken views in my perceptions of the manner of this requirement," &c.

Not so with him, who, in all succeeding generations, has been termed the "father of the faithful." No; his enlightened perceptions of the immutable nature of him who had promised, forbade views so dishonoring to God. We shrink from the supposition of what would have been the inevitable consequence, had he practiced, as many Christians do, under this dispensation of light. And yet we hear them speak of their unbelief, with a seeming complacency, much as though it were an unavoidable evil.

O that all who are seeking this blessing were

fully aware of the sinful inconsistency of this unbelief! If Abraham had been guilty of even this one supposed act of distrustfulness, would he have been placed so prominently before us, as the father of the faithful? And yet the Christian, with a clear revelation of the will of God continually open before him, is, day after day, practicing upon the same principles of unbelief. The younger Christian looks to the example of those older in profession; the member, to the class leader; and the class leader to one whose faith he has been divinely admonished to *follow;* and each deems himself in a manner excusable from the example of the others. The mention of this reminds me of the dilemma of a devoted individual not long since. She was but a lamb of the fold, and young in the experience of the blessing of holiness. Returning from a meeting one evening, where her beloved pastor, in the recital of his experience, had said, that he did not enjoy the witness of holiness, she remarked, in distressing perplexity, "Can it be that I enjoy this blessing when Mr. —— does not?" It was a well-circumstanced temptation; and the enemy made it the means of nearly robbing her of her confidence, though grace eventually triumphed.

But is it of small account to be destitute of that faith whereby we may be enabled, momentarily, to realize the entire consecration, and purifi-

You will find it in this Exercise.

cation, of body, soul, and spirit? Is it a small thing to keep back any part of that price which so sacredly belongs to God? And just as truly may it be kept back by the fearfulness of unbelief, as from an unwillingness to comply with any other requirement. Upon such as do not esteem it a subject of momentous interest, may the Holy Spirit impress the force of that solemn truth, "Without holiness no man shall see the Lord." But to such as are waiting at the foot of the cross, feeling that the excellency of the knowledge of this grace is better than life, I would say, You will find it in this exercise.

Bring the offering of all your redeemed powers; not only *to* the altar, but, through Almighty grace, lay the sacrifice *upon* the altar. Do not delay, because nature shrinks from making the surrender *now*. Now is God's time: 2 Cor. vi, 2, "Behold, now is the accepted time; behold, now is the day of salvation." The acceptance of the gift does not depend upon the worthiness of the *offerer*, or the *greatness of the gift*, but upon the sanctity of the ALTAR: Matt. xxiii, 19, "For whether is greater, the gift, or the altar which sanctifieth the gift?" It is by *virtue* of the altar upon which the offering is laid that the gift is sanctified: Exod. xxix, 37, "And it shall be an altar most holy; whatsoever *toucheth the* ALTAR shall be holy." CHRIST IS THE CHRISTIAN'S ALTAR. Lay body, soul, and spirit,

A Living Sacrifice. Covenant that you will believe.

upon his merits. Let the sacrifice be a *living* one. Rom. xii, 1. Remember, that it is not left optional with yourself whether you will believe. "This is the *command* of God, that ye believe." Believe steadfastly that the blood of Jesus cleanseth. Not that it *can*, or that it *will*, but that it *cleanseth now*. Covenant with God, that you will believe this, his revealed truth, whether your *feelings* warrant the belief or not. The just shall *live by faith*. Be willing to live by the moment. You cannot breathe to-day for the morrow, neither can you believe now for any future period. Bear in mind that Christ is a *Saviour*, and the salvation which you receive must be in the present tense, and of course must be received *momentarily* from above. Ask the Lord to write upon your heart the deep spiritual meaning of the expression, "a *living* sacrifice:" the blood of Jesus *cleanseth*: for though you may live days, months, and years, in the possession of this faith, you will find no other way than that of living by the moment; and though you were the veriest sinner that ever existed, or were the accumulated guilt of the whole world laid upon your head, such is the all-sufficiency of the atonement, that it is but to place yourself upon this altar, that sanctifieth the gift, and you *must* be cleansed. The crimson stream, unbounded in its efficacy, is ever flowing.

Reject the simple way of faith, and the most

violent efforts of body or mind—rivers of tears, or the devotion of a martyr—will not bring you to the point. *"One act of faith will do more for you than twenty years' hard toiling without it."* You cannot receive the full efficacy of the atonement, apart from this faith; neither can you recommend it so successfully to others; and the debt of gratitude you owe the purchaser *demands that you be a witness of his power to save unto the uttermost.* If you live short of full salvation, you may, perhaps, at the last moment of life, cast yourself upon the infinite merit of the atonement, and be saved; but O, what a risk do you run, and what an infinite loser will you be, if you leave the reception of this grace till the hour of death!

It is this implicit trusting in God, with a resolute determination not to proportion *faith* to *feeling;* believing, if he permit your faith to be tried, by a seeming delay, it is only that you may be accounted worthy of being a more victorious example of its power; which will produce a fixedness of purpose, and an established state of experience, beyond expression glorious. Look well to the terms. Holiness and sanctification most expressively signify the state intended. You cannot consistently expect it, until you make up your mind to live in the *continuous act of unreserved consecration.* Consequently, you *cannot* believe that there is an entire acceptance on the part of

God, until you come to this point, even though you were as desirous, and should shed as many tears, by way of imploring the acceptance of your sacrifice, as did the ancient Jews, who covered the Lord's altar with tears, until he became weary, and regarded not the offering any more. (See Malachi ii, 13.) It is *unreasonable* not to live in the entire and continuous surrender of soul, body, and spirit, to God. All are *already* his, by the right of redemption. If you withhold aught, you keep back part of the price. It is, therefore, *unreasonable* not to be holy. O then enter at once into the bonds of a covenant never to be broken, to be wholly the Lord's! Count the cost fully, and then lay the offering upon the altar. *While you present it, the blood of Jesus cleanseth.* In the strength of Omnipotence venture *now*, and you will find, what you had thought to be the mystery of faith, simplified.

Yours, in the bonds of perfect love.

THE END.

CPSIA information can be obtained
at www.ICGtesting.com
Printed in the USA
LVHW08s1414050918
589222LV00018B/706/P